The Johnny Chronicles

Excerpts from the life and times
of a ne'er-do-well

This account is entirely true and reasonably accurate except for the parts where the Statute of Limitations may not have run or may not apply owing to the nature of the crime, or where offense may be taken by relatives, friends, authorities, acquaintances, former lovers, etc. in which case it is entirely fabricated, totally false, and a complete figment of Johnny's imagination.

John Peterson, A.K.A. "Johnny"
Honolulu
2021

"Life should not be a journey to the grave with the intention of arriving safely in a pretty and well preserved body, but rather to skid in broadside in a cloud of smoke, thoroughly used up, totally worn out, and loudly proclaiming - Wow! What a Ride!"

Hunter S. Thompson

Contents

Chapter 1

The Ocean

"It's bumpy and it's sour and I'm never going in there again." That's all Johnny had to say about that upon exiting the Pacific Ocean for the first time in the summer of '49. He was three years old with a snoot full of water and a suit full of sand. Aside from the time a few days earlier when he had dropped a sledge hammer on his toe, and the time before that when he'd stuck a nail in an electric socket, this was his earliest memory.

It was a shaky start to a love affair. But love is a funny thing, and for reasons unknown and unknowable, the Ocean was to become a big frickin' deal. It would consume his thoughts and most of his spare time. It would shape his identity. The inhabitable portion of the earth's surface came to be defined by its distance from the sea. It would thrill him beyond anything there ever was or ever would be except perhaps sex (which he would later find out was really great but didn't last very long) and cocaine (way too expensive). And it would afford him with many and sundry opportunities to expire prematurely (Evel Knievel would be proud).

Standing there on the shore, glaring back at the sea, Johnny was completely oblivious to the fact that his fate had already been sealed.

Chapter 2

The Quarry

It belonged to them, it being the abandoned granite quarry a quarter mile from his back door, them being Johnny and those no good dirty rotten Aarons boys, Mike and Ronnie, the only other kids for miles in their collective rural neighborhood/universe.

This was some quarry. Cut into the side of a granite mountain at the turn of the century by Italian immigrant stonemasons, it spanned many football fields in length and width. At the end furthest from the mountainside, it was only a few steps down into the belly of the beast, which was littered with hundreds of huge slabs of granite (like 2001 A Space Odyssey except bigger). At the other end, cut into the side of the mountain, the sheer granite walls rose majestically several hundred feet straight up. This end was dangerous, for a fall from here was likely to ruin your day. If Johnny's parents had known of the existence of this quarry, much less it's finer attributes, they would have packed up the family and moved to Death Valley. Mike and Ronnie's folks were glad it was there because it gave them a place to send 'em when they misbehaved, which was often.

The boys reasoned those slabs had been methodically cut away from the sheer wall and were somehow slung and lowered gently to the quarry floor, then carted out the low side and away to Los Angeles on the train tracks that ran nearby. Also, apparently, many of 'em got away and dropped hundreds of feet to the ground where they joined the other slabs that preceded them. Or maybe all of them were allowed to fall freely – the mechanics of working with twenty-ton slabs of granite were unknown and unfathomable to a nine-year-old, a ten-year-old, and a twelve-year-old. In any event, by the time the quarry was abandoned, there was a hell of a pile of slabs down there.

This was the kind of pile that drove kids crazy. For one thing, the scale of it was remarkable - it made you feel like an ant. Years of accidental or intentional slab bombs had created a labyrinth of caves and tunnels underneath and through the precariously perched granite. You could hide in there for a really long time or until dinner depending on how serious a spelunker you were.

And Johnny, Ronnie, and Mike (the boys) had it all to themselves, until one fine autumn day somebody had the grandkids over, and those grandkids took a little walk and........discovered the quarry.

This would not have been so bad if they had gone undetected. However, they had the misfortune of timing their discovery to coincide with the exact moment the true owners happened by. Shocked and appalled that someone else had intruded upon their personal private property, the boys huddled in the shadows and made their plans.

"Fuck those guys," said Ronnie. "Yeah, fuck 'em," concurred his younger brother Mike. Johnny, being the youngest, had nothing to say. "Here's what we do, we climb up the other side of the mountain to the top of the far wall, and we bomb 'em with rocks." Ronnie was the kind of guy who enjoyed pulling the wings off butterflies, but at this moment, his plan, the only plan, sounded both plausible and reasonable.

And so, they climbed the mountain slowly and quietly, until they reached the top of the sheer wall. This was the first and last time they would ever do this. The mountain sloped downward at a steep angle, then dropped sharply away into the void. So, to peer over the edge, it was necessary to lay flat (while the blood rushed to your head), slide toward the edge while digging the toes of your tennis shoes into the exposed rock, inhale, and open your eyes. It was a long way down. Unfortunately, they had forgot to consider the part where they would need to back up. This

5

made things quite a bit more "interesting" and became a standard component of nightmares for years to come.

And down there, climbing around and enjoying the boy's private property, were these kids from out of town, these interloper trespasser bastards who were going to get theirs.

Ronnie and Mike picked up a couple stones about the size of grapefruits. The only one Johnny could find was a monster the size of a pumpkin (like the ones on steroids that get blue ribbons around Halloween) which he had delicately rolled down to the edge of the cliff.

On the count of three the rocks were launched (Ronnie and Mike throwing theirs well out into the air, Johnny rolling his off the edge which, it turned out, was actually hanging out beyond vertical, like the north face of the Matterhorn).

The boys began to scream profanities at the intruders. The speed of sound being seven times faster than the speed of a rock (or boulder) accelerating to terminal velocity, the interloper trespasser bastards were afforded the opportunity of looking up and watching for several seconds as two rocks and one very large boulder fell silently from hundreds of feet above.

As Johnny watched his pumpkin boulder drop away into the abyss, he noticed a kid down there peeking out from underneath one of the slabs, looking up, as it were, into the barrel as the hammer fell.

They say at the moment of death your life flashes before your eyes. Well, it happens that it works similarly from the opposite perspective; at least it did for Johnny. "Oh shit, this guy is gonna die and I'm gonna be the guy who killed him – my parents are going to be very upset – I'll spend years in juvie, and when I get out people are still going to be pissed and I'll live out my life alone and hated – this guy is going to die and it's my fault, oh shit, oh shit..." And the pumpkin/boulder continued to drop straight down, approaching 120 miles per hour as it honed in like a laser guided missile on this kid's forehead.

At the very last moment, with a fraction of a second and a few feet to spare, the kid ducked back into the shadows and the boulder exploded on the ground in front of him. For a few moments it looked like that kid was a goner, but to Johnny's relief he peeked out from underneath the slab with a horrified look on his face.

They never saw those kids again and Johnny decided never to throw any more rocks (at least not big ones).

Chapter 3

The De Anza Theater

Johnny learned a lot about life at the De Anza.

It was a bitchin' ol' movie theater in "Downtown" Riverside (a ridiculous honorific given the size of the municipality and the prevailing mentality of its citizenry, some of whom wore tee shirts proclaiming "Suicide, Homicide, Genocide, Riverside"). When it was new back in 1939, they had Hollywood opening nights there. By the time Johnny arrived on the scene in the late 50's, it was pretty seedy and obviously spiraling toward its ultimate reward (conversion to a health food store). But it was where you went to see movies.

It was a frickin' long peddle to get there on a bike, playing cards attached with clothes pins to the frame to make that throaty Harley sound as the spokes slid over the aces, deuces, and one-eyed Jacks. Johnny went there often, since he had not yet discovered girls or surfing and was not prone to suicide, homicide, or genocide.

He took in a few regular movies before he ran into "The Blob" on a Saturday afternoon. Although he did not know it then, this would be his introduction to paranoia. For weeks after that movie he suffered delusions of alien persecution, waiting in the night for a slimy substance to ooze under the bedroom door.

He would later expand and refine his psychosis as the tetra hydra cannibinol content in marijuana increased with the advent of hybrid strains and hydroponic gardening. At one point in later life, there would be a knock on the door immediately following the consumption of a particularly egregious dubie. At a reasonable distance it was probably possible to hear the teeth stripping off Johnny's cerebral gears. Helped along by a pavlovian response (Pavlov's principles of classical conditioning have been found to operate across a variety of experimental and clinical settings) and whatever smoking embers remained in his otherwise shattered mind, he found the door. Upon opening it, he stared at an assembled throng of gaily-attired carolers and, just as they broke into "Hark the Harold Angels Sing," he closed it. Upon reflection, this was not very neighborly, but at the time it seemed wholly appropriate and absolutely necessary (paranoia strikes deep).

He was sitting in the first row of the balcony at the De Anza on a Sunday afternoon when he learned about mistaken identity and injustice. He had splurged his paper route money on a ticket and a box of popcorn. He was feeling guilty, since he had a load of homework and a test on Monday, and here he was watching a movie. Upon reflection, it was a good movie but a bad move - however, it was too late now. Plus, he rationalized, his grades weren't all that great anyway, and so one more screw up probably wasn't going to have a major impact on the arc of his academic career. He does not remember the movie, but it was one of those suspense thrillers where the guys on the sound track playing the violins start screeching in ever higher octaves as the camera moves closer to the shower curtain which suddenly opens and somebody gets stabbed.

It was at the moment the curtain flew open and the violins were going "rrreeeeek rrreeeeek" that a large fat guy sitting next to Johnny threw his box of popcorn (hot and buttered) over the railing. Normally, this would be pretty funny, but there was a busload of really old people immediately below who flinched mightily, clutched their chests in unison, and began gasping loudly.

Someone called the cops. A minute later, Lester the pimply-faced steroid abusing sadist usher came charging down the balcony aisle and grabbed Johnny by the neck. Lifting him up out of his seat so that only the tips of his black high top Keds touched the ground, he perp walked Johnny up the aisle, down the

10

stairs, through the lobby and out to the street where he body slammed him onto the sidewalk in front of the De Anza for all to see.

Lying there under the disapproving gaze of an assembling crowd, he wondered what the hell just happened. It was then that he experienced the shocking realization that he had been unjustly accused of a crime he did not commit and summarily executed without the opportunity to mount a defense. It hurt. He cried on the way home. He would take this lesson with him.

But other things happened at the De Anza that weren't quite so bad. He was fifteen when he noticed this girl in his freshman Spanish class. He took Spanish because he thought it would be easier than French or German and might come in handy if he ever made it to Tijuana, not because he foresaw it becoming the official language of the United States. She was Mexican, and may have been there for similar reasons plus she was already fluent and therefore destined to ace the class. She was, uh, unusually well developed for her age, with bodacious tatas and a smile that just said, "fuck me." She was the first girl he had ever noticed with lips so full (years later he would see other women with similar lips, but these were attained only through extensive plastic surgery or enormous injections of collagen). She was, to put it mildly, stone beautiful. He got a boner just looking at her. The thing that REALLY drove him crazy was that she was looking back at him.

But Johnny was excruciatingly shy and could neither introduce himself nor jump her. Unrequited love's a bitch, and for weeks they stared at each other across the room. She sat in the front row when he gave his famous "mountain speech" which consisted of standing on a chair (her lips mere inches from Big Joe) and proclaiming "Pois, aqui esta en la montana" ("Well, here I am on the mountain") which earned him a solid C- and the horrific embarrassment of standing on a chair in front of the entire class with a ridiculously huge woodie.

When the theater's financial situation got particularly bleak, they would show all night movies at the De Anza. On a good night they could make $100 on ticket sales and $200 on popcorn and candy bars.

One Friday evening Johnny went there to take in a film about gang fights in New York. Imagine his surprise when he discovered that "Westside Story" was a musical. At the 2 am intermission, he wondered out to the snack bar and there, in all her magnificent glory exuding sex from every pore, was Consuelo, the girl from Spanish class. Their eyes met. Locked in a licentious stare, she bent forward to pick up a box of Junior Mints. Her skirt slipped up over her beautifully proportioned derriere and her breasts nearly fell out of her blouse – holy smokes!

It would be exquisite to say that they fell into each other's arms and fucked in the back row till dawn. But, unfortunately for Johnny, this was not the case. He stammered "Buenos noches," picked up his popcorn, and stumbled back to his seat, kicking himself all the way for he knew he had blown the best chance he would ever get of kissing and perhaps having sex, his first sex, with Consuelo. She never looked at him again. At the end of the semester, she transferred to another school and was gone forever. It had been his first painful lesson in love, lust, and loss. He would never forget her.

Chapter 4

The Perfect Vacation

The folks would take everybody on vacation once a year. In the beginning, it was just the family nucleus (Dad, Mom, Johnny, Glen, and Jackie in chronological order). Everybody'd pile into the car and take off for parts unknown. The first car was a shitty old '49 Packard with a top speed of fifty and a turning radius of almost a quarter mile. Later, the folks popped for a bitchin' '54 Chevy station wagon. Johnny would later destroy this car on his 16th birthday when he and his girlfriend du jour pulled outta Tuxies' burger joint into oncoming traffic and got T-boned by a fully loaded '63 Cadillac, a very uneven match.

Being that they lived in Riverside, California, the great unknown consisted of the Desert to the East, the Mountains to the North, and the Sea to the West. The South consisted mainly of Mexico, which was out of the picture, being a foreign country and all.

The first vacation was spent in the desert. It was so hot it was ridiculous – the tires would stick to the asphalt so ya had to keep moving. Jumping directly into the fire (why mess around) they drove east for half a day across the scorching wasteland, ending up several hundred feet below sea level in a place called

Death Valley (aptly named). This first trip into the unknown may have been inspired by a television series called Death Valley Days that hit the airwaves in 1952. However, this imposter was actually filmed in Apache Junction, Arizona which is a god damn Garden of Eden compared to Death Valley. Had the folks checked this out ahead of time, they would have skipped the desert all together. But it was too late now.

The temperatures range between a toasty 134 degrees at high noon and a nippy fifteen degrees at night, so a tee shirt and a pair of shorts (what Johnny packed) didn't cut it. You know you're in the bottom of the oven when you look out across the horizon and all you see is shimmering heat waves and the occasional dead animal. It was freakin' hot and then it got freakin' cold.

To amuse himself (there is nothing, absolutely NOTHING to do in Death Valley – at least back then although there may be bars and strip clubs now) Johnny would lay in the sand and look straight up, imagining the surface of the ocean 282 feet overhead, which is where it actually was a million years before. Then he would hold his breath and imagine floating to the surface. Unfortunately, he'd turn blue well before the half way mark, and although he never passed out, he did manage to work up a series of ferocious headaches, which are the perfect compliment to a 134-degree day lying on the scorching sand in a pool of sweat under a blazing sun.

Even Dad realized that he had made a mistake on this one, and that was the last time Johnny ever saw Death Valley (although years later he would drive by it often on the way to Las Vegas in a vain attempt to win his money back).

Pop committed another blunder the following year, striking out toward the East once again, this time taking the crew to Palm Springs, which is Death Valley with buildings and swimming pools. Johnny floated around until he pruned up, then lay out until his skin started to slough off. His brother and sister wisely stayed in the air-conditioned hotel room watching TV. An emergency run to the pharmacy for burn medication got Johnny back on his feet (he could not lay down) and he spent the rest of the vacation in agony, standing like a mummy in the corner of the room watching TV with his brilliant siblings.

With two disastrous trips under the ol' belt, Dad threw a change up, driving this time North into the San Bernardino Mountains and 5,000 feet straight up (you could see friggin Catalina) to a place called Lake Arrowhead. The ultimate destination (much like the Griswald's Wally World) was Santa's Village which, according to the sign, was "a fairyland setting where Santa's gnomes, elves, and little animal friends make up a children's and grownups' paradise the year round." This tourist attraction opened in 1955 and some how continued in operation for forty more years before imploding all over it's lame self. The experience is summed up well by the name of the state-run gasoline outlets in Ghana – Agyp.

There were, however, several other aspects of the trip that were actually pretty good. One of them was the lake itself. Lake Arrowhead is a man-made reservoir with a surface area of approximately 780 acres and a capacity of 48,000-acre feet of water, meaning this is one deep mo' fo'. In the summer it's actually "refreshing" after the ice pack melts. Johnny was a little disappointed to learn the thing was man made and that Indians hadn't been camped around its shores for thousands of years.

In 1904 somebody got the idea that they could irrigate San Bernardino if they built a dam on top of the adjacent mountain to catch the melting snow. They forgot about all the people on the other side who depended on the run off to sustain life in the high desert, and the legal feathers hit the fan. Several decades later, a savvy group of businessmen thought they could make a pile of loot by building a resort. Since they needed a lake to compliment a dock, they quietly enlarged the dam in 1922 (screw those guys on the wrong side of the hill) and the hole filled up.

Besides swimming around for a few minutes until your extremities went numb, you could also rent a row boat equipped with forty pound oars. On a particularly windy day, Johnny and his mom started off across the lake, Johnny pulling easily on the oars with a wind aided trajectory, enjoying the voyage. One stroke would take you about twenty feet in the ripping wind, and Johnny made it half way across the lake before pooping out. Then it was mom's turn. Oh boy, was she in for it. Turning the boat around (nearly capsizing in the wind and pounding white caps) she gamely started rowing back from whence they'd come. On the first few feeble strokes she lost about two feet. Picking up the pace, she was able to actually gain a foot or so on every pull. Johnny thought this was pretty funny, noting "It only took me ten minutes to get us here – you've been rowing for twenty minutes and we haven't moved."

Johnny had never heard his mother swear before, but at that moment she let go with a string of expletives that would have embarrassed the crew of the York Town, then kicked it into high gear. It was like one of those movies where the slaves are down in the bowels of the ship pulling on the oars as one guy beats the drum and the other guy beats the rowers. Johnny just sat there, dumfounded in the newly acquired knowledge that "you don't mess with mom." Two hours later they pulled into the dock – no more row boating – ever.

Another thing that was way cool was the ice rink. This slab of ice was nearly as big as a football field. It looked like all ya had to do was strap on the blades and off you'd go. There were pretty girls out there leaping and spinning and ripping around with graceful aplomb – how hard could it be? Johnny stepped onto the ice and immediately injured his coccyx.

Regaining a modicum of composure, he pushed off again, noticing an odd sensation as his ankles scraped the ice – first the inside, then the outside. It was not possible to hold the blades perpendicular, so it was a wobbly affair. He noticed the horrified expressions on the faces of onlookers each time he crashed into the railing or took out one of the prima donnas in mid-air, but he thought it was all part of the game. He managed to wreak havoc for nearly an hour before he was asked to leave, which was probably a good thing since he had difficulty walking for several days thereafter and might have suffered permanent damage if left to his own devices.

They would return the following year to Lake Arrowhead, but since Johnny was banned from most of the attractions, it was not all that much fun, at least for him.

Then, inexplicably, Dad turned West and headed for the Ocean. It was there they found Shangri La. Lazy summer days lounging on the beach and playing in the sparkling waves, cooking fish over a fire at night, watching the grunion run (Johnny would later apply this knowledge to good advantage when he and some of his fellow dorm mates caught enough one evening to fill a room – oh man, those things stink). Johnny surprised himself and absolutely shocked his parents by voluntarily reading his first book – "Knights of the Round Table." Years of misbehavior and a train-load of pakalolo later, he can not clearly recollect the details, but he's pretty sure it had something to do with guys in armor sitting around a table.

Having perfected the vacation thing, the folks returned year after year to the sea, renting little beach houses on the shorefront for a week of bliss. They even started taking Grandpa and Grandma. Grandpa Rozmarynowski (one word) was a 5-foot Polish dentist with a great sense of humor and an affinity for whiskey, cheap cigars, and big women. Grandma was a six foot plus size German who looked like a prize fighter (she scared Johnny's friends) and liked to joke that she was "Polish by injection." During Prohibition, Grandpa used to drive to Canada, strap a load on Grandma, and drive back – nobody, not even border guards, messed with Grandma. They lost everything in the Great Depression, and life had been a struggle, so vacations at the beach were a real treat.

Grandpa was a great kidder and a hilarious guy. Being around him was always fun and you never knew when he was going to do something unexpected, only that it was definitely coming and you'd better be ready. He embarrassed Johnny to the point of crawling under the table when he ordered "bosom berry pie" from a particularly well-endowed waitress. They fished off the pier and he'd tell great stories. They hung out – they were buddies.

One day Grandpa was sitting on the lanai in a beach chair, enjoying an adult beverage and a very large cigar. He said, "Ya want one?" Johnny, not wanting to wimp out, graciously accepted a stogie the size of a cucumber, and proceeded to smoke the bloody thing down to the nub, in between occasional shots of Jack Daniel's. This was his first experience with projectile vomiting, and he amazed himself and everybody else at how far he was able to hurl the contents of his stomach.

Aspiring film directors were just then starting to make surf movies. They would show them on Friday nights at weird little venues. The folks took Johnny to one – it was a grainy 16-

millimeter film, maybe a half hour long with dozens of surf-action montages. It was at The Crab Cooker in Newport Beach. They slid the tables out of the way, hung a sheet on the wall, and showed the movie – admission was fifty cents.

What a mind blower. To realize for the first time that it was actually possible to ride on the waves instead of just getting mowed down by them. And there was something about the surf culture that appealed to him – maybe it was the part where you got to hang around the beach all day with scantily clad beach bunnies, or maybe it was the wild parties at night. Johnny knew one thing for sure – he wanted in!

It took quite a long time to talk the folks into getting him a surfboard. But his constant whining finally paid off, and there, under the tree in 1957, was a gleaming new Hobie – 9'6" with a $\frac{3}{4}$ inch stringer and a big ol' fiberglass covered wooden fin. The thing was pink, but Hobie said it was "coral."

Anyway, Johnny had a new surfboard and the rest, as they say, is history.

Chapter 5

The Biggest Wave Ever Ridden

It is generally accepted in surfing circles that the biggest wave ever ridden (until quite recently) was attempted by Greg Noll at Makaha in the winter of '69. They say it was 35'.

In those days the height of a wave was purposely understated to discourage "townies" (surfers who lived in Honolulu) from driving all the way out to the Country (North Shore) and flocking to all the good spots where they would royally mess things up. Which is to say, on any wave, large or small, the last thing you want is for some floundering goon to take off in front of you and execute an over-the-falls-tip-roll-snowball-wipe-out as you try to slide by underneath in the barrel.

Johnny had experienced this many times, and on one occasion caught a fin in the back of the head. There was lots of blood and all his buddies were concerned (not about the enormous gash on Johnny's noggin but rather the elevated probability of sharks in the water with all those feet dangling down).

Johnny was able to make it to shore under his own steam and got to a beach-side shower which he turned on full blast to wash out his wound. Unfortunately for a young lady standing nearby, a significant portion of Johnny's scalp flopped back which caused her to faint, knocking herself unconscious on the concrete shower floor, and necessitating an ambulance which took her to the hospital. Fortunately, the driver saw Johnny standing in a pool of blood, expressed incredulity ("Jeeezuss Christ what happened to you?!") and made room in the ambulance for one more.

The wave that Mr. Noll took off on was probably quite a bit bigger than the reported thirty-five feet. Those in the know usually cut the size of small waves in half so anybody phoning from town to check the surf would hear "three feet" when the waves were actually firing at six feet, so the Townies stayed in town. On bigger days, the size was usually cut by a third, so a thirty-foot wave would be reported as twenty feet. Since most Townies weren't really keen on risking their lives on anything over ten feet, everyone felt a little better about reducing the magnitude of their lie in the knowledge that nobody from town was going to show up anyway.

Later, they attempted to legitimize the falsehood by claiming that they were measuring the backside of the wave, not the front. The TV weather people bought it and continued falsely reporting to millions of tourists "The waves today are five feet" when in actuality they were dangerously large ten footers. As a consequence, many tourists drowned and many lawsuits were filed claiming the drowndee had been falsely misinformed. A couple years ago, after millions of dollars had been paid out as a result of adverse verdicts, the City, State, and all television and radio stations began to report wave heights based on actual size (front of the wave from trough to crest). However, old habits die-hard and most of the OG's (original gangsters) still underestimate the size of waves.

So, Mr. Noll's "thirty-five foot wave" probably had an actual face measuring forty-five feet or more from crest to trough – a very large wave indeed (which perfectly matched the size of his cahones).

There were no photographers, no other surfers in the water and the waves were breaking so far out people on shore wouldn't have been able to see him eat shit anyway. Someone with binoculars did see him lunge over the edge and head straight down so it is known that he made a gallant attempt to drop in (hence is given credit for "riding") but got obliterated at the bottom, where he stayed for quite some time. Mr. Noll gave up surfing shortly thereafter and moved to Alaska.

Not to take anything away from the modern surfing heros/daredevils/crazy people who tow behind a jet ski into extraordinarily large waves, but that's not surfing, that's tow-in surfing. There's a big difference.

Surfing is when you paddle into a wave using your own two arms and as much juice as you can muster, ya huck it over the ledge with your eyes full of spray, and you take the drop into the belly of the beast come what may.

The problem that pops up in surf over fifty feet has to do with the laws of physics. At that height and larger, it becomes practically impossible for mortal man to produce enough paddling energy and translate it into board speed to be able to overcome the rush of surface water that climbs up the face of such a wave as it moves forward in a stationary sea. Any attempt to go there (like the movie 2001 a Space Odyssey "Attempt no landing there") usually results in an awkward and occasionally fatal dismount as the lip pitches forward and the surfer is catapulted into thin air. The predictable sequence of events is (a) life flashes before eyes (b) there's a few seconds of silence as gravity prevails (c) the world explodes and (d) the lights go out.

With the recent discovery of ridiculously huge surf spots such as Jaws on Maui (aptly named), some surfers have now paddled into larger waves. However, it is important to note that these surfers pursue extraordinary training regimes and are in superb physical shape. They never surf alone. They wear inflatable vests that pop them to the surface in the event of a bad hold down. They ride modern big wave boards (Rhino Chasers) with space age designs and materials, they are observed by cliff-side onlookers with cell phones, have rescue jet skis and helicopters at the ready and hospitals near by.

Mr. Noll, on the other hand, was alone with only a pair of trunks and a prayer. His training regime consisted almost entirely of twelve-ounce curls (lifting a beer from bar to lips). His only buoyancy was provided by blubber. He was riding a surfboard that was ancient by modern standards. The closest hospital was an hour away in Honolulu. He preceded all other big wave riders by nearly half a century. We must, therefore, pay homage to Greg Noll and accept that, at least until recently, he is the man who surfed, or at least attempted to surf, the largest wave ever ridden.

But that's not what we're talking about here. We're talking about the largest wave Johnny ever rode. That's somewhat different, but of equal importance, at least to Johnny.

You know how, when you're a little kid, things seem bigger? When you go back to the house you grew up in, it seems so much smaller. You can now touch the ceiling which once looked as high as the sky (as Jimmy Hendrix put it "excuse me while I kiss the sky"). Well, Johnny rode his biggest wave when he was forteen years old; at least that's how he remembers it. This is his story and he's stickin' to it.

He had hitched a ride to the beach with his good buddy Brian and Brian's sister Kerry Jo who was older and could drive (gawd, she was beautiful – sweet sixteen with enormous protrusions and a smile that could melt rocks).

He had only been surfing a couple years and his surfboard was already pretty beat up, but it was a doozy – coral (ok, pink) with a white stripe down the middle and a big fat wood fin. His parents (bless 'em) had no idea what surfing entailed or where it would lead and, therefore, had no reservations about buying him a surfboard for Christmas. From his parents perspective it was a twofer - it made their son very happy, and it shut him up since he had been whining about a new board ever since they made the mistake of taking him to a surf movie and then to Doheny beach for his first surfing experience.

The initial surf odyssey consisted mainly of paddling out into one-foot chop and riding back prone since standing up looked pretty much impossible. By the end of the day, however, he was on his feet and, with arms flailing like the Great Wallenda just before his final fall, he wobbled toward shore. He was STOKED.

Jack Nickolson (Johnny's idol from One Flew Over The Cookoo's Nest) was quoted as having said about golf, "Once you're bit, that's it." Well, the same thing applies to surfing. Johnny had been bit.

So, there he was, at 5:30 in the morning with Brian, Kerry Jo, and a couple other surfers lying on their boards in the back of a Woodie heading for Cotton's Point. (Nixon would later build the Western White house there and screw the whole thing up, but that's another story). In those days, it was great to have other guys to surf with since there weren't many surfers in the world – maybe a few thousand in California, a thousand or so in Hawaii and another thousand or two in Australia. You could fit all the surfers in the world into Aloha Stadium with room to spare.

They were a loosely knit fraternity by virtue of their shared passion. There was Johnny, hangin' with a couple of the select few, and it felt great. When word of adventures like this spread through his junior high school, he was transformed from a frog into a prince and girls started to notice him (whoopee!).

But right now, his mind was on the surf (except every sixty seconds he'd take time out to fantasize about Kerry Jo naked with a come-hither stare). There was no way of knowing what you were going to get when you pulled up on the beach since there were no surf reports on the radio, no publicly available buoy readings, no information at all. So, you paid your money and you took your chances.

To get to Cotton's Point, you had to go through San Onofre Marine Base. It was commonly believed that if you tried to sneak in there and got caught, you would be summarily executed. As they found out later, the MP's didn't actually kill you but instead occasionally they beat you with their nightsticks and confiscate your board. The beatings weren't so bad, but losing your board really hurt.

Fortunately for the guys in the Woodie, Kerry Jo was not only stone gorgeous but a military dependent as well. As such, she was afforded a card attesting to this fact. That, a wink, and a little shimmy (gawd, how that girl could shimmy) would get them through the front gate and home free (pretty much). If you were later mistaken on the beach for one of the guys who snuck in, you were toast.

But this day, there were two things that tended to rule out an incident of mistaken identity. First, there was no one there. It was a weekday and yes, they had ditched school and stolen ("borrowed" sounds so much better) the family Woodie, but it had to be done. Second, and perhaps more important and pivotal to this story, it was foggy. We're not talking about a wussy little fog like you might find in Glendale at noon, we're talking about dark grey fog as thick as Campbell's soup (Andy Warhol comes to mind – many years later Johnny sold pot to Andy until he got shot by his girlfriend, but that's another story).

Visibility was about thirty feet. They almost drove into the ocean. They piled out and stood transfixed. The vista from the beach was uninteresting - you couldn't see a thing. But they could hear rumbling out to sea. It sounded like thunder on the mountains - maybe God was mad about the school and the Woodie thing. Then reality set in. Oh dear, it was monster waves crashing somewhere out on the horizon.

"I'm not going out there," said Kerry Jo (not only beautiful but intelligent as well). "Me neither, at least not right now," said her younger and very wise brother Brian (exhibiting excellent survival instincts). The rest of the guys just stared at their feet "Well, the heck with you guys – I didn't ditch school and steal a car to come all the way down here and not paddle out – see ya." And with that, Johnny grabbed his board and waded into the icy Pacific Ocean.

The bottom was covered with slippery round rocks, punctuated by the occasional razor-sharp shell or spiney sea urchin. It was impossible to walk here for a normal person. Surfers, however, were used to it, having had to make the journey many times, both out to get to the surf, and back in to retrieve their boards. There were no board cords in those days – or, as they were referred to when they first appeared on the scene, "goon leashes" – so when you lost your board, you had to swim in to get it, usually all the way.

All that surfing and swimming made just about every surfer very fit (have you ever seen a fat surfer – me neither). Later in life Johnny put a sign on top of his refrigerator that said, "Have you ever felt like you've had too much wine? Me neither." Anyway, most of these exquisite surfing specimens were intensely recruited by high school coaches for various sports, particularly ones that had to do with water (except Kerry Jo who was on the Varsity Cheerleading Squad and later Playboy and a little bit later Penthouse) - Lordy, that girl was photogenic!

The surfers pretty much swam the 200 and 400-yard freestyle (since they were the only kids in the whole school who could actually swim that far without drowning) or played water polo (where they kicked the living snot out of every other unsuspecting inland empire team unfortunate enough to find themselves in the same pool).

Walking over the slippery rocks became a sort of dance that only surfers knew. You had to put one arm out for balance while clutching your board in the other, walk lightly but with purpose, and have faith that the next time you put your foot down it would be on another slippery stone and not a shell or urchin. This was not always the case, and Johnny suffered many gashes and punctures including a grim encounter with a big purple Mexican sea urchin when he flipped over the falls at San Miguel and landed feet first on a spike that pierced the bottom of his foot and came out through the top. He limped for a while after that.

Notwithstanding the fact that you couldn't see a thing because of the fog, and they were the only ones on the beach for miles and had permission to be there, a large Marine deuce and a half pulled up and a dozen marines in bright red speedo's jumped out. Surfers called 'em Lawrence Welk trunks because they had "make believe ball room."

Hearing the commotion, Johnny turned around just in time to see a dozen brawny marines run into the water and eat shit not more than twenty feet from where he was standing. They were in a pile screaming profanities and holding their feet. Blood was beginning to pool. Johnny turned around and sprinted across the next twenty yards of shallow water, finally throwing himself onto his board and paddling out to sea, toward the thunder on the unseen horizon.

There is a physical phenomenon, which probably has a name. How it manifests itself is that something very large but far off seems to move in slow motion. For instance, a huge airliner flying at 30,000 feet looks like it's hardly moving. As the fog momentarily broke, what Johnny saw was very large waves moving very slowly.

As he paddled further out, well beyond what he thought was supposed to be the normal take off point, he found himself being lifted into the air by massive quantities of water that rolled by underneath him. He knew it was getting serious when it took nearly five seconds to paddle up the face and another three to coast down the other side. The sound of the waves breaking hurt his ears.

Waves generally come in sets, usually three to a set, some times more. In between the sets there is a lull and the water is flat and glassy. When there's a lull and you're inside, you want to paddle like a mad man to get outside before the next set shows up with predictable results. Johnny paddled as if possessed.

Miraculously, he found himself outside at last, alone and completely spent. He was not in the shore break or anywhere near it. He was not in Kansas anymore. He was on the high seas. He was halfway to Catalina. He expected to see the Queen Mary roll by any moment. It was calm. It was the calm before the storm.

He couldn't see it but he knew it was coming because the water was receding rapidly, much like an artificial lake when the dam breaks. And when the fog momentarily broke again, he saw the horizon rising. Oh dear, that looks like a wave. And what a wave it was.

This was not your ordinary wave. In fact, it is highly unlikely that anybody has ever seen a wave like this and lived to tell about it. Think of the movie Perfect Storm, then instead of a fifty-foot trawler, put yourself on a ten-foot slab of fiberglass and foam. And instead of a whole boatload of friends to share the experience, you're all alone in the fog. And then think about that wave and add twenty feet. This was the picture that morning at Cotton's Point, and Johnny had a starring role.

Sometimes the best thing you can do is get it over with. If you're gonna lose a finger, make it fast. If the nurse is gonna stab ya with a six-inch needle, get 'er done. If the doctor is going to ram a garden hose up your ass, run.... And that's what Johnny did.

He began to paddle really fast, perhaps faster than anyone had ever paddled before, toward the expanding horizon in the fervent hope of being able to get over this mother, slide down the other side, apologize for everything he ever did wrong, and get safely back to shore... It didn't quite work out that way.

As you get closer to a 747, it flies faster. When you're standing underneath it on the tarmac, it flies really fast and you can sense the power by the way it blows you off your feet. The same goes for a cork in the sea before the largest wave any living person has probably ever seen (except for those crazy guys at Jaws fifty years later on much better equipment including blow up vests, life guards on jet skis, and rescue helicopters).

Johnny realized that he was in a tenuous situation. A strange calm came over him as he accepted the fact this was probably it. He would never have a chance to get intimate with those junior high school girls who were just now starting to notice him. And Brian's sister was now clearly and forever unattainable. His board would be shattered into a million pieces and spread all over the Southern California coast line. They would never find his body. There would be no witnesses and no wake.

And then, for no apparent reason, he turned his board around and began to paddle toward shore. This was either his last colossal mistake or a stroke of sheer genius. The wave began to pick him up, the water was sliding underneath him way faster than he could paddle, and although he was trying to move forward, he was being dragged rapidly and inevitably backwards up the face of this monster to meet his fate.

The wave crested shortly thereafter. If you had your eyes open and the fog subsided, you might even be able to see Pasadena. Johnny's were shut, and he was therefore denied the pleasure of this one last vista. Instinctively and with reckless abandon, he stood up. What an idiot.

The wave crest, now probably towering over Mount Palomar, pitched forward and Johnny began his last ride, free falling into the maw for a full ten seconds (a normal macker at Waimea is good for a three second drop but this was no normal macker). He instinctively opened his eyes but couldn't see the bottom for the fog. Amazingly, his rail touched the vertical face, and then his fin. His arms were up over his head but his feet were planted firmly on the deck and he felt a slight tug as the board caught hold.

There are only two kinds of waves – lefts and rights. If you are a regular foot, meaning your left foot is forward as Johnny's was, you prefer rights because you are facing the wave and it is easier to know when to bail if it looks like you're going to get cleaved in half by the lip. If you are regular foot and you are on a left, you are facing away from the wave and, at an amateur level anyway, you have no idea what's going on behind you or when the axe is going to fall. This wave, unfortunately and on top of everything else, was a left.

Assuming a crouched position and spreading his arms out to the side, he began the part of the drop where he was actually in the wave, not free falling in front of it. And still the elevator plunged straight down.

The mass, volume, and speed of what was under, over, and behind him pushed the fog out of the way. It was now possible to stare down the elevator shaft and see the bottom far below as it curved out majestically into flat water. It would be several more seconds before he reached the bottom. At warp speed (the fastest he had ever gone or would probably ever go on a surfboard) you don't want to make any sudden moves. Although Johnny was a complete fool for being in this predicament, he knew enough to lean ever so gently to the left that slung him in a huge arc perhaps thirty feet out into flat water in front of you know who.

Regaining a tiny sliver of composure, Johnny held his arc and headed back up into what would become possibly one of the largest barrels ever surfed (at least for another half century - apologies to Mr. Noll and all those guys with helicopters and jet skis).

As he began to ascend back up the face he leaned ever so gently to the right, beginning the second part of an extremely large S turn. Centrifugal force held him to the face of the wave and for a time he was staring straight down at certain death until the turn was complete and he had miraculously slotted himself into a high line, streaking down the face backside (this was decades before "the pig dog" was invented where you crouch down, throw your left hand back into the face of the wave and stabilize your ride by holding the rail of your board with your right hand), so Johnny just stood there.

The barrel was like nothing he had ever or most likely would ever again experience. You know the feeling you get when you're walking around in a huge empty airplane hanger? It was like that except the hanger is moving thirty miles an hour and wants to kill you.

So, Johnny just stood there and waited for the axe to fall. The sun burned through the fog and illuminated the roof way up there as hundreds of tons of water pitched out overhead and exploded in flat water beyond as he sped left down the line with his back to the wall inside the barrel from hell. It was like being in church and looking up at the biggest stained-glass window that ever was. And then he was overtaken by and disappeared into..... the foam ball.

When a particularly hollow wave folds over onto itself, it explodes from within. All the water and air that has been trapped inside the barrel must escape, and it does so at high velocity out the open end of the wave. Surfers call it a "foam ball" – when the foam ball overtakes you, you're in trouble. To disappear into the vortex of the foam ball on a very large wave is pretty much the end of the party.
He was not at all religious, but in that moment, deep inside the foam ball as the whoosh of escaping air and spray made his ears and trunks flap, he laid one on the likes of which would not be surpassed until Martin Luther King saw the top of the mountain.

And his "prayer" was answered. Or maybe he was just the luckiest guy on the face of the earth as he exploded out into the foggy morning humbled but unmolested - still upright, knees shaking, wrapped in a type of euphoria unknown to mortal man (far beyond even that experienced a decade later by those few Woodstock revelers who doubled up on the purple acid).

He proned out and held on tight (they say Greg Noll, when proning out on a big one, would actually crush the fiberglass and foam on the rails of his board, leaving impressions of his fingers). The remnants of the breaking wave (the soup) pounded him unmercifully, periodically shooting him far out in front, then overtaking him and then repeating the cycle. Johnny, at the tender age of forteen, had not really matured much so he was by no means a muscular guy. In fact, his arms were closer to pencil size and his hands often slipped off the handlebars after a speed bump. But he nonetheless somehow held on.

At last he was spit up onto the sand. He rolled off his board and laid there at the water's edge for quite some time. When he finally regained his senses, he picked up his board and walked into the fog. When he got back to the Woodie, his buddy Brian asked, "Where've you been?" And then Kerry Jo said "What happened to the rails on your board?"

For the first time in his life, Johnny was speechless.

Chapter 6

Brothers Grim

Mike and Bob were brothers and part of Johnny's core circle of friends, which included Wags, Bill, and Brian. Mike was marginally handsome (he presumed it to be true and never missed a mirror or a chance), and the girls sometimes swooned when he walked by. Bob, not so much. Bob, however, was bigger and meaner than just about everybody – ok, everybody.

They all surfed together, and a typical Saturday morning would find them wedged into somebody's Woodie at 5 am heading down to Trestles with a pile of boards in the back or on the roof.

The boys were beholden to Mike and Bob, for they were military dependents and among the first (along with Kerry Jo) to introduce them to the front door of Trestles (one of the best surfing spots on the coast of California).

Prior to Mike, Bob, and Brian's lovely sister Kerry Jo, Johnny used the back door exclusively. This meant being dropped off approximately a mile away and running with your board through the underbrush hoping not to get caught by the military police who zealously guarded the seventeen mile stretch of beach where Trestles (and several other great surf spots) happened to be located. This was Camp Pendleton Marine Corps Base and the Marines who lived there did not take any shit, especially from lowly surfers. It later became clear to the boys why the enemy would piss their pants when the Marines came over the hill, but back then, long after WWII and Korea and a while before Vietnam, nobody had a clue.

One thing was certain - you did not want to get caught by the MP's sneaking into Trestles. The consequences could be severe and occasionally long lasting.

Mike and Bob had a father who was a general or something and they therefore had a Military Dependent I.D. with some kind of sparkly shit around the edges which screamed "My dad's a general". With this, a truckload of surfers could pull up to the front gate at Camp Pendleton with impunity and seek, nay, demand admittance. It used to piss the MP's off something fierce, and they would display their displeasure in many ways (usually by pretending to ignore them), but in the end the guards knew they were going to have to let these bastards in.

So Mike and Bob were understandably included on every surf trip (mainly because Brian's outstanding sister Kerry Jo had moved on to bigger and better things and could no longer be bothered with driving her younger brother and all his goofy surf buddies to the beach, although Johnny always suspected that she enjoyed the way they stared at her large breasts, but this was just his hypothesis).

There was a hitch. Both Mike and Bob were, for lack of a better description and before anybody knew the meaning of the word, sadists. That is to say, they derived abnormal pleasure from cruelty. Behind their backs they were referred to as the Brothers Grim. Unfortunately for Brian, they had their eyes on him.

Brian was a couple years younger than the rest of the guys, but he was a good surfer and a pleasant dude – plus his aforementioned sister Kerry Jo was a stunningly beautiful babe (with large breasts – was that previously mentioned?) and a '32 Ford roadster that her father had cherried out and given to her for Christmas. On more than one occasion as Johnny trudged to school, she would glide by in the '32, give a wink, and disappear in a cloud of smoke and dust. Gawd, she was hot. But she was several years older and far more sophisticated, although in his dreams she was accessible. So, Brian was IN.

Unfortunately for Brian, the Brothers Grim fixated upon him – he was a piñata full of candy and they were the sweet tooth fairies from Hell with baseball bats. They beat him unmercifully at every opportunity and for any reason. In retrospect, the general consensus of opinion was that Mike probably had deep-seated homosexual proclivities and felt that flailing away on Brian was a way to banish the beast. Bob, on the other hand, wasn't getting any and, as an alternative, just liked to watch people bleed. Years later Bob unwittingly scored with a transvestite who had a very large Adams apple and a mighty surprise.

It is a wonder Brian survived, although a couple of times it was close. Because he was the youngest and the smallest, the process of natural selection consigned him to his lot in life as the sole occupant of the lowest possible rung on the surfer food chain. The other guys turned a blind eye to the carnage because "there but for the grace of God go us."

So poor Brian got the shit kicked outta him all the way to the beach and all the way home. It was "What did you say?" - POW, "What did you call my mother?" – BAM, "You lookin' at me?" – THUD. But, to his credit, he took it like a man knowing that someday he would get his revenge. And revenge he eventually got, although it was strange and a long time coming.

A typical Saturday started early with a one-hour drive down to Camp Pendleton, fifteen minutes at the guard house getting hassled by the MP's, ten minutes more on the winding road down to the beach, and six hours of surfing and goofing off. By this time, everybody was starving so it was back in the Woodie for a drive to the nearest store (a Safeway in San Clemente) where they would disembark and hunt for food. "Hunt" is perhaps not exactly the correct verb. Most of the guys had five-dollar appetites and thirty-five-cent bank accounts. It therefore became necessary for some of them to purloin consumables, which is to say, steal stuff.

Now Johnny NEVER stole anything (that he can remember), and Brian was flush so he was buying stuff for himself and several of the other guys as well, but those freakin' Brothers Grim were gonna have to fend for themselves.

And so, it happened on one fine Saturday afternoon that Mike slipped a package of cheese down his pants and got instantly popped by the store manager (who had had his eye on all of them from the moment they walked in).

Now normally this would not be a big deal. He'd get lectured and banned from the store or, in a worst-case scenario, booked at the San Clemente police station and released on his own recognizance. But this was not a normal situation since Mike aspired to a career as a Naval aviator and a bust like this could sour his chances of admittance to West Point, or the Naval Academy, or wherever it is that you go to become a jet pilot. Also, his father, a stickler for prudence and military bearing, would probably knock several teeth down his throat if he ever found out.

They were all in the Woodie chowing down when somebody said, "Where's Mike?" They went back to the store and peered through the glass into the Manager's office where Mike sat, getting lectured and eating cheese. Then the cops came and took him away.

So, they drove on home, discussing among themselves how to handle this delicate situation while Bob pounded the crap outta Brian.

It was decided that Johnny should be the one to break the news to Mike's parents (Johnny stupidly went along with this idea). So, upon arriving at their house, Johnny walked to the front door accompanied by the rest of the motley crew, and knocked.

Unbeknownst to them, Mike's dad and mom were hosting a bridge tournament for the officer's wives, and when the General opened the door (in full regalia), they were confronted with two-dozen ladies holding cards and chatting amicably.

"Uh, General, Mike got arrested for stealing cheese." The room went silent. If a pin had been dropped, it would have been heard. The General turned red and it appeared for a moment as though actual steam was swirling out of his ears. The metals on his chest began to clank.

They had never seen the look of death before in a grown man's eyes, and they steeled themselves for they realized that Johnny (and possibly the rest of them as well) was about to face an early demise since as far as they knew it was customary in situations like this to kill the messenger.

Thank God for witnesses. It took the General nearly two minutes to regain enough composure to speak. Whatever he said is lost to antiquity, but Johnny remembers that his voice was squeaky with a kind of warble that you might expect to hear at a yodeling competition.

The General went down to San Clemente, retrieved Mike, and somehow talked the police into expunging the arrest from his records. Sadly, the cheese would have saved his life if they had only let it. But it was too late now.

There were a few more years of Saturday surf trips and sock hops before they went their separate ways. Mike ultimately became a jet pilot. On his first take off at sea, the launch catapult failed and he went down with his plane in the path of his aircraft carrier. The only recognizable wreckage left floating in the wake was a cellophane bag containing a cheese sandwich.

Bob became a nightclub manager/bouncer. Twenty years later, on a vacation to Kauai, he chanced to meet Brian on the shore fronting a dangerous surf spot (Kalihiwai) during an epic swell.

Brian helpfully directed him to the outside line up where he was immediately mowed down by a monstrous rogue wave. The rocky cliff fronting the impact zone devoured his board. Small pieces of foam and fiberglass cluttered the shoreline.

Bob was last seen bobbing around and yelling something like "You bastard, if I ever get my hands on you..." Brian responded with a classic "Go Fuck Yourself!" flipped him the bird and drove on down the road.

Who was it that said, "Revenge is a dish best served cold?" In homage to that person and as an indication of success, Brian stopped at an ABC Store and bought a bright red ski cap and a matching pair of ear muffs, which he wore around Hanalei for several weeks.

Chapter 7

Meat Packer

In the summer of 1960, Johnny got his first real job (if you don't count that friggin paper route – the whole concept of peddling a funky Schwinn around at four in the morning with a hundred pounds of newspaper hanging off the handlebars really sucked). This new job was for Saturdays and Sundays only, but Johnny was fourteen years old and thankful for any opportunity to actually earn money instead begging the folks for it.

Johnny's buddy Tommy had a cousin just out of prison who had recently landed a job at the local meat packing plant and asked if they would like to be similarly employed. Apparently this particular meat plant was on a roll because they sold the cheapest hamburger patties in Southern California (there was a reason for this). Business was so good they had run out of ex-cons and were looking a little further down the unemployment line. Johnny and Tommy, who were theoretically standing pretty close to the end, were hired immediately.

The situation at the plant was grim. There was no air-conditioning on weekends so the inside temperature matched the outside temperature which was usually around one hundred degrees. There was a small cooler room packed to the ceiling with a week's worth of boxes containing freshly ground Grade B hamburger patties (legally prepared under the supervision of FDA inspectors). There was also a large walk-in freezer where they kept frozen meat. The temperature there hovered around zero. This was the place where everybody went to cool down. Ten minutes in there would precipitate frostbite so the visitation intervals were short but frequent. There was blood everywhere in the main part of the building and the concrete floors were quite slippery. It smelled really bad in there.

The intellectual caliber of the employees was dreadful. Most had not finished high school and some had not even finished grade school. Everyone smoked, drank, spit, swore, lied, carried knives, and picked their noses. They viewed Johnny as an "expendable clueless summer hire" who was there for the sole purpose of doing the "dirty work" on weekends when the FDA representatives were not present. This was the first time Johnny comprehended the benefits of higher education.

The owners of the meat packing plant had developed an ingenious business model wherein hamburger wrongfully labeled grade A and illegally "blended" with a large amount of inferior beef by-product was sold at a steeply discounted price.

How it worked was basically a four step process:

1. On weekdays, they made bonofide legal Grade B hamburger patties under the watchful gaze of FDA inspectors.

2. On Saturday, when there were no FDA inspectors around, they reground a week's worth of Grade B patties, combine them with questionable "beef by-product", and made them back into adulterated patties (thereby expanding volume by approximately one-third).

3. On Sunday, they relabeled Saturday's work as Grade A and reloaded the freezer trucks.

4. On Monday, they'd deliver these adulterated and mislabeled hamburger patties for cheap to hundreds of Mom & Pop hamburger joints all over Southern California.

It should be noted here that the Federal Meat Inspection Act of 1906 was passed by the United States Congress in an effort to prevent adulterated or misbranded meat from being sold as food. The law was partly a response to the publication of Upton Sinclair's *The Jungle*, an exposé of the Chicago meat packing industry. However, the rigorous inspections required by the 1906 Act only applied to meat that crossed state lines or went to foreign countries. Consequently, local meat packing plants that did not ship to other states or foreign counties were scrutinized by inspectors who were much less rigorous.

Predictably, these plants were "pushing the envelope" of what they could get away with. Noticing this, Congress passed the Wholesome Meat Act of 1967, which required that states have inspection programs "equal to that of the federal government." This would have been bad news for Johnny's employer, but the new law would not come into existence for seven more years. Well before that time the jig was already up, the company had already been shut down, and most of the owners and executives were already several years into their prison terms.

Between 1960 and when they went to prison, Johnny's employers were killing it. The only product they legally produced was a Grade B hamburger paddy.

To understand the egregious nature of the lie perpetrated on the hamburger consuming public by Johnny's meat packing plant, it is helpful to note that hamburger is made from beef which is labeled Prime, Choice, Select, and Standard. At the low end of the scale there is "meat" labeled, utility, cutter, and canner grades. These last three grades are never sold at retail but are used to legally produce; you guessed it, Grade B hamburger and other "processed products." Johnny's employer created an imaginary ladder to the meat-packing basement and produced "hamburger" that was unworthy of any grade whatsoever.

A typical Saturday would start at 6 am. The boys were ordered to march into the freezer to retrieve unlabeled boxes containing miscellaneous cattle parts, which were hidden in the corner under a tarp. These were transported out to the parking lot so the contents could defrost in the sun. When these boxes began to leak blood and emit an odor that can only be characterized as foul, it was time to drag them back into the plant to be processed. There, Tommy and Johnny rolled up their sleeves and took their places along side the ex-cons.

First, they helped open the freshly defrosted boxes of cattle parts (mainly hearts, lungs, livers, and some things that look suspiciously like assholes and sex organs). These were fed into a large grinding machine, which disgorged a huge pile of what the ex-cons were instructed to call "beef product." Then they would retrieve the reground FDA approved Grade B hamburger that had been processed during the week and load it into the machinery along with the "beef product." These two components were then ground together into a horrendously disgusting mass containing every part of a cow except teeth and hooves.

This "modified hamburger" was then smashed back into patties and loaded back into the original Grade B boxes, and then loaded into a couple huge freezer trucks ostensibly for Monday delivery. This all happened on Saturday. Sunday was a "whole nother deal."

Sunday was the highlight of Tommy and Johnny's weekend. They dutifully reported at 6 am to a vacant meat packing plant (the ex-cons had Sundays off). Although they were only forteen, they were allowed to drive fully loaded freezer trucks out into the desert to be "attended to." There were no dash-mounted rear view mirrors and the side view mirrors were mounted so far out they could not adjust them. So, Tommy and Johnny drove 30,000-pound freezer trucks half way to Palm Springs essentially blind. Every once in a while they would pull the overhead strap that activated a very loud bull horn and people would get out of their way (sort of like Richard Pryor's observation "When you're running down the street on fire, people get out of your way!")

When they arrived at a secluded location, they would unload the contents of each truck and spread the boxes out across the prairie for easy access. Then, the sticker on each box, which proclaimed "Grade B Quality Hamburger," was removed and replaced with a new sticker incorrectly (laughably) proclaiming "Grade A Quality Hamburger." This took most of the day in the sweltering heat and although some of the boxes bled out, the trucks were usually reloaded prior to sun down.

Working in a meat packing plant has its drawbacks. Around 1960 the manufacturers of detergent began experimenting with various additives that would take the toughest stains out of soiled clothing. Since the job at the meat packing plant involved a lot of blood sloshing around, Johnny talked his Mom into buying a newly enhanced Tide product that had "active enzymes" (a substance produced by a living organism that acts as a catalyst to bring about a specific biochemical reaction). Unbeknownst to Johnny, he was violently allergic to enzymes. Upon arriving at work the next Saturday, he immediately began to itch all over. By noon he had ballooned to the size of a refrigerator and it was necessary for the ambulance crew to cut his cloths off with a scissors. He was, however, excused for the rest of the day.

They had been told that they would be paid $2 for each hour of work (a princely sum in those days for idiot fourteen-year olds). When pay envelopes were finally distributed, Tommy and Johnny noticed that they were actually paid $1 per hour because an unspecified amount had been deducted for "taxes." When they timidly inquired about the discrepancies, they were brutally reprimanded and ended up trudging through the balance of the summer underpaid and covered in blood.

Then there was the specter of getting caught. The freezer trucks containing the bogus "Grade A" hamburger were sent out on Monday mornings across Southern California. Surprisingly, the truck drivers with this really awful "Grade A" hamburger got away with it for a long time although there were a few complaints about the peculiar smell emitted by patties on the grill.

But one day the feathers hit the fan. As it turned out, the problem could be (and actually was) directly traced back to Tommy and Johnny and their lackluster efforts in swapping labels in the desert. They had reasoned that it was just too much trouble to take off the existing labels and replace them with phony new ones when all they had to do was slap phony ones OVER the real ones. This worked fairly well until they got a little sloppy and started only partially covering real labels.

One of the proprietors of a hamburger establishment taking advantage of the very reasonable prices offered by the meat packer noticed that several of the boxes he received had been relabeled. The truck driver (having been paroled on a manslaughter rap a year earlier) was "shocked and appalled" and promised to get to the bottom of this. The proprietor, not entirely convinced, called the FDA which arrived in force, confiscated the load, and descended on the packing plant.

Tommy and Johnny were fired and the packing plant was shut down. But it was a good thing. They had learned many valuable lessons about being cheated, lied to, and made to do highly questionable work under trying circumstances. But it was all behind them now.

Their efforts to maintain a hamburger free diet lasted for several months.

Chapter 8

Girls League Assembly

Johnny could just not stay out of trouble. He knew enough to surround himself with like-minded people, and high school turned out to be a lot of fun.

There was a flagpole in the middle of the grassy student commons there at Riverside Polytechnic High School, which, owing to a territorial imperative, belonged to whatever class Johnny and the boys happened to be in. They made a point of getting to school early so they could hang around and shoot the breeze. The pole happened to be strategically located next to the main access road and adjacent sidewalk, which curved around and down a steep hill to a parking lot. No one could enter or exit campus without seeing or being seen (which seemed important back then).

It was 1962, and somebody had just figured out that it was possible to put a bottle cap between your fingers, raise it up next to your ear, and SNAP it. The snapping motion imparted a spin to the cap enabling it to fly like a Frisbee (homage must be paid to Fred Morrison who actually invented the first prototype Frisbee by tossing an inverted pie pan on Santa Monica Beach in 1938). At first, five feet was a pretty good bottle cap snap.

Then ten. With a little practice, it became possible to launch a bottle cap twenty feet or more.

This rage hit campus when one guy with too much time on his hands (it should have been Johnny but it was not) pulled a bottle cap out of his pocket and limply sent it out there three or four feet. For everybody standing around watching, it was like that moment in 2001 A Space Odyssey when the gorilla starts tapping the dinosaur skull with a large bone and ends up bashing it to smithereens as the music crescendos and the penny drops.

Johnny looked at his buddy Tommy, and it was a foregone conclusion that right after 6th period they were going to visit every single coke machine in the greater Riverside metropolitan area for the purpose of acquiring an awesome arsenal of bottle caps. It took nearly five hours but they ended up with a garbage bag full of pure gold (approximately thirty pounds worth – Coke, Pepsi, Orange Crush, RC Cola, 7-Up – they had 'em all).

The next day they strolled to the pole early, set the bag down, and waited until everybody had assembled, whereupon the contents were emptied onto the grass. It was as if someone had dumped a wheelbarrow full of quarters and everybody desperately needed lunch money. It was a friggin' frenzy as several dozen testosterone fueled teenagers dove for the treasure. They had a high ol' time, snapping bottle caps in every direction, basically covering the area around the pole to a radius of twenty feet. They then advanced outward, picking up and re-snapping caps to a radius of forty feet, then sixty, until finally the whole place was covered in a sea of bottle caps. Then the bell rang and they went to class.

Shortly after all the students were safely ensconced in first period, Pedro, the school janitor/gardener, fired up the riding mower (among other things) and cut the lawn. The "spoon in the garbage disposal" sound generated by the whirling mower blades as they sliced the bottle caps in half did not bother Pedro who, scrupulously observing the safety manual, was wearing ear muffs and singing to himself.

When the students reappeared for lunch on the commons, it was covered with extremely sharp shards of metal resembling Gillette razor blades. The entire student commons had been rendered a disaster zone, and Johnny and Tommy were starting to feel like the hapless Russian sailor holding on to the steering wheel when the U-Boat captain yelled, "Dah submarine iss ssinking und every boody iss blambing YOU!" This episode earned them each thirty demerits and thirty hours of detention hall (which was tacked on to their already lengthy obligation).

This unfortunately led to more trouble when the detention hall supervisor correctly deduced that the number of hours owed exceeded the number of hours available in a given year. So, he devised an ingenious form of punishment, which did not require his presence - all he had to do was show up on Monday and inspect the results. His brainstorm was to require Johnny and Tommy to report on Saturday morning and paint all the benches on campus green (his favorite color – that guy was weird).

This was bordering on child abuse. There were over a hundred friggin' benches scattered all over campus, which they were expected to paint...green...by Monday. Since they were already hanging by a thread, the boys dutifully showed up on Saturday morning, found the brushes and the paint, and started in.

They reasoned that it would be faster to pour the paint on than it would be to brush it on, so that's what they did. Fortunately, the maintenance shed was stacked to the ceiling with cans of green paint, so they had plenty of material to work with. And that's how it went – they'd throw a can of paint on a bench, smear it around a little with the brushes, and proceed to the next bench. In this way, they were able to paint approximately one hundred benches by noon.

What they didn't know and could not even have guessed, is that paint, when so applied, does not dry. The surface layer fogs up and basically forms a thin leathery outer skin, which seals in the rest of the wet paint below. As they were later informed, it would take weeks for the wet part of the paint to finally dry to a wrinkly mass, rendering all the benches on campus useless during that period, and exceedingly ugly thereafter.

But that Saturday at high noon, stepping back to admire their work, they felt a certain sense of pride and accomplishment for a job well and efficiently done.

They returned on Monday morning to pandemonium. The guys around the pole were fine, since there were no benches there. However, as it turned out, many of the other kids actually used the benches in their areas for sitting. The sitting part was no problem. The getting up part was where it got serious.

As it turns out, when you get up from a bench with wet paint, it adheres to your clothing. Nearly a hundred kids were sent home that morning for a change of clothes. The principal's office was inundated with screaming parents seeking refunds and wondering what the hell was going on. It was a black day for Tommy and Johnny. There was a substantial penalty to pay in demerits and detention time, but they were already so far in the hole it was academic. The principal noted that one more screw up would result in the termination of their high school careers. The thread they hung by was now badly frayed.

They tried to be good. But it was hard. They stood by the pole, watching the kids drive up and down the hill. They inevitably pondered the question - what if you were to take a 55-gallon drum of waste oil and pour it on the curve and down the steep part of the road leading to the parking lot? It would be a kind of science experiment. Perhaps they could get extra credit.

Tommy and Johnny actually found such a drum around midnight behind the Standard Oil Station on Main Street, and drove straight to campus to deposit the contents in strategic locations. It was hilarious to watch all those cars spin on the turn and continue sideways and backwards (some did 360's) all the way to the bottom. No one was hurt or killed, property damage was minimal, and they never found out who did it, although the Principal had his suspicions.

It was calm for several weeks (the calm before the storm) until somebody from the administration made an announcement over the loud speakers, "This year's Girl's League Assembly will be bigger and better than ever before – girls, mark your calendars." The hair on Johnny's neck stood up.

Every year one day was set-aside for the girls. There was a big assembly in the auditorium to which the boys were not invited. The girls, who were deprived of just about everything else, cherished this special day. The female teachers (come to think of it, except for Mr. Pyle in wood shop and the athletic coaches, ALL the teachers were female) spent months preparing for this glorious event. And it was all a big mystery since the girls would not reveal to the boys what it was that went on in that sacred and secret assemblage.

This struck Johnny as just plain wrong, so he floated a rhetorical question to the guys standing around the pole that went something like, "What if some guys dressed up as girls and went to that assembly?" The straight A students, kiss ups and wimps all looked at the ground. But Johnny noticed there were about a half dozen ne're-do-wells looking at the sky, pondering with fingers on their chins.

It was a suicide mission, and they all knew it. But still they came forward – Tommy, Bob,

Glen, Brian, and Charlie (who once called the English teacher Daddy-o). The others just shook their heads and melted away – they wanted no part of this.

So, the Suicide Six met that evening at Charlie's house, and developed operational details. Since Johnny's Grandmother was over six feet tall and built like Hulk Hogan, he would be responsible for clothing. Glen was in charge of melons for the braziers. Tommy had cosmetics. Bob was on wig detail. Brian and Charlie were responsible for mapping assault and retreat routes, respectively. In hindsight, they never should have put Charlie in charge of how to get out of there. But, as it turned out, it didn't matter.

The week leading up to the Assembly was fraught with peril and excitement. If the plan leaked, they would be screwed. The girls were ecstatic that they had something to lord over the boys "Nyah, nyah, you can't go" and the like. Boy, did they rub it in. But Tommy, Bob, Glen, Brian, Charlie, and Johnny stoically took it in, knowing that the Girls League Assembly was, at last, going to be "penetrated," the secrets would be revealed, and they were the guys who were going to do it.

The day came a lot sooner than they expected. They were learning one of life's lessons early -

it is one thing to think about doing something, another thing entirely to do it. There was a little bit of angst and the boys had that Michael Corleone look (like in the Godfather when Michael returns from the bathroom with the gun and sits there waiting to make his move).

The Assembly was scheduled to start promptly at 10 am. At 9:30 the boys moonwalked out of class and rendezvoused at Tommy's car. There, they retrieved several suitcases loaded with everything they would need and headed up the back way to the auditorium. At 9:45 they reached the boys bathroom, where they stripped down and suited up. As they were peering into the mirrors applying lipstick and rouse, Pedro, the school janitor/gardener, walked in.

The boys froze. Johnny knew that Pedro had taken a ration of shit for mowing the lawn that day with all those bottle caps, and that forgiveness was probably not on the top of his list. So, there they were, looking into the mirror at Pedro's reflection, wigs askew, lipstick poised, melons hanging out over the sinks, waiting for the hammer to fall.

God bless Pedro. He started laughing like a hyena (there was a reason for this – he was high as a kite). Apparently figuring that the boys were part of a skit for the Assembly, he wished them well, and headed back out the door. Their hearts were pounding.

With minutes to spare, they filed out of the boys room in ones and twos, doing their best to blend in with the horde of girls streaming into the auditorium. Part of the assault plan was to break up into small units and sit at random locations so, if something went wrong, only some of them and not all of them would get mowed down by the powers that be.

This was an excellent strategy as far as it went. There were, however, two problems. First among these was that the boys were the most bizarre looking girls in the world, which is to say, they stood out. Secondly, what they did not know and had not figured on was that women in general, and high school girls in particular, apparently have some sort of invisible radar which enables them to pick up on seemingly innocuous situations, such as boys dressed up as bizarre looking girls.

They had not been seated for more than a few minutes before a wave of recognition swept the auditorium. The timing could not have been worse since Ms. Sawyer (the unmarried spinster senior teacher whose entire life revolved around this moment) launched into the welcoming speech she had been working on for the past several months.

Girls were staring, girls were screaming, girls were laughing, girls were peeing. The whole place came apart. It was like a series of explosions. Each time another cell of interlopers was identified there was a crescendo of screaming, laughing, and whatever.

Ms. Sawyer was sobbing and the other ladies on stage were yelling "SHUT UP, SHUT UP," pointing fingers and shaking fists – some were just shaking. Several dozen teachers stepped over Ms. Sawyer, who was now lying on the floor in front of the microphone, and streamed into the audience. Help was called. The Principal, Vice Principal, and all male employees (except for Mr. Pyle who had caught his hand in the jig saw and Pedro who had been arrested for possession of marijuana) appeared in mass to administer the coup de grace. It was sort of like a pig hunt, where you get cornered by the dogs until the hunter saunters up and puts one through your eye.

They were dragged by their necks up the aisles and out of the auditorium – there was laughter and applause, but it was lost on the boys as they contemplated their fate.

The Girls League Assembly had been ruined, Ms. Sawyer would retire early, Pedro was fired and they had to air the auditorium out for several days.

It looked pretty bleak. But Johnny had an ace up his sleeve. The Principal of Riverside Polytechnic High School was Mr. Wrentmore. His son, who coincidentally was attending Poly and unbeknownst to his father had fallen in with a bad crowd, was Bob. Bob's mother, Mrs. Wrentmore, had an extensive collection of wigs and was wondering at that moment where they were.

And so, when the boys were lined up before the principal, he did a double take when he realized that standing before him as if he belonged among all these idiots, was his son in a dress and his wife's favorite wig. Thus insulated, the boys hoped that justice would be administered evenly, and that whatever they got Bob was gonna get too, so maybe there was an outside chance at leniency.

Mr. Wrentmore was so bent he was unable to mete out an instantaneous sentence. Deep down, he may have shared some sense of male pride in the caper, but he did not let on. His lecture that day went on for approximately an hour. It consisted of threats and bluster, homosexual insinuations and discussions of permanent black marks and ruined careers. When he had run out of things to say, he told them all to go home and await his decision.

But an interesting and unexpected thing happened. The girls came to their defense. Not just some of the girls, but most of the girls. A large female contingent was on hand the next day to plead for leniency. Mr. Wrentmore, apparently sensing a way out for his son, relented. The final verdict was one week of suspension and one hundred demerits, a small price to pay.

Things were looking up!

Chapter 9

Woodie

It was 1962 and the surf craze was sweeping the nation, or at least the West Coast of it. Johnny lived in Riverside, California which is approximately fifty miles from the beach which was a friggin' long way to go to get in the water. The first Surfer Magazine had been published and when it arrived, he stayed up all night reading it, looking at the pictures, and fantasizing about taking the drop at Makaha or Sunset Beach – sometimes till dawn when his good buddy Wags would bang on the window and tell him to "Get up, we're going surfing!"

Johnny had gotten a jump-start on the whole thing by discovering surfing at an early age when his parents took the family to the beach for summer vacations. By the time the other kids took notice of the sport, Johnny was already out there doin' it.

The uniform of the day was a plaid Pendleton long sleeve shirt, Levi's, and black high-top Ked tennis shoes (these things were actually very uncomfortable since the soles were just a slab of hard rubber and the black high tops absorbed the sun's rays and made your feet sweat).

Blond hair was in and the guys and girls who actually had it were admired. The rest of 'em turned to Peroxide which would scorch the crap outta your scalp and turn your hair into unpredictable colors of green, orange, or yellow depending on how much you used and how long you could stand to leave it on.

Johnny's decision to "go blond" had been perversely influenced by the swim coach who advised "Anybody bleaching their hair over spring break is off the team." Johnny pondered this for several minutes. On the one hand, as a surfer he was cannon fodder since very few of the other school kids were able to swim long distances. This meant that Johnny and his surf buddies were forced to swim both the 200 and the 400-yard sprints since nobody else would or could. Unfortunately, the way the swim meets were set up, the 400 immediately followed the 200. So, by the time you finished 600 yards, you were puking your guts out and gasping for air. On the other hand, if he got kicked off the team, he would no longer have to get into the proverbial cannon. This had a certain appeal. Also, chicks seemed to dig blonde hair. So, there it was.

The guys assembled on the beach (T Street in Laguna Beach) at high noon, peroxide in hand. They poured it on, rubbed it in, and sat there in the sun as wisps of smoke wafted off the top of their heads and the skin on their hands turned white and sloughed off. Johnny may have overdone it. The root damage inflicted in conjunction with this process probably had more to do than genes with his baldness in later life.

The results, however, were spectacular. Fourteen surfers with really blonde hair reported for swim practice Monday following Spring Break, and fourteen surfers went to the showers early and for the last time. Coincidentally, the Riverside Polytechnic High School Swim Team plunged to last place in the Inland Empire rankings, where they stayed for the rest of the school year.

The Beach Boys had gotten together a few months before and were doing little gigs here and there. One of the guys involved in the planning for the Junior Prom contacted them to see if they would be willing to drive all the way out to Riverside to play. They allowed as how they would if the money was right. In this way, the Beach Boys played at Poly High's Junior Prom exposing a whole room full of kids to the surfer sound. It was a gas. Later that night, as Johnny and the guys were driving around looking for something to do, the Beach Boys pulled up in a bitchin' 49 Ford Woodie. Brian Wilson leaned out the window and yelled "Which way to the Beach?" It was a classic moment. The Beach Boys followed them to the freeway entrance, waived and were gone. The next time they would see them in person was thirty years later at Aloha Stadium where they played live before 50,000 fans.

What stuck in Johnny's mind was that bitchin' woodie. Gawd, that thing just exuded "surfer." A woodie is basically a station wagon where the rear bodywork is made of wood. The vast majority of woodies were produced before the end of the 1950's at which time safety regulations and changing automotive fashions meant the effective end of that style.

A regular car in those days generally had a wood or metal frame onto which they bolted aluminum or steel panels which then had to be fitted, finished, and painted. Woodies, on the other hand, didn't need the panels so they were way cheaper to build. Railway stations started to use them to haul luggage, hence the name, station wagon.

US woodies (the Europeans were makin' 'em too but they were wussy imitations) were large and powerful but not very luxurious. By the 1960's most people thought woodies were undesirable and unfashionable. California surfers, on the other hand, realized the potential of these cars - they were cheap, large enough to carry lots of people and surfboards, and could be fixed up with the type of basic skills you'd learn in woodshop. Thus, the woodie became the archetypal surfer vehicle, and The Beach Boys would later refer to them in many of their songs.

Johnny had to have one. There were two problems – he had no money and his parents would disown him if he went against their wishes and got a car (he was supposed to be studying). Nevertheless, he scoured the want ads daily and, in the back of his feeble surfer mind, devised a plan that would enable him to raise cash without having to rob a bank AND avoid having to tell his parents of his gross misbehavior.

And then one day, buried in the classifieds was a simple one liner, "'48 Mercury Woodie for sale cheap – needs work." Johnny responded immediately, and an hour later was standing in the back of this old guy's barn looking at a real live woodie. It was in pretty sad shape, covered with dust, flat tires, and rotting wood. But by gawd it was a woodie and Johnny knew he must have it. He would find out later how really bad it was, but in that moment, he didn't even care if the thing was missing an engine, it was going to be his.

Johnny, "How much do you want for it?"

Owner, "How much you got?"

Johnny, "I don't have anything right now but I think I can get my hands on.... $25."

"Sold!" That was all there was to it.

So, he implemented his scheme to produce wealth out of thin air by basically going around school the next day begging for money (which he falsely promised to pay back). Surprisingly, kids started giving him nickels and dimes. As he got closer to the goal, he was even getting the occasional dollar bill. In a half day he collected $26. He immediately bought the woodie and put a dollar's worth of gas in the tank and air in the tires.

It was complicated, however. He couldn't take the thing home cause his folks would freak. So, he took it to Tommy's and the two of 'em worked through the afternoon to spruce the ol' girl up. He could not raise suspicion with his parents that he was even THINKING of getting a car, so mum's the word. That evening, the phone at his folk's house rang off the hook with "investors" seeking a ride in "Johnny's woodie." When he came home later, he knew by the look on his parents' faces that his goose was cooked. There was a lot of hand wringing and stern lectures, and his Mom even teared up at one point. In the end Johnny had to promise to sell the thing at the earliest possible moment.

He got to drive it around a little the next day, and while attempting a right turn on Magnolia was surprised to see the right rear tire and axle pull away (along with some break lines and other mechanical devices) and wobble down the road on its own separate path. He came to an embarrassing halt with the help of the rear bumper which gouged a huge rut in the asphalt. Surprisingly, he was able to jack it up, push the axel back in and drive away. He made it all the way to Tommy's house on left turns only.

One of his "investors" came by that night and gave him $20 for it. But it was OK – Johnny had owned a woodie for a day, and she had been a beauty.

Post Script –

Fifty-nine years later Johnny still yearns for one. This summer, he plans to fly over to Huntington Beach and pick up a brand-new custom job with a blown injected 502 cubic inch Chevy big block, tuck and roll leather, fire engine red fenders and satin finished oak. That's what Johnny's talkin' about!

Chapter 10

Menlo College

Johnny had not really been concentrating on his studies. It was just too much fun hanging out with his buddies and wasting time. At school, he realized that all ya needed to do to matriculate was put one foot in front of the other, sit in the back of the room, and keep your head down. So, he was on cruise control, watching it all go by but not really taking a lot in.

By the summer of 1962, he had just finished his junior year in high school. It was clear to his parents they'd better do something to enhance his chances of getting into college or he'd end up living on the couch. So, in a stroke of genius, they decided to send him far away for the whole friggin' summer to a place called Menlo College. This was considered the "back door" to Stanford (for unknown reasons which may have had to do with reciprocal expectations of generous institutional support). Their hope was that the penny would drop and Johnny would become a serious student (riiiiiiiight).

This was both complicated and painful since Johnny had recently taken up with a sweet young thing named Nancy. Unfortunately, she was pure as the driven snow and some kind of fanatical religious person (Catholic), so he wasn't getting any, although he tried every Friday night to no avail. He sensed that he might be wearing her down, and if he just had some more time, he might be able to advance a couple bases. Just as things were looking up, June came, school was over, and the folks stuffed Johnny in the car and drove him 500 miles to Menlo College just down the peninsula from San Francisco. What he didn't know but would have surmised if he had read the brochure is that Menlo College is for men (boys) only. That is to say, there are no girls. What a gyp.

Actually, it wasn't so bad. For one thing, a majority of the guys there were in pretty much the same boat – under achievers who just needed a source of ignition to take off (or so their parents thought). There were a few guys who had that blank stare (like when you look into a cow's eyes). But most of the kids were just like him, full of fun and lookin' for a good time.

Over that summer Johnny was the beneficiary of a number of extraordinary first experiences. These can be loosely grouped into the following categories:

Pool
Combustible Farts
Muscles

Self-Awareness
Homosexuality
Cigarettes
Booze
Sex

Pool – There was a really big pool table in the student commons. The friggin' thing was huge – it looked like a tennis court with legs, all green and felty with these bitchin' leather pockets and ivory balls (somewhere an elephant was short a tusk). It didn't take more than a few hours after arrival to make this discovery. Fortunately, helpful fellow students who already knew the game were more than happy to teach Johnny how to wield a cue, and within a few weeks he actually started winning his money back. He found he could wile away many hours a day here working on his hand/eye coordination and pool became a pleasant diversion. By the end of summer, he was a stone cold pool shark, and could hardly wait to get back home to teach HIS buddies and take THEIR money.

Combustible Farts – The way the dorms were set up was two men (kids) to a room with six rooms in a wing. You got to know everybody within a few days, and the mob seemed to rotate from one room to another for intellectual conversation (bull sessions). In one of these rooms there was a wild and crazy guy named Willy who postulated that it was possible to light farts on fire. Everybody else said he was out of his mind. It turned out he was pretty smart after all, cause he bet everyone in the room a dollar that he could prove his theory – eleven guys, eleven dollars. Incredulous, they all crowded around as Willy worked up a good one, pulled down his pants, fired up a Zippo, and held it near his ass. They were startled to see a jet of blue-green flame perhaps two feet long leap from his rectum under pressure. He fell forward and lay on the floor as the hair on his ass sizzled. It was worth a dollar for the floorshow and the wisdom that came with learning about the flammable properties of methane gas.

Muscles – There was a weight room in the gym full of all kinds of equipment including a lot of free weights (bar bells and such). Out of the whole student body that summer, there was one guy who was into bodybuilding. Johnny had the misfortune of walking into the gym when that guy was there. He had kind of a hard edge and, in retrospect, weight lifting was probably his only talent. It turned out he was a bit of a sadist as well, since he goaded Johnny into one weight lifting contest after another, knowing the final outcome. Unbeknownst to Johnny, the way you get big muscles is to tear the livin' shit out of little muscles and, when they mend, the scar tissue makes 'em bigger. So, Johnny and this sadist mo' fo' were pumping every kind of weight as many times as possible to complete physical exhaustion. Looking in the mirror at the end of that session, Johnny thought to himself "Jeez, my muscles DO look bigger." He did not realize that the blood from thousands of torn muscles had engorged just about every part of his body, but particularly his biceps, which now resembled over inflated balloons. He was unable to lift or bend his arms for the next several days. In fact, he remained in bed in a stationary position and came close to getting bedsores. Another valuable lesson learned.

Self-Awareness – His folks insisted that he work his way through the summer, so he took a job in the cafeteria. It was hard work but, in a way, kind of rewarding. The manager would remark favorably on his performance from time to time, and he lapped it up since these were, perhaps, the first encouraging words he had ever received from someone in authority. He washed dishes, mopped floors, cleaned tables, and performed any other task necessary to pick up after 500 dinners three times a day. He found that he could do this cheerfully with a sense of purpose. Instead of just wandering around in a daze, he felt like maybe he was doing something worthwhile. And he noticed that while he was working, experiencing some vague form of fulfillment and earning money, his classmates were all hanging around in the parking lot goofing off.

He started to think that maybe working was better than goofing – the penny had dropped.

Homosexuality – He had never even HEARD of a homosexual person before, so it came as quite a shock to find that some of his professors were mahus (Hawaiian for homosexual). At first, he didn't know what to make of their demeanor or the weird topics they discussed in class, but his dorm mates filled him in. According to them, it's the quality or characteristic of being sexually attracted solely to people of one's own sex. This seemed a little strange to Johnny, but he began to vaguely understand by virtue of his observations there in the sweltering classroom. Apparently, in addition to the professor there were a few students who also broadly fit into this category. The topics of conversation (homo sapiens, Vikings, and nude sun bathing) seemed to illicit a different response from this group. He also noticed that the professor paid more attention to them and had a tendency to grade their papers on a higher scale than Johnny or the rest of his classmates could achieve. The idea of missing out on being attracted to the opposite sex seemed like you'd be losing out on a lot of fun. On the other hand, this would reduce competition and increase opportunities for the rest of us. In the end, Johnny developed his own perspective on the issue, which is "Whatever floats your boat."

Cigarettes – Unfiltered Chesterfield Kings. That was the brand he would become addicted to. In those days, just about every Hollywood star smoked like a chimney, and almost every film glorified the smoke ring. Johnny was there approximately ten minutes before his new roommate offered him a smoke. Not wanting to appear prudish, he took one, smoked it down until his fingers blistered, then asked for another (he was pretty dizzy by this time). Pretty soon they were pooling their allowances so the guy with the most chest hair could slide on down to the corner market and get a few cartons. Johnny was a three pack a day man in no time. He could take a drag, inhale down to his shoes, and exhale pretty much nothing but clean air. All that smoke, all those carcinogens, all that nicotine stayed right there in his lungs. It got to where he didn't know what to do with his hands if he didn't have a cigarette to fiddle with. He would dangle one off his lips at night when he was supposed to be studying, and squint through the smoke as it curled up into his eyes – it was impossible to read under these conditions but it seemed somehow cool in a James Deanie sort of way. He smelled like a paper mill in August. He spent just about all the money he had on cigarettes (this is back when cigarettes were $0.25 per pack – the good ol' days), which didn't leave much left over for anything else. And then, abruptly and without warning, summer was over and it was time to go home.

Johnny got to thinking "Oh shit, I can't go home and light up in front of my folks – they'll disown me." Deep down he knew the reason he really couldn't continue smoking is that he would disappoint his parents who would know then for sure that he was an idiot. So, on that last evening at Menlo College, he had his last unfiltered Chesterfield King – GAWD it was good! And then he found out what it must be like to stop shooting heroin after a three-month binge. Holy shit, the craving was unbelievable – if he could just have one more cigarette, but no, he didn't dare. It took almost a year before he was free of the yearning. Another lesson learned – don't smoke and for Pete's sake don't do heroin.

Booze – Of course you have to experiment with booze. His previous experience was pretty much limited to working up enough nerve to take a swig outta the folks bourbon stash. Later, his Mom would stock a second refrigerator in the garage with beer (she loved that Coors beer) from which he would partake freely every Friday night. They had a tacit agreement – he could have as much beer as he wanted as long as he didn't rat Mom out for how much beer she was drinkin' during the day. But that was later. Now, here at Menlo, it was all pretty new. So, they would pay some wino to stagger into the liquor store and get 'em some beer, and then they would go down to the park and consume it with gusto. There's some pretty disgusting beer out there, but they tried 'em all anyway, with predictable results. He learned he liked flopping around in a state of delirium, but he definitely did not like feeling the way he did the next morning. By the end of the summer he had intoxication and hangovers down pat (not really).

Sex – Of course, no summer odyssey would be complete without sex. In this case, Johnny's first. Him and this other guy Phil across the hall resolved that, no matter what, they were gonna get laid. So, one evening, they steeled themselves with a few beers, then hopped in Phil's car (Johnny was not only clueless but carless as well), and headed for San Francisco. Actually, they headed for Oakland thinking that their chances of finding a sporting woman would be amplified in reverse proportion to the socio-economic strata of the neighborhood in which they might find themselves.

Holy smokes, they found some pretty seedy neighborhoods. And, as luck would have it, an aging brother with a curly white goatee was sitting out in front of a dangerous looking bar when they drove by. He gave 'em a nod, waived 'em over and said, "You boys lookin' for a little pussy?"

BINGO! He disappeared into the bar and a few minutes later emerged with the hottest looking black girl either of them had ever seen. She said, "Hi, I'm Shaquilla - you boys wanna come to my place?"

DOUBLE BINGO! So Shaquilla and the pimp with the goatee got in the back and they cruised around Oakland. Subconsciously, Phil and Johnny were waiting for somebody back there to pull out a forty-five and start blazing. Fortunately they were a pretty happy group (read stoned) and had no interest in gun play or mass murder for a couple skinny wallets. They exchanged pleasantries until they found Shaquilla's house. As they walked in Shaquilla said, "Who's first?"

HOT DOG! Since Phil was a year older and it was his car, he got to go first while Johnny and the goatee man chatted idly, trying to ignore the grunts and groans coming from the bedroom. Five minutes later Phil comes out with a shit-eating grin and says, "It's your turn."

THIS IS IT! Johnny walks in and there's Shaquilla layin' naked on the bed, lookin' real good. She says, "Come on ova here." The next thing he knew he was starring in his own porn movie, so to speak. Pretty soon Shaquilla is screaming "DO IT, DO IT, DO IT" and Johnny is giving it his all. The guy with the goatee was probably getting nervous, particularly when she started flat out screaming "OOOOOOHHHH, OOOOOHHHHH, OOOOOHHHH MY GAWD." Ol' Shaquille was shakin' like a leaf. Johnny held on tight for an extra few minutes, and finally collapsed into a pool of extraneous bodily fluids.

After Shaquilla caught her breath, she looked up at Johnny and said, "Yo betta get yo sef a girlfriend." Wiser words were never spoken.

Chapter 11

Motorcycle

Johnny's first encounter with a motorcycle occurred in 1963 – it was glorious. It belonged to one of the guys at school who fell somewhere on the outer fringes of the greaser crowd (those who got to take auto and wood shop instead of freeking calculus and chemistry). But this guy, Jerry, was cool in a Fonzie sort of way. Johnny, your basic surfer ner' do well, would never have guessed that they would, in the course of their senior year, become friends.

There may have been some sort of mutual admiration (both distant and denied) between surfers and greasers. The mere idea of taking an engine apart, actually understanding how it works, and then putting it back together again was astounding, probably (to a lesser degree) what frolicking in the ocean might have been for a non-swimmer. There was also a sort of begrudging admiration for the guys who actually got to have fun in high school building things vs. getting headaches from quadratic equations.

About the only time that surfers and greasers intermingled was gym class since everybody was thrown together and required to behave (or "No Diploma For YOU!"). So, the beach bums and greasers formed a team. And to everyone's surprise, they found that they could not only get along, but their counterparts from another world were actually pretty good guys. And Jerry was one of them.

Somewhere along the line, they actually spoke to each other. It is not known who made the first effort to communicate. To this day, they will probably say it was the other guy. But words were spoken. Maybe it was something as simple as "hike" or "throw the friggin' ball," but it was tangible communication nonetheless. It took a while, several weeks, as they appraised one another from a distance, circling cautiously like pit bulls eyeing a turkey sandwich.

But as they got to know one another, they found that neither was the demon the other had thought. In fact, it was just like talking to a regular person. They would still just faintly raise their eyebrows in acknowledgment as they passed in the halls so as not to raise suspicion among the others in their respective gangs, but on the playing field they got along, finding themselves on the same team frequently, and frequently winning.

And then one day Jerry simply said, "I got a new motorcycle."

Johnny said, "Get out of town!"

Jerry said, "No, really."

Johnny replied, "You're putting me on!"

Jerry said, "Well, if you don't believe me, why don't you come over Sunday and I'll show ya."

These few sentences far exceeded their entire historical repartee. Not only that, but the words were uplifting and laden with promise.

Sunday finally came and Johnny rode across town on his Schwin. It was totally embarrassing to be a senior in high school and be stuck on a Schwin. Normally, he would hitch a ride with one of his buddies or, in a pinch, walk. But it was a long way across town and none of his buddies were going that way.

So, he rolled up to Jerry's house and, just as he was stashing his bike in the bushes so no one would be the wiser, Jerry rolled out of his garage on a brand-new Triumph dirt bike (gawd, it was beautiful) and said, "Follow me to the hills." In those days, there weren't a lot of houses around and the hills were pretty much everywhere you looked, so it wasn't too much of a peddle and Jerry went mercifully slow.

And then he saw something he could not have imagined. Jerry cranked the throttle back, the engine screamed, the rear wheel dug in and he climbed ten or twelve feet straight up the side of a mound, pausing at the top for a moment, then gliding straight down the other side.

It was friggin' fantastic. It was a revelation. It was like surfing in the dirt. It was to become a whole new chapter in Johnny's life – in fact, many chapters. It would impact both his health and his well-being. He would break a few bones and visit the hospital many times (where he became known as "a frequent flyer"). Later in life he would walk with a slight limp and could not wear Levi 501 jeans with the button fly because his broken thumbs caused him to look like Joe Cocker on acid in the men's room at the movie theater when he tried to button up.

But it was a small price to pay, for he would derive extreme pleasure in pegging the throttle, flying through the air and basically defying gravity at will. It became a parallel universe to surfing, and he would ultimately spend nearly thirty years of Sundays "surfing in the dirt."

That day Johnny would just watch as Jerry did wheelies, roared up impossibly steep hills, and got airborne off the tops of smaller ones.

But on other Sundays, Jerry would let him take the bike out (under close supervision), and Johnny quickly got the hang of it.

They continued shredding the hillsides through the summer. But when September came, Johnny went off to college and Jerry stayed behind to work in his dad's garage. They never saw each other again, but Jerry knew he had launched his weird surfer pal in a whole new direction, and Johnny was forever grateful.

Chapter 12

Cal Western - Introduction

Johnny arrived at college in September of '63. In the first month he burned through two potential roommates before a "long hauler" showed up. His name was Bill Tucker and they shared the same dorm room for the full length of Johnny's stay, which was a remarkably short one and a half years.

The College they found themselves in was called Cal Western University, a small nondescript campus off to one side of San Diego on a barren peninsula called Point Loma. They had been thrown together by serendipity and an overriding concern on the part of their parents that they be protected from the larger State and Private Colleges where freethinking and wild parties might negatively impact the learning experience.

It was hilarious, then that they should end up at Cal Western with all those other bored and uninspired sons and daughters from modestly wealthy families. For one thing, the college was built on a bluff overlooking the Pacific Ocean and one of the finest surf breaks in Southern California whose name is so sacred it dare not be mentioned here (Newbreak). For another, it was only twenty miles from Tijuana (that pretty much sums that up). And finally, what you had was a critical mass of wild and crazy teenagers amping on their newly found freedom, ripe for experimentation and fully versed in the art of making their own fun.

Johnny had picked up on the potential of this place immediately upon disembarking from the car. His parents had taken him on a gawd awful but well-intentioned trip around Southern California to visit college campuses, which, in their view, would be "appropriate" for their son who they worried a lot about (rightly so and for good reason). You should have seen those places - some so small you could fit the entire student body in one bus, some so religious you could almost hear the choir singing, some so remote it would have taken an hour to walk to the nearest bar, and (if you can believe this), some with no girls.

So, when he looked around at the panoramic view of the Pacific Ocean, the new buildings strewn across the hilltop, and the pretty girls passing by giggling, he knew he had found his college.

But this was a delicate matter. He could not be seen to exhibit undue enthusiasm for this would surely raise suspicion which might well result in his being sent off to some other college which would likely have been small, religious, remote, and male. So, recalling a fable from his youth, he pulled the ol' "please don't throw me in that briar patch" routine, and son of a gun, it worked!

His father later informed him that, after due consideration and notwithstanding his objections, his mother and he had determined that Cal Western was the best and only option for him, and that he should fill out and mail his application right away. YES!

Although he did dutifully fill out the application, he put it in a drawer and forgot to mail it (out of sight, out of mind). The folks would periodically ask if he'd received any word to which Johnny would respond in the negative. They were incredulous, since the fix was already in – they had pledged their undying support to the appropriate university officials, who were delighted to accept another marginal student in return for what looked like a down the road bonus and possibly a new library wing.

With only a few weeks to go, Johnny, without having applied, received an acceptance letter from Cal Western. University officials would later rue this day, but it was too late now - the rat had hit the cheese without regard for the trap.

So, the folks delivered Johnny to the dorm on the appointed day, and gave him a generous check, which they said was his allowance for the semester, noting that he was now in an excellent position to acquire the skill of "budgeting."

He wandered to his room and was there confronted by a crazy person. He was some random guy who had been assigned by the administration in its infinite wisdom to that room and who, as theory goes, was supposed to live with Johnny for the school year.

He does not remember this guy's name (we'll call him Gonzo). He was a basket case from the get go. He had never been away from home, apparently had never had a friend (and certainly not a girlfriend), did not know what to do, and basically didn't have a clue. It was clear in the first three minutes that this guy was not going to make it. But Johnny made every effort to bring him out of his shell, taking him on a tour of the campus which terrified him, sitting with him at the cafeteria where he could not or would not eat the food, and volunteering to turn off the lights which met with hysterical rejection since he needed them on "to preserve my sanity."

The next day Johnny hitched a ride into town to look at some used mopeds that a rental place was selling cheap (his check for the semester would just about cover it). On the way back (on his new used moped), he passed

Gonzo heading down the hill toward the harbor with a wild look in his eyes. Johnny's loony roomy did not return that night, nor the next day – in fact he was never seen again. The evening paper had a small article about an apparently insane person who untied several dozen boats at the yacht club and pushed them out into the bay where they crashed into one another repeatedly and for some time. Damage was estimated in the hundreds of thousands. No mention was made of his disposition.

While Johnny was at class, somebody retrieved Gonzo's belongings and another guy moved in. His name was Willy Wildman and he was late to the party, having spent the first few days of the new school year skiing in Aspen (his story was he "missed the train"). Willy was a really fun guy and his last name perfectly described his demeanor. He was definitely a wild man. He loved to drink, smoke, carouse, and get in trouble (Johnny's kinda guy). Unfortunately, Willy only lasted three weeks.

The circumstances of his demise were these: He met a girl. He asked her out. She said yes. Willy returned to the dorm room to change. He couldn't open the door.

It is important to elaborate on why the door would not open. The older guys in the dorm were always playing pranks on the freshmen. Somebody discovered that it was possible to pull out the built-in drawers and lay them end-to-end across the room from the far window wall to the door. Amazingly, they fit perfectly and if you dropped the last drawer on your way out, it would be impossible to open the door, which swung inward.

Willy, frantic to pick up his new girlfriend, lost it. That is to say he chose the most immediate path conceptually available to solve the problem. This turned out to be the firebox on the hallway wall, which contained both a hose and an axe (a big axe). While Johnny might have chosen the hose, taken it up to the next floor, slid down and busted in through the window (nobody would be the wiser), Willy chose the axe.

A fairly large crowd gathered as Willy turned the door into firewood, slapped on a clean shirt, and presented himself to his date (only fifteen minutes late). The police and fire department were called, Willy was apprehended upon his return to the dorm at 6 am, and by 6:02 he had been expelled. There goes roommate number two.

As coincidence would have it, his third and final roommate appeared the next day. His name was Bill Tucker but everyone would know him as "Tucker." He was mildly curious about the door as he explained his reason for being a month late to college – he had been on a surf trip! (No, really!)

Johnny liked this guy right away. A fellow surfer and all-around wild man, they were meant to be roomies. The University administration had unwittingly committed another colossal blunder – they had put too much plutonium in the bomb.

They quickly scoped out the other surfers in the dorm who, like themselves, could not believe their good fortune at having been consigned to this place over looking, dare we say it (Newbreak) and the rest of the Pacific Ocean. They quickly realized that newcomers (freshmen) were relegated to Mountain View rooms on lower floors, and set about to correct this injustice.

It was the great misfortune (and first mistake) of Abdul Azziz, an unfriendly senior foreign exchange student from Saudi Arabia, to occupy the end room on the top floor next to the fire escape overlooking you know what (Newbreak). They approached him first in a congenial manner, asking what it would take to exchange rooms. He mumbled something about "filthy infidels" and waived them off. That was his second mistake. Since he was a very obnoxious guy, he would be afforded no further civilized opportunities.

That night, one of the surfers noticed it was a full moon and mentioned that the grunion might run. Grunions are a type of small silver fish that live off the California coast and are notable for the regularity with which they come ashore to spawn under a full moon. Johnny had seen them once before many years earlier while lying on a beach at midnight with a fair maiden. It was quite a sight since they came by the thousands, slithering up the beach to deposit their eggs. He had picked one up to examine it (it smelled a little fishy) and released it back to the herd.

Johnny looked at Tucker, Tucker looked at Johnny, and, finishing the gallon of Red Mountain Vin Rose they had smuggled in earlier (the only wine apparently made without the benefit of grapes), they assembled the crew. Equipped with buckets, shovels, and rakes purloined from the maintenance building, they headed down the hill to a secret stretch of beach (Newbreak). They were rewarded with the biggest grunion run in the history of California. There were millions of 'em. It was a receding tide, the beach was fully exposed, and they were flopping around three deep as far as the eye could see.

They worked most of the night collecting the fish and putting them in buckets at first, then pillow cases, trash cans, wheel barrows, a stretcher donated by a student nurse, and finally into several large open sand pits above the high-water line. By day break, they had collected approximately six (maybe seven) thousand pounds of grunion.

By now Abdul had gone to class and the fatwa had commenced in earnest. When the other kids found out what was going down, it was as if a pharaoh had decided to build a pyramid in a day and required all hands-on deck. The line stretched nearly a quarter mile from the beach to the dorm, and the fish, every last one of 'em, were passed along all the way up to Abdul's room. When the pile, now beginning to ripen, covered the floor to five feet, they realized they had a rare opportunity to fill an entire dorm room with fish, and possibly set a new Guinness World Record in the process.

Approximately half the student body worked throughout the morning and, by noon, the last fish was slipped over the top of the door before it was inexorably closed by the weight of what lay within. Then everybody split.

It is not known how Abdul reacted when he could not open <u>his</u> door (the administration had removed both the hose and the axe from the fire box). What is known is that the maintenance crew ultimately had to retrieve the fire axe and later produced a rather large chain saw to gain entry. The fish, now capable of inflicting severe damage nostril-wise, spewed out into the hallway and down the fire escape. It was, apparently, beautiful.

Abdul got the message and was not seen on campus thereafter. He went on to become a prominent figure in Saudi Arabian history, and is rumored to have been the co-founder of an anti-American organization, which later evolved into a politically active group called Al Qaeda.

Johnny and Tucker bravely volunteered to move into the newly vacated dorm room. Since no one else could stand the smell, their request was granted. It took about two weeks and twenty gallons of Lysol to get the place back in shape, but from then on it was smooth sailing.

Oh my, what will we do now?

Chapter 13

Cal Western – Intoxication

Well, let's begin with Johnny's first encounter with complete and utter intoxication. He and Tony Dean, one of the guys down the hall, thought it might be a good idea to get a gallon of Red Mountain – EACH – and see what would happen.

The experiment commenced in the house a dozen of them had rented in Mission Beach, a few miles down the road from the campus. They were good until about three-fourths of the vino had been consumed and their blood alcohol level reached double digits. It was then they realized they were blind drunk and needed a little air.

So, they staggered out onto the boardwalk and weaved along until Johnny noticed a sweet young thing peering out a picture window at them. Naturally, he dropped his nearly empty gallon jug and crawled head first through the bathroom window, landing awkwardly in the commode but nonetheless intent on properly introducing himself.

The young lady, a teenager at the local high school who was house sitting that evening, was horrified. Johnny did his best to calm her down. After some pleasant banter, it became apparent to her that she wasn't going to be raped and/or murdered, and she began to relax. When he pledged his undying love for her (it had worked for his folks on the school administration and he was a fast learner), she melted and blurted out that he needed to flee immediately since she had called the police while he was trying to get his head out of the toilet during his botched entry.

Sensing a clever ploy, Johnny declined and moved a little closer. Just then there was a loud banging on the front door. She held on to him, begging him not to open it, but he did anyway.

It was Tony Dean, utterly incapacitated and wondering what had happened to his Red Mountain soulmate. Just as Johnny was introducing him to his future wife, two policemen burst through the back door while another two ran around front.

Alas, Tony was not a surfer and, therefore, lacked the reflexes necessary to deal with a situation such as this. Johnny sprinted through the front door just ahead of the cops, down the boardwalk, up an alley, over a fence and, two hours later, collapsed on his dorm room floor. The world was spinning and he was exhibiting all of the classic symptoms of acute alcohol poisoning.

Tony was not as lucky. He was instantly collared, handcuffed, and thrown into a squad car. This was before police were forced by an adverse ruling in an expensive lawsuit to put their hand on your head when they invited you to sit in the back seat of their car. So, on top of several hours in jail and the beginnings of what was to become the most serious hang over of his life, Tony had a bloody knot on his forehead the size of a softball.

The surfers rallied, taking up a collection which included Johnny's last $2 (six weeks into the semester and he was flat broke – excellent budgeting indeed). They (except for Johnny who was practically comatose) went down to the police station, bailed Tony out, and brought him back to the dorm where he was gently laid upon the floor next to Johnny. Tony, by now, was exhibiting similar symptoms.

What neither of them knew was that the intoxicating agent in fermented and distilled liquors is really ethanol, a colorless volatile flammable liquid (C_2H_5OH), one of a class of organic compounds that has a tendency to dry you out ("when your mouth gets dry, you know you're high"). This is what in large part precipitates the disagreeable physical effects that inevitably follow unreasonably heavy consumption of alcoholic beverages.

Many hours of projectile vomiting ensued. Later, they progressed to the "dry heaves," convulsing mightily but regurgitating nothing even though their bodies sincerely wished they could. As they were to find out eventually, if you dry heave long enough, the blood vessels surrounding your retinas explode and your eyes turn red.

They were a sorry lot, and every so often one of their dormie buddies would peek in and thank God it was Johnny and Tony and not them lying there dying. Dinnertime passed and the night lasted forever. Finally, the sun came up and it was a new day. But still Johnny and Tony dry heaved, convulsed, and generally writhed in agony. They did not, nay, could not consume anything. This included water, the one thing they desperately needed to counteract the severe dehydration that would very nearly kill them.

Breakfast, lunch, dinner, and another night passed. The morning of the third day found them in a pool composed primarily of sweat, urine, diarrhea, and stale puke. They were weakened to utter exhaustion. If they had not been young and healthy, they would surely have expired by now. Sometime before the dawn of the fourth day, they were able to hold down small thimbles of water. It took another day before they were able to make it to the cafeteria for their first solid food in nearly a week.

The experiment thus concluded, they deduced that alcohol was probably not good for you, and abstained for nearly a month before falling off the proverbial wagon.

Chapter 14

Cal Western – Silverware

Cal Western had no fraternities or sororities in keeping with the theory that the school administration would have to put up with fewer shenanigans. Ergo, the freshman did not get hazed in the conventional sense. It was, therefore, necessary to devise other ways to torture incoming students.

One of the many loony ideas they came up with was to deny the freshman class the use of silverware for the first week of school. While all the other students were politely eating with utensils, freshmen were reduced to eating with their fingers.

Johnny was up early that morning to check the surf. It was flat so he decided to shift his attention to his college predicament and trudged up the hill to the cafeteria for a little breakfast before class.

The cafeteria manager smirked as Johnny entered and took his place in line. The all-knowing sophomores, juniors, and seniors looked at him and then at each other as they shared their pitiful little secret.

When he got to the end of the line with a bowl of oatmeal and a plate of fruit, a pudgy Latino cafeteria worker with a very weird fish net on her head slapped his hand as he reached for a spoon "No spoon por YOU!"

Johnny, "Beg your pardon?"

Fish net lady, "De preshmen, day get no spoon."

Thinking that she was just putting him on, he grabbed one anyway, she grabbed back, and they started a tug of war that nearly precipitated an international incident. At last, when it became clear that she was really serious, he relinquished the damn spoon and went to sit at the freshman table where some, but not all, of the other new recruits were admiring his resolve.

"What the heck is going on here?" Johnny asked.

"We're being hazed, isn't it exciting?"

To which Johnny diplomatically responded, "Are you really going to sit there eating oatmeal with your fingers and let them get away with this?"

Down at the end of the table, a tanned blond-haired dude (obviously a surfer) spoke up, "Hell no – waddaya think we should do about it?"

That bit of encouragement was all that was needed. Within ten minutes a dozen freshmen had enrolled in the cause, and a meeting was held in Johnny's dorm room an hour later.

"It's pretty simple – we steal the silverware and let 'em ALL eat with their fingers." There was unanimous agreement that this was the proper course of action and they proceeded to work out the details. The parents of one of the guys had required that he work in the cafeteria to get some real-world experience (that would be Johnny) and he was to report to work that evening to clean up the mess created during the day. So, Johnny reasoned that it shouldn't be too difficult to malinger a while and open the back door for the dirty dozen who would come armed with pillow cases and be ready to take it all. The blond tanned surfer guy had a bitchin' new '63 Thunderbird convertible and volunteered to keep the silverware in his trunk until such time as they might decide to give it back, if ever.

Around 8 o'clock most of the workers went home, and by 8:30 the cafeteria manager left as well. Johnny, lurking in the freezer, was overlooked and, at precisely 9, he opened the back door. In streamed not only the original twelve core group members, but also a third of the freshman class. It took less than thirty minutes to bag and drag every single piece of silverware in the joint. Not just the forks, spoons and knives, but every single utensil even remotely associated with food consumption or preparation (that fat chick with the hair net should not have slapped Johnny's hand).

When the Latino cafeteria workers reported for work the next morning, there were no pots, no pans, no ladles, no rollers, no spatulas, no egg beaters, no prongs – no nothing, and most certainly no forks, spoons or knives of any type or description.

The workers did the best they could with what they had – their fingers – and managed to whip together a bizarre but reasonably consumable breakfast line. The concept that unwashed hands and dirty fingernails could pass on potentially lethal bacteria was unknown and/or disregarded at this time. So, the fact that Jose (who had crossed the border hours earlier after a wicked all nighter at the Blue Fox) had used his filthy hands to stir just about everything. This did not raise a flag with the cafeteria manager who was already so overwhelmed with the enormity of what he was facing that a couple of dead students was the last thing on his mind.

The entire freshman class came to breakfast that day. It was freakin' glorious. Pandemonium reigned. The cafeteria manager was close to a nervous breakdown. The Mexicans had lightened up a bit and seemed to actually enjoy what was happening. The rest of the student body, those prissy sophomores, juniors, and seniors, were not amused.

By noon they had made plastic spoons available – it was like eating lunch in prison except nobody got shanked.

The campus was equipped with a fairly serious intercom system, and the administration used it to good advantage that morning. They warned of the dire consequences facing those who had stolen the cafeteria silverware, and pointed out that this had risen to the level of a felony since the value of the booty exceeded the statutory limit for misdemeanors.

Some of the Group of 12 started to wobble. The blond tan surfer guy was one of them, since the front wheels of his T-bird were off the ground owing to several thousand pounds of silverware in his trunk (which was actually a mere fraction of the haul, the balance having been stashed in just about every freshman dorm room on campus).

Surfer dude sought the advice of a counselor who, it turned out, was gay and very attracted to young tan blond surfers. The counselor, thrilled to be in on the caper, volunteered to act as an intermediary with the administration. The terms of the deal were that the silverware would be returned if there were no questions and no recriminations.

The administration mulled this proposal over for about five minutes before unilaterally and unconditionally accepting. Slowly but surely, the silverware, the pots, the pans, the spatulas and all the rest began to appear mysteriously in the vacant classroom of the homosexual counselor who, by now, had become a hero to his peers and a popular figure on campus, particularly among the students who were thankful they hadn't been expelled or arrested.

The next day, as Johnny entered the cafeteria, the manager walked up to him, and with his face mere inches away, said, "I know you had something to do with this" to which Johnny responded, "Really?"

Chapter 15

Cal Western - Baja

Since Cal Western was a mere twenty miles from the border, it became fashionable among the surfing segment of the student population to cross it with impunity. There were two basic destinations – Tijuana and surf spots further down the Baja Peninsula.

Tijuana got its name from a cattle ranch that existed there in the early 1800's called Rancho Tia Juana (Aunt Jane's Ranch). It was located in the middle of Mexico, which, at the time, extended up through California, Nevada, Utah and parts of Arizona, Colorado and Wyoming. However, in 1848 the United States kicked the living shit out of Mexico (the Mexican-American war) and, to use an earthquake metaphor, the top part of Mexico slid into America and Tia Juana became "beach front property." Aunt Jane was not happy.

But Mexico adroitly turned this misfortune to advantage. In 1889 they changed the name to Tijuana and positioned it to serve a unique function as an international border town. They packed it full of bars and whores, added gambling, drugs, and the occasional photo op donkey cart and dog meat taco stand, and called it "a tourist destination." They made a killing.

The surfers of Dorm 2, anxious to do their part for the Mexican economy, went to Tijuana often. The things that went on there are not fit for publication, but typically involved alcohol, drugs, and fornication. Friday nights would find the boys at the Long Bar, which, during prohibition, was advertised as the longest bar in the world. By the time they got there, however, suspicious fires and periodic explosions had reduced it to a mere eighty feet – still further than it was possible to slide a beer without spilling.

After a dozen pitchers of Dos Equis and a few tequila shooters, it was off to the Blue Fox for some interesting/amazing floorshow entertainment, rounding out the evening with a street taco and hopefully a willing lass. It is a wonder none of them got a sexually transmitted disease or a severe case of the Mexican two-step.

On occasion they would lose somebody and have to go back the next night to find them. This happened twice to one individual, and it became standard policy thereafter to forcibly eject him from the car whenever they were loading up for another border crossing.

One of the guys developed a theme for his Sociology term paper that coincided nicely with the Tijuana forays – "Why Mexican Girls Become Prostitutes – Interviews With Twenty Subjects." That guy got laid more than all the rest of them put together. But, hey, it was a brilliant stroke of genious and he deserved the A he got.

When they ran out of beer/girl money, the guys developed a secondary strategy. They would stay up most of the night "studying" in their dorm rooms, then around 3 am, load up the car, blow straight through Tijuana, and head for various surf spots down the Baja Peninsula (K-38 and San Miguel were favorites).

This had both advantages and disadvantages. On the plus side, you got some studying done. Also, they would occasionally hit really good surf. On the negative side, however, you had to drive through Tijuana at four in the morning just as all the bars and whorehouses shut down. This was quite dangerous since there was a lot of gunfire and car crashes, and there were surly Mexican Police everywhere with their hands out just itching to bust somebody and forcefully extract money. On one of those early morning transits a car load of really _really_ drunk Mexicans followed them very closely for about mile, crashing into and ricocheting off of dozens of parked cars. Also, when you finally did get to a Baja beach, you had to deal with the sea urchins.

Sea urchins thrive on the Baja coast, and they get quite a bit larger than their cousins in California, possibly because of the "nutrients" (raw sewage) in the water. They are round, purple and covered with sharp spines that can grow several inches long. This is a problem for surfers who must traverse the shoreline out to get to the waves and back in to retrieve their boards after a wipeout. It was not uncommon for several people in the car to step on at least one per trip. On one occasion, Johnny got caught in a shallow barrel, was sucked up over the lip and deposited feet first on the rocky bottom – squarely on top of a large urchin. He carries with him to this day evidence of that encounter. Fortunately, this was the only time a spine entered the bottom of his foot and came out through the top.

There were cliff-hanging restaurants up and down the Baja coast, and they welcomed surfers as well as drug dealers, escaped prisoners, pedophiles, and anybody else with an American dollar. They were courteous, attentive, and the food was great. So, they would load up on lobster and enchilada rancheros on every trip and rarely got sick. The whole idea of being treated well was completely foreign to them, since surfers at that time were viewed pretty much as scum by most of the people in America. It got progressively worse the further east you went from Malibu, and for this reason most of the guys had never even been to Arizona.

The innocence of the early '60s waned with the discovery and acceptance of pot as a desirable alternative to blind drunkenness. It was noted that a room full of drunks would almost inevitably explode into a brawl with associated abrasions, lacerations, and the occasional loss of life, whereas a room full of stoners would just lie there (Texans later developed a saying that was apropos to this situation – "Well, are you gonna cowboy up or just lay there and bleed?"). It should be noted that food tasted GREAT. So, Johnny took to bringing back a little herb.

This was a risky proposition, because if you got caught, you were fucked. On the other hand, if you made it, you were a campus hero and likely to have more than one girlfriend. In consideration of those who wished to accelerate and improve their study habits, he also made a point, while the other guys were boozing it up at the Long Bar, of visiting the friendly back-alley Pharmacia where the guy behind the counter was more than happy to fill your hand written prescription for "a thousand bennies." On one occasion the pharmacist actually took the time to correct his misspelling of "Benzedrine." It was not lost on Johnny, his peers, or his parents that his grades definitely spiked as a by-product of this budding cottage industry.

However, you felt like crap after a Benzedrine fueled all nighter, and Johnny reasoned there must be some type of medicine to counter act this. The Tijuana pharmacist was very helpful in this regard, suggesting a thousand red secobarbital capsules for starters. Unbeknownst to Johnny, seconal, or reds as they are commonly known, is a barbiturate ($C12H18N2O3$), which, while outstanding as a hypnotic/sedative, is also highly addictive. Johnny spread these around the dorm liberally, and pretty soon guys were banging on his door at all times of the day and night looking for a "bag" (as in Papa's got a brand new...).

Johnny finally realized that this might not be a road down which he should either walk or run. He had successfully smuggled a huge quantity of drugs across the border without apprehension/prison and reasoned that he may be running out of "luck." So, he eventually gave up his seat in the car if Tijuana was the final destination (he still went on all the surf trips), and Baja became merely a footnote on his resume.

With the sudden subsidence in the flood of drugs, things settled back pretty much to normal at Cal Western. However, Johnny was only able to retain one girlfriend (who, ironically, he lost, found, and later married).

It should be noted that, for the rest of Johnny's life, Mr. Seconal remained discretely behind him at a distance, softly calling his name.

Chapter 16

Cal Western - Coming of Age

When Johnny was initially thrown into the public-school system, they had a simple rule for what grade you got placed in. If you turned six anytime prior to December 31, you got put in kindergarten for the school year starting in September of that year. So, if your birthday was on January 1, you were an old six by the time you got to class in September. If your birthday was, say, November 24 (as Johnny's was) you hadn't even turned six yet but were nevertheless hurled into the cage with the rest of the older "students."

The bottom line was that all the older kids were gonna pick on you all the way through thirteen friggin' years of school. This wasn't so bad in grade school since nobody had matured to the point where they could actually inflict bodily harm.

When ya got part way through junior high, it got weird. Girls sprouted breasts and were hustled off to the restroom when they started bleeding all over their dresses. Guys started getting pimples and muscles and hair and unintended boners.

The pimples and the hair were not so bad – it was the muscles that posed a problem. For when two combatants squared off behind the gym and only one of them had muscles, the other guy was in for a dirty lickin'. Johnny got more than his fair share.

He yearned for the day when he too would have muscles, but he was not only a year younger than most of the other guys, but he was also a late bloomer. And so, he was "invited" to several trips behind the gym and hence the nurse's office (where he became known as "a frequent flyer"). It got to where he looked strange if he DIDN'T have a black eye. The beatings went on and on. Johnny, it turned out, had invented the Ropa Dope long before Cassius Clay would change his name and take credit for it.

He got all the way to High School with skinny arms and a 140-pound frame. Desperate for an edge, he showed up for the first day of wrestling practice. The coach rolled his eyes and the rest of the guys just laughed. At least the beatings that were administered there were governed by certain rules that prevented really bad injuries (no intentional eye gauging, no intentional breaking of arms or legs, like that). If they knew you were gonna get your head ground into the pavement, they made you wear a set of headgear to cover your ears so they wouldn't fill up with blood. Some of the guys who didn't wear headgear sported gawd awful cauliflower ears for the rest of their lives. So, Johnny was grateful for his set.

He was a pathetic sight out there on the mat. The standard issue wrestling uniform hung limply off his frame, and whenever photographs were taken or they assembled as a team at away games, he was always put way in the back. He cannot remember winning a single match that entire first year.

But, to his credit, he kept at it and concentrated on learning the moves. As it turned out, if you knew the moves you could really surprise your opponent, particularly if he was a non-wrestler with a leather jacket and waterfall hair-do waiting for you behind the gym.

And then, almost imperceptibly, it happened. He slowly started to gain weight and muscle mass. He was moved from the 140-pound weight class to 152, then 160. His chest started to swell, but not his waist. His arms started to develop beyond string beans. He grew hair down there. His voice cracked on occasion (usually in embarrassing situations involving girls). He got taller by nearly half an inch a month. Barbells that previously had been impossible to even get off the ground were now mere child's play. By the end of his junior year he could (in his mind) bend quarters between his index finger and thumb.

It was, to a certain extent, anti-climatic, since invitations to appear behind the gym all but dried up, and in tense moments the other guy usually blinked (Johnny was always thankful for that). In fact, he never really got a chance to pick on anybody cause his heart just wasn't in it. So, he cruised through his senior year unscathed, won a few wrestling trophies, and went off to college with a modicum of self confidence and the knowledge that he would probably never have to worry about getting picked on again.

This misconception was short lived. He fell in with a bunch of other surfers and they got to drinkin' wine and getting crazy (in a good sort of way). Intercollegiate football games were a big thing, and they went to all of 'em. Cruising around after a particularly vicious mauling (San Diego State 67, Cal Western 3), Johnny wound up behind the wheel of Brian's car (Brian was preoccupied at the moment in the passenger side back seat, window down, anticipating a violent episode of projectile vomiting). As they attempted to negotiate a sweeping left turn the car, overloaded with inhabitants and low on air, swerved into the adjacent lane, and part of Brian's stomach contents found its way through the rear window of the adjacent vehicle which appeared to be full of large college students from another school.

This precipitated a disagreeable exchange of opinions and a challenge to pull into the next alley to discuss it more completely. Inasmuch as everybody in both cars was completely wasted, the concept of a lively discussion in a dark alley seemed not only fitting but also proper.

So, they turned into the alley, slowed to a stop, and piled out. Johnny and his surfer buddies found themselves looking up at the underside of the chins of the front line of the San Diego State football team. Since Johnny had been driving, he became the focus of the debate, which lasted about five seconds before he caught a fat high velocity knuckle sandwich in the snoot.

There was dead silence as blood poured out of Johnny's face. The very large football player with the big hands smirked and said, "What are you going to do about it, fag?"

"Did that guy just call me a rag?" Johnny asked rhetorically. "OK mother fucker, you're goin' down." Johnny pulled out all the stops. Utilizing the basic "slam your man" wrestling move, Mr. Varsity Football Guy immediately kissed the pavement with a leg and an arm cocked at extreme attitudes. He screamed for mercy. It was embarrassing. "Please don't" and a lot of "aaaaaaaaahhhh, AAAAAAAAAHHHH!"

That guy should never have called Johnny a rag. It was over in an instant. The other football players stood there in shocked disbelief as their captain lay on the ground whimpering. The surfers couldn't believe it either (Johnny was also quite surprised). Everyone just got back in their cars and drove slowly away.

Johnny's jaw swelled shut and he had to suck baby food through a straw for several days (little did he know that he would get a lot of practice a few years later when he kissed the underside of a Cadillac). But it was all worthwhile since he was now a stone rock star around campus, and even assholes made an effort to be friendly.

It's been over fifty years now, and expect for a couple guys at the office (who really truly deserved it) and some guy on the freeway who cut him off, Johnny has abstained from physical violence. However, you never know what tomorrow may bring.

PS – Oops, shortly after his 75th birthday, Johnny was involved in a fight on a bus in Hilo – it turned out "Slam your man" was still a valid concept. Please see the Chapter entitled "Get Off the Bus Gus"

Chapter 17

Cal Western - Out Late

In order to prevent unbridled fornication, there were two sets of dorms – the guy's dorms overlooking you know what (Newbreak) and the girls' dorms way on the other side of campus overlooking some sort of uninteresting forest (although part of the Pacific Ocean was visible through the leaves).

So, when you wanted to go out on a date, you had to go all the way over there to pick up the girls. Fortunately, some of the guys had cars, and Johnny was able to double date or borrow a car when needed, which was frequently.

Early on, twelve surfers in Dorm 2 had gotten together and, realizing the necessity of an off-campus party house, had chipped in to rent a place right on the boardwalk in Mission Beach. It was a smelly old beach house that had seen many parties before they arrived on the scene, but it had four bedrooms (excellent!) and rented for $120 a month, which was conveniently divisible by twelve. Johnny met his first FBI man at the door one morning who presented his badge and inquired as to the whereabouts of a previous occupant. Although the badge looked real, the guy was skinny and sweaty with a pencil mustache and a large gun under his unbuttoned coat. Johnny guessed he was more likely on an errand for the mob.

Word spread like wildfire, and soon the hottest ticket on campus was an invite to "the surf house." Imagine hundreds of nubile young coeds yearning to meet a surfer, and then add tequila, a 5,000-watt record player and four bedrooms. What we're talking about here is fun, fun, fun. This went on for nearly the entire school year - they got their money's worth and then some.

And so, it happened that a dozen scruffy surfers found themselves in considerable demand. They could not go anywhere on campus without "coincidental" meetings with debutants of every kind and description fawning all over them – it was weird but wonderful.

Later in the year, the situation reached extreme proportions and went entirely off the rails when Johnny and his buddy from Hawaii Jim Davis were walking up the road to the cafeteria. The road circumnavigated the playing field, which had been dug into the hillside. The makai or ocean side was flush with the existing terrain overlooking the ocean, while the mauka or mountainside faced a huge sloping cut, perhaps a hundred feet tall, on top of which the road to the cafeteria had been built.

They were walking along, admiring the view, which was exceptional that day since it was sunny and clear and the women's archery class in their skimpy little uniforms was underway on the playing field below. Jim took a step and an arrow shot through his foot. The projectile passed just above the sole of his shoe and just below the arch of his foot, but this was not immediately ascertainable. They stood there in silence for a few tense moments, looking down at the arrow protruding from Jim's Florshiem. Then, with Jim slipping into shock, they sat down and tried to take his shoe off, hoping that the flow of blood would not be too great.

As Johnny gingerly removed Jim's shoe, the entire women's archery class arrived on the scene, apologizing profusely and offering any assistance they could. And, if it was possible in any way to make it up to them, they would be pleased to show up at "the surf house" tonight to perfect their apologies.

Jim ended up dating the girl who had shot him, and Johnny ended up with two really outstanding archery participants. The party that night reached near epic proportions, but midnight loomed and there was still tequila in the bottle.

The problem with midnight was that the girl's dorm imposed a strict curfew – if you were even a minute late, they'd lock the doors and call your parents. The girls, understandably, were very attentive to the idea of returning to the dorm on time.

So, Jim and Johnny had to take the girls back to the dorm before consummating their, uh, friendship. A problem arose, however, when Johnny's two dates allowed as how they would be willing to return to the party if he would be kind enough to come around the back and bail them out.

Johnny, ever the bon vivant, readily agreed to this proposition and, upon depositing the girls at the front entrance, went around to the back and jumped through the window (the wrong window) to free the fair maidens.

The sixty-eight-year-old dorm mother screamed to high heaven. Johnny thought there was a hint of "please don't, please don't.... give it to me baby" in her voice, but that was just too gross to contemplate so, as he lay on the floor amid the broken screen material, he expelled the thought from his mind. Jumping to his feet in preparation for the drop, he leaped back through the window, found the ground, and repeated the exercise, this time at the proper location. The girls were glad to see him, and made their appreciation known upon returning to "the

134

surf house" with the four bedrooms, three of which became superfluous.

The next morning, frazzled and hung over, the Three Musketeers returned to the girl's dorm where they found the parking lot full. In addition to a few student cars, there were police cars, ambulances, and a fire truck (they could not figure that one out). There was also an unmarked FBI car (they stand out with government plates and dash mounted multi colored lights) since this was an investigation involving student kidnapping and rape PLUS attempted rape of a senior citizen on top of all the other charges.

They realized that they were screwed, not only in the biblical sense, but in every sense. There was no use turning back now - it would be best to face the music. As Johnny walked them to the door, they both noted with some reservation that their parent's cars were also in the lot. Johnny kissed them both, pivoted abruptly, and high-tailed it outta there.

Later that morning, he received a message to report to the Dean's office. It might have been illuminating here to relate the details of that conversation, but it was blunt, humorless, and very short indeed. A minute later, Johnny was a free agent.

Johnny's education at Cal Western had come to an end (he lasted nearly a year and a half). His parents drove down to get all the sordid details. The Dean (who was later arrested and jailed for absconding with tuition funds) was kind enough to describe their son as "one of our more colorful students" and wrapped it up with "He was a charming rogue – we'll miss him."

PS – Johnny returned several weeks later and took a gigantic dump on the Dean's desk.

Chapter 18

Diamond Head

After he had been kicked out of Cal Western, and then another college after that, he decided to try his luck at the University of Hawaii so he hopped a plane with a couple of surf buddies and ended up in Honolulu. It was 1965 and he was twenty years old.

He was financially destitute, but managed to scrape enough capital together to buy a used Triumph dirt bike off a sailor who was shipping out "tomorrow."

As far as is publicly known, he is the first and possibly only person to ever have scaled Diamond Head on a motorcycle. It happened the day he got the Triumph. He was tooling around, enjoying the breeze in his face, when he noticed a little used road leading to the base of Diamond Head. It was probably little used for two reasons:

1. Everybody congregates at the "front" of Diamond Head, meaning the Waikiki side – this road was in the back.

2. There was a highly restricted military installation inside Diamond Head to which this road led.

Curiosity got the best of him as he turned onto the forbidden road and soon came to a giant tunnel big enough to drive a tank through (it turns out there was a reason for this). It looked like something you might find at Disneyland. It was just too perfect not to drive into – and although there were lots of menacing signs, there were no armed guards.

So, Johnny took the plunge. The bike sounded good as he throttled up through the tunnel – it was like a huge megaphone that amplified every exhaust note – it sounded bitchin'.

Exiting at high speed into the sunlight, he realized that he was (a) inside a volcano and (b) in the middle of a formidable looking military installation. There was a lot of hardware in here, some so large it was a wonder that they fit through that tunnel. This was not a place a civilian would want to spend much time. Nor were civilians welcome.

It was high noon, and as luck would have it, the entire Diamond Head Branch of the United States Army was in the mess hall having lunch. This was a very good thing, for if they had been at their stations, he might have been mowed down in a hail of 50-caliber gunfire.

But, without a soul in sight, he blew directly through the center of the installation. In front of him rose the interior wall of the volcano.

Being a rather feeble student of history, he knew only that Diamond Head got its name in the 1800's from a drunken British sailor who, hanging off the yardarm, saw the calcite crystals in the lava rock glimmer in the sunlight and understandably deduced that there must be diamonds in that thar hill.

He later learned that when the United States annexed Hawaii in 1898, the US became instantly paranoid about defending Honolulu's harbors. It was determined that the best place to lob cannon balls onto enemy ships was from the top of Diamond Head. In 1910 a trail was cut to the top where several gun emplacements were built (hats off the guys who dragged all that stuff up there) and manned 24/7/365 by rotating crews prepared to pull the trigger. Guns got better, ranges longer, and destructive force substantially larger. Those who may have been tempted apparently figured all this out, and Honolulu's Harbors remained unscathed until December 7, 1941 when the bastards used planes instead of ships.

After WWII the site was abandoned when it was found much easier to locate sea faring invaders by radar/satellite and vaporize them with missiles.

As Johnny screamed through the far end of the vacant encampment, he found himself on a dirt trail that led up the volcano wall. Holy Smokes! A dirt biker's dream! And up the trail he went, zigging and zagging, standing on the pegs for technical riding through steep and rough spots and around switch backs, ever higher, the 760-foot summit still towering overhead. "I think I can, I think I can." But the shear cliff face was getting impossibly steep, and he began to wonder how this was going to turn out. Rounding a corner, he came to a screeching halt. He had discovered "the staircase from hell" as it must surely have been known by the men who built it and hauled cannons up it the last few hundred feet to the top.

The staircase from hell has ninety-nine steps at an incline of fifty-five degrees which, when you are sitting on a motorcycle at the bottom, looks perpendicular. This was the end of the line. There would be no further dirt bike adventure. But, by god, he'd come this far - he was going the rest of the way on foot.

He shut off the bike and started to climb. In the distance far below, he could hear sirens and many people yelling. This was not a good sign. He was screwed and he knew it. But he was going to the top first. Even traveling light with revolvers and billy clubs, it would take a platoon of MP's at least thirty minutes to get to where he was. So "The heck with those guys, I'm goin' all the way up."

He was wheezing by the time he got to the 99th stair. There, he entered a long steep unlit tunnel, which came out at the base of a **second** set of stairs ("For Pete's sake!"). By the time he got to the last of those seventy-six stairs, he was delusional. He held on to a railing in the dark, which spiraled upwards (picture a lighthouse on steroids).

He emerged blinking into the sunlight and was greeted by a spectacular view of the entire south side of Oahu - from Koko Head in the East, through Waikiki directly below, on out to Barbers Point and the Waianae Range to the West. He knew he was going to jail for this, but it was worth it.

He stayed for perhaps twenty minutes, drinking it in, then turned and headed back down to face the music (they wouldn't kill you for trespassing – would they?). The stairs were a lot easier going down but you had to be careful not to pitch forward because if that happened you weren't gonna stop tumbling till you got to the bottom.

His bike was still there. The MP's had not been able to reach and destroy it before he could climb back on. It was eerily quiet below. He knew they were laying in wait somewhere along the trail. Rather than fire it up, he turned and started to coast around the switchbacks, through the hard parts, down to come what may.

He was almost back to the military installation when he noticed that there were no formal lines of Army personnel waiting to confront and abuse him. To this day, he does not know why that was. Maybe they thought he'd fallen and died when his motorcycle went silent. Maybe they'd lost interest (doubtful). In any event, there didn't seem to be any organized resistance.

Not wanting to look a gift horse in the mouth, he dropped it into gear, popped the clutch, and roared head long into the center of the installation where soldiers, frantic soldiers, emerged from every door shouting and waiving, some with guns.

He did not stop. Ducking down on top of the gas tank, peering out over the handle bars, he pegged the throttle and made a beeline for the tunnel as several jeeps joined in pursuit.

Apparently, there is something in the military code that precludes making arrests on non-military property for, as he hauled ass through the tunnel down the access road and out onto the public street, the jeeps slowed and stopped.

Johnny looked back only once, thanked his lucky stars, and headed on down the road.

Chapter 19

Pali Cruiser

They needed a station wagon real bad. You can only fit so many surfboards on the roof of a regular car (the record so far was fourteen). Beyond that, the roof of a normal car would sag, and you'd have to lay down on the back seat and pop it back out with your feet which left weird wrinkles in the sheet metal. Also, boards on the roof had a tendency to fly off at inappropriate moments, usually in sharp turns (such as the Haliewa Round About) or at high speeds (such as the hill leading down to the Haliewa Round About). Plus, you have to make three trips to the dump to get rid of your crap instead of piling everything in there and taking care of the whole mess in one load. Also, sleeping on the beach in the rain was getting old. Stretching out in the back of a nice dry station wagon had a certain allure.

So, they looked in the Honolulu Advertiser and there, on D-19 in small print was the following message "1954 Buick Station Wagon for sale cheap."

Inasmuch as it was 1965, we're talkin' about practically a new vehicle here (in surfer years). Johnny was the only one with a job and short hair. The other three guys (John Wagner, Bill Lewis, and Mike Stearns) were

144

pretty much surf bums and looked like it, although everybody was, by some miracle, successfully attending the University of Hawaii on a part time basis. Johnny was accordingly nominated to handle the transaction. They dropped him off in Kailua and said "good luck."

It turned out that the seller was a really nice guy, a pilot for United who had just been transferred to Florida. He was asking $200 for this righteous vehicle and probably could have cleared a grand if he had held out. Johnny had just gotten paid ($159 which was supposed to last until next pay day, a distant two weeks away). The other guys said they would "pay him back later" so it was necessary, for the purposes of survival, to negotiate.

With a quavering voice, Johnny weakly implored, "Would you take $150?" It never hurts to ask. The guy folded immediately (he must have been in a real hurry to get outta town) and the deal was struck. The seller mentioned that since the registration, safety check, and insurance had expired the buyer would have to take care of that. Johnny thought to himself "Riiiiiiiiiiiiiight." And then, inexplicably, he handed over the keys and the pink slip and said, "I gotta run, could you handle the transfer for me?" This later proved to be one of the biggest bonehead maneuvers the pilot had ever made, except for clipping the Honolulu Airport control tower, which had something to do with his transfer.

Driving away in that shiny beige '54 Buick Wagon, Johnny felt like the cat that just swallowed the canary. It was sweet. It had a big ol' V-8 engine and purred like a kitten (what a coincidence). When ya put the rear seat down, it was cavernous – you could park an ice cream truck in there. With expert judgment, Johnny guessed it would accommodate perhaps twenty boards.

The jungle in Waikiki (so named because it was a bad address where prostitutes, professional wrestlers, mahus, and surfers hung out) was separated from Kailua by the Ko'olau mountain range. On the Kailua side it's pretty much straight up and down, owing to some sort of disastrous land slide 100,000 years earlier where that half of the island slipped into the sea (no, really). Standing there at the top of the Pali and looking down was quite similar to hucking it over the ledge on a Waimea macker, except here a misstep resulted in instantaneous death whereas at Waimea you could look forward to a horrific hydraulic beating and several minutes of prolonged agony prior to your demise.

Kamehameha the Great, the Hawaiian warrior who united all the islands by going to each one in turn and slaughtering anyone with a spear (expect Kauai which just said "it's all yours brother") had thrown some 20,000 Oahu spear bearers off this very cliff. Several months earlier a despondent mental patient had leaped from the same spot. In his case, however, the trade winds were blowing really hard and were compressed with added velocity up the side of the sheer cliff so he floated like a butterfly to the bottom, got up, dusted himself off, and walked back to the asylum.

Johnny fired up a big one, smooshed back into the comfortable seat, and drove slowly and deliberately over the Pali back to the jungle. It occurred to him as he was passing through the Pali Tunnel that (a) this is one freakin' long tunnel and (b) I think I'll call her the Pali Cruiser. And so, that's what it came to be known far and wide by most of the inhabitants of Oahu and the entire Honolulu police force.

The great thing about an unlicensed, unregistered, uninsured station wagon legally held in somebody else's name is that you have "diplomatic immunity" so to speak. In other words, when you get a ticket, you can just put it in the glove box and forget about it, because they're going to chase the owner, not you. It wasn't long before we (did I say we, I meant they) had to start stuffing tickets under the seat because the glove box was full. Somewhere in Florida, the FBI was looking for a pilot who was apparently flying back and forth to Honolulu and engaging in outrageously irresponsible behavior behind the wheel of a car, which he presumably kept there in a warehouse or under a tarp in somebody's back yard.

The trick, of course, is not to get caught driving the thing. They, or more accurately Johnny since none of the other guys would even touch the wheel, had many close calls. The police giving parking tickets began to tire of the pile under the windshield wiper and started to leave personal messages, which cannot be repeated here. Fortunately, in 1965 the cops didn't have all the sophisticated communications equipment that later came into vogue, so all they could do was watch you pass by with their mouths open if they were on foot or attempt to chase you down if they were driving. With a big V-8 and a low center of gravity, the Pali Cruiser was hard to catch.

They had been in Hawaii for several years now, and there was talk of actually returning to the Mainland to enroll full time at a "real" college (ironically, the University of Hawaii compared well with its Mainland counterparts). Also, Vietnam was heating up and those 2-S student deferments had become the most valuable piece of paper a surfer could own.

There was time for one last surf. Johnny took his good buddy Pokii (pronounced "Po-key-ee" meaning "little one" since he was the youngest in the family) Kahualanimaumaukamalii Vaughn (really, that's his name) and his father Frank down to the beach at Waikiki to get in the water one last time before leaving.

Johnny had met Pokii the day he had arrived several years before at the very same surf spot. Johnny was paddling out and Pokii was surfing in, tucked into a high line on a big one. There was a spectacular collision. Johnny dove to save himself and thought "Son of a bitch, I'm here three hours and I'm already in a fight with a Hawaiian." He came up apologizing profusely. Fortunately, so did Pokii.

They became instant friends. Later that day, Pokii took him to his home in Manoa Valley for dinner. It was Sunday. His brother Palani and some friends were in the garage playing music as they did every Sunday. They later formed a band and called it "Sunday Manoa." Pokii's Mom and Dad were pure Hawaiian. They were the most gracious people he had ever met and from that day forward he had a new and lasting respect for Hawaiians and Hawaiian culture.

So, on this last day in Hawaii, it was important to Johnny that he make a good final impression on Pokii and his father. Unfortunately, it didn't go well. As they drove down the street toward the water, a cop with a gun started running after them, waiving his revolver and yelling "You bastard, if I catch you, I'm gonna shoot your legs off." Johnny had a lot of explaining to do, but it was really a hard one to gloss over.

The Pali Cruiser by this time had violated just about every vehicular traffic law and had been abused beyond all reason - it was hotter than a thermonuclear accident. It was, therefore, dangerous even to be around. Johnny knew there was only one thing left to do, and the rest of the guys solemnly concurred. The last act for the Pali Cruiser was about to commence.

That evening they drove up to the University of Hawaii, being careful to take back roads and drive slowly. They stopped next to Sinclair Library where they had spent many hundreds of hours high on amphetamines trying desperately to make sense of the irrational proposition that debits should go on the left and credits on the right – who thought that up?

Students began to crowd around, as pretty much everyone knew that when the Pali

Cruiser showed up, something was goin' down. The boys did not wish to disappoint.

The windows, doors, and tailgate were opened and a brick was placed under each wheel. The windshield wipers were bent outward and turned on, as were the lights. The engine was left running. The excitement was building and students were now three deep in a circle. It began to look like a mob scene, and there was an overriding concern that the attention of the authorities might be prematurely attracted. Pulses began to race.

The three others ceremoniously held out the last brick, which was given to Johnny in recognition of his outstanding performance over the past several years as the captain of a ship that would not sink and could not be caught.

With poise and dignity, Johnny layed the brick on the accelerator and that big V-8 started to scream. Not just a regular scream, but an ear splitting, guttural rod knocking howl that could be heard for quite some distance.

Anyone who has ever attended a drag race knows that engines sometimes blow up, sometimes spectacularly. It has to do with exceeding the physical limitations of the metal that the engine is made out of. The pistons, which go up and down, are connected to the crank shaft (which goes round and round) by rods. Up to the "red line" i.e., the calculated maximum revolutions per minute of the crank shaft beyond which danger lurks, the rods can pretty much be depended upon to hold onto the pistons as they go up and down.

Exceeding the red line (never a good idea except when being pursued by a squad car) can and quite frequently does lead to catastrophic failure. In bigger engines, such as the one in the Pali Cruiser, we're talking about something approaching a midget version of the first atomic bomb. As the vehicle manufacturer might say, "All bets are off and your warranty is void."

Well, the brick on the accelerator precipitated an inevitable chain reaction and the immutable laws of physics inexorably manifested themselves. The four musketeers, having attended many drag races, pretty much knew what to expect and, therefore, bid a hasty farewell to the Pali Cruiser, waived to the crowd, and sprinted down University Avenue at maximum tilt. The crowd, sensing an aura of impending doom, rapidly disbursed.

To the Pali Cruiser's credit, she held on for a full two minutes. Then, somewhere in the distance, there was an explosion, and the lights of Sinclair Library blinked out.

Chapter 20

Military Career

Johnny's military career commenced in 1966
(he was twenty-one) and apparently has
continued for more than half a century. Why,
you may ask. Before we get into the details, it
might be helpful to explore a little history.

On November 24, 1963 when Johnny turned
eighteen, he was "encouraged" to go down to
the draft board and "register." Although he
did not know it at the time, this is similar to
what happens to a pig on its way to becoming
a sausage. It struck him as the patriotic thing
to do – also, if he DIDN'T, he would likely end
up in prison or Canada. After careful
consideration, he dutifully reported to a
sterile government office in a deserted
shopping center with his birth certificate and
a recent hair cut (no sense aggravating the pig
farmer).

On that very same day, President Johnson
called a meeting of advisers and allowed as
how he would be willing to provide his support
to help win the Vietnam war, if only an
opportunity presented itself. Although in the
history of the world this does not rank up
there with, say, the Titanic meeting the
iceberg, it was, as far as Johnny was
concerned, a good example of very bad timing.

On August 2, 1964 the USS Maddox, cruising along North Vietnam's coast, fired upon and damaged several "torpedo" boats that had been "stalking" it in the Gulf of Tonkin. Two days later, the USS Turner Joy did the same thing. The circumstances were murky, and no one really knows what happened except perhaps the machine gunners who gave 'em the "whole nine yards," meaning the entire twenty-seven foot long fifty caliber ammunition belt.

One theory goes that two separate sampans loaded with Vietnamese fishermen trying to sell fish to US sailors were unlucky enough to find themselves respectively in the vicinity of the Maddox and Joy when deck hands decided to have a little fun. Even Lyndon Johnson commented to Undersecretary of State George Ball that "those sailors out there may have been shooting at flying fish." It was noted that the price of fish in many coastal Vietnamese villages spiked shortly after this incident.

These "skirmishes" led to retaliatory air strikes and prompted Congress to approve the Gulf of Tonkin Resolution which gave the president power to conduct military operations in Southeast Asia without declaring war. In the same month, Johnson pledged that he was not "...committing American boys to fighting a war that I think ought to be fought by the boys of Asia to help protect their own land."

Johnny put his hand over his mouth and coughed "BULLSHIT," but his pathetic attempt at derision was unnoticed and ineffective.

By the end of 1964 the number of guerrilla fighters in South Vietnam exceeded 100,000. The military model at that time was that ten soldiers were needed to deal with each insurgent (now, with the advent of remotely operated drones and highly sophisticated weaponry, the correct ratio of soldiers to insurgents would be more along the lines of 1 per 1,000).

This was bad news for Johnny since the total number of U.S. troops in 1964 needed to defeat the insurgents based on the ten to one ratio exceeded the entire strength of the United States Army. The Army was lookin' for a few good men, and Johnny was a deer in the headlights.

It is widely held that the average U.S. serviceman was nineteen years old. The idea was for each nineteen-year-old to "visit" Vietnam for a one-year "tour of duty," then return home and resume as normal a life as possible after a healthy dose of mayhem and agent orange. This rapid turn over resulted in a dearth of experienced leadership, and one observer noted "we were not in Vietnam for ten years, we were there for one year ten times." One problem with this scenario is that nobody knew what the hell was going on. In the confusion it was easy to get shot to pieces or end up a heroin addict. Several of Johnny's friends who had earlier been herded on government sponsored flights to Saigon came back both ways.

Fortunately, there was something called a "2-S" student deferment. As long as you remained enrolled in college full time, you were shielded from getting your ass drafted. Thus, it was critical to keep up with your studies. Thank Gawd for amphetamines, or Johnny might have been on an early plane. He was able to maintain a minimally acceptable grade point average (to really excel it would have been necessary to cut back on surfing and partying - it was important to establish your priorities).

Things were going swimmingly until he came face to face with Accounting 101, which demanded that you accept the irrational proposition that debits are on the left and credits are on the right. Johnny might just as well have enrolled in a Theoretical Physics class taught in Chinese. He wasn't going to cut it, and his trajectory was as clear to him as Evel Kinevel's had been when he let go of the rocket throttle on his Snake River Canyon jump. Which is to say, Johnny was going down. He held out valiantly until the last week of class, when his professor kindly informed him that if he withdrew now, he could avoid a "big fat F" and could reapply for another go at the Accounting Piñata the following year. This seemed like an excellent plan, and Johnny made a hasty exit flanked by a credit on his left and a debit on his right.

Unfortunately, somebody down there at the Selective Service Office was on the ball to the extent that they noticed Johnny was three credits short of a full load. He or she accordingly prepared and sent a letter inviting him to attend a free Army pre-induction physical. It was 1966 and the jig, as they say, was up.

One good thing about surfing was that you got these huge knots on your feet and knees from knee paddling. Johnny, who had been knee paddling almost daily for years, had especially gross looking ones – particularily on his feet. Those mothers were BIG and required extra-long shoe laces. In the surf world, these were considered a badge of honor and a thing of beauty, much the same as in Africa where the bigger the plate you could stuff in your lower lip or the more rings you could stack up your neck, the better. It occurred to Johnny that he may have an edge on all the rest of the land lubbers who would be reporting with him for a physical next Saturday. Just in case, he beat on his feet with a two-by-four to accentuate the positive.

The day came and Johnny reported (with flip flops). He made his worse guesses at what was bigger, a division or a squad, and what do you see when you look at this ink blot, a mother kissing a baby or the devil stabbing Jesus. Apparently, he guessed wrong because, to his horror, he passed every single segment with above average scores. It was down to the last line up – thirty guys standing in a row waiting for the axe to fall. The drill sergeant says, "Is there any man here who is aware of any issue that may infringe upon his ability to serve in the United States Army?" Johnny stepped bravely forward and said, "Yes sir – I've got these knots on my feet that prevent me from wearing boots." To which the sergeant replied, "Get back in line."

And that was that. They advised that within two weeks he would receive his orders and be off to Fort Ord for a "shake and bake." That's what they called accelerated military training. They were funneling tens of thousands of kids through there on a weekly basis, so all they could do was give 'em the ol' shake 'n bake, hand 'em a gun and put 'em on the plane.

Johnny preferred to be neither shaken nor baked. So, he devised what to him seemed like a logical, some might say brilliant, plan – join the Hawaii National Guard and protect the shores of Waikiki! So, he went down to Fort DeRussy and signed up. When the notice came from the Army, it was too late – he was already betrothed to another.

This was more of a lateral move – he avoided the fire but merely exchanged pans. It turns out you had to attend these week end shindigs once a month, and sooner or later you were going to have to get a hair cut and go to basic training on the Mainland. The weekends at Fort DeRussy were bad news. They'd give you a toy gun, you'd fall in, then out, then be subjected to two days of mind-numbing activity complimented by excruciating boredom.

It only took one weekend to figure it out. From then on, Johnny would show up in a neatly pressed uniform, grab his rubber gun with gusto, fall smartly into formation, yell "Here SIR!" when his name was called, then break with the rest of the boys and head, in the confusion, for the hedge which surrounded the parade grounds. Deftly stuffing his gun in it and leaping over it, he was home free until Sunday afternoon when he did the whole thing in reverse. This worked quite well for nearly half a year until the accident.

Johnny survived by pumping gas on the night shift at the Standard Oil station on Kuhio Avenue. It is now a Chinese restaurant with a hotel above but, back then, it was a combination gas station and multi-level parking structure. It was directly behind the

International Market Place which was and still is the epicenter of Waikiki. Between midnight and 7 am it was a wild scene down there, especially when Don Ho's show let out and all the drunks staggered into the elevator, found their cars and attempted to drive home.

In those days being blind drunk was not seen as an impediment to good driving, so just about everybody was totally wasted. As they weaved down the ramp toward the little stand where Johnny sat with his ticket stamp and cash box, he would grit his teeth and hope they would miss him. The stand got taken out a few times, but anticipation and excellent reflexes enabled Johnny to side step the bull.

It was pretty entertaining talking to these people, many of whom were utterly incoherent. There was, however, one draw back. Every night at least one and some times several of the drivers and/or passengers would puke their guts out on the pavement next to his little stand, and Johnny would have to clean it up.

One evening Don, drunk as a skunk with a girl under each arm, arrived just in time to witness a particularly egregious episode. He stopped, fished around in his pocket, and came up with a five-dollar bill which he gave to Johnny and said "Clean it up." Five dollars in those days was like almost a hundred dollars today, so we're talking big money. Don was in the habit of coming by every night after his show let out, usually around three or four in the morning and usually with a different female member of his audience. So, Johnny would just leave that evening's mess on the concrete, wait for Don, graciously accepted $5, and get out the hose. He had a good thing going.

But then a guy with a 1960 Cadillac taxi pulled in and said, "I think I've got a leak; would you get under there and check it out?" The 1960 Cadillac is generally considered to be the largest car ever produced, with the possible exception of the Abrams tank which technically is not a car.

Johnny rolled the twin arm jack under the Caddie's front bumper (which was a big curved chrome affair) and pumped 'er up. Unbeknownst to him, the arms on the jack were not long enough to reach all the way under the curved bumper. He lay down on a dolly, slipped under the front end, and just as he raised his wrench to the oil pan, the lights went out – **BAM**.

It was an ugly scene. Suffice it to say, Johnny got really messed up. He spent the next three months in the hospital attempting to get better, but it was a long row to hoe. In an effort to restore order, they straightened out and wired up his teeth, inserted plastic disks in the bottom of his eye sockets to "even things out", then wired his skull back together from the bottom of his jaw to the top of his forehead. It was there that the wires protruded about four inches on either side. The purpose of this bizarre set up was that if he had to throw up someone could theoretically cut the wires and open his mouth before he drowned in his own juices. It made him look and feel like a grass hopper (somewhere a surgeon was laughing).

He lay in the hospital bed, periodically ringing the buzzer when he ran out of morphine or when the i.v. was improperly inserted and his arms swelled up like Popeye. Breakfast, lunch, and dinner was Gerber baby food (his favorite was apricot) which he sucked through his teeth. He nearly bought the farm when they mistakenly gave him apricot mixed with tapioca which clogged up the works. When it came time to remove the wad of gauze they had stuffed into his bleeding sinuses, it got stuck on a bone shard. You know how a dog flails around when he's playing tug-o-war? It was like that except the doctor was dragging Johnny around by his nose.

The very farthest thing from his mind was how things might be going down there at Fort DeRussy. It turned out, not very well. They immediately noticed the absence of the sharply dressed gung-ho recruit who had missed several weekend hoe downs, and deduced that he was apparently AWOL (absent with out leave). This precipitated a frantic man hunt – they did not think to look for him in St. Francis Hospital's IC unit.

When he finally got out, he was a shadow of his former self. Lack of exercise and three months of a strict baby food regiment had "trimmed him down" as the nurses liked to say when they would periodically glance in horror at the needle on the scale (which had gradually declined from 190 to 140). Lack of sun light had resulted in a pallor that eerily resembled the color of a dead person.

It was in this condition that he showed up at the Surgeon General's office at Tripler Army Hospital clutching the letters he'd found stuffed in his mail box regarding his status as a deserter and the long list of punishments he would be subjected to if they ever caught up with him. The Surgeon General recoiled and said, "Whoa son, you don't look too good – why don't we give you six months to, uh, get better." It turned out the wire "feelers" were a nice touch.

Johnny reregistered at the University of Hawaii, and basically wandered around campus scaring people. He would occasionally disappear for plastic surgery but, like the Hunch Back of Notre Dame, if you're not out there swinging on a rope ringin' bells, you're not gonna be missed. Towards the end of the six-month reprieve, as he slowly began to once more resemble a homo sapien, he started thinking about the future. He concluded that it might be a good idea to further his education at some Mainland college, and began to pack his bag.

Before he left, he dutifully reported to his National Guard unit at Fort DeRussy, and advised them of his intent, providing his parent's mainland address where he could be reached. His orders were terse "Wait for us to contact you." In theory, they would transfer his records to the folks at Central Command who would identify an appropriate Mainland Guard unit to which he would then be assigned.

Life returned pretty much to normal. He enrolled at USC, cut way back on booze and pot, and started (for once) to apply himself. He was sitting on the couch one Sunday morning reading the paper when he came across an article about a huge conflagration at the Army's central records facility which had destroyed "tens of thousands of vital documents." At the time, he did not grasp the significance of this. But as days stretched into weeks, then months, then years without word, he began to think that maybe his folder had gone up in smoke along with all those other valuable documents.

A half century later he still waits, like a Japanese soldier in a jungle bunker, for orders that have not yet come. When he turns seventy-five (wait, he's already seventy-five – let's make that eighty) and is damn sure he will be of no practical use whatsoever to the military, either foreign or domestic, he plans to march into the VA on a walker and demand his pension.

Chapter 21

Nail 'em

Miraculously, Johnny graduated from college in 1969 with a Master's Degree in Business Administration, which astonished him, his parents, and everybody else who ever knew him (upon hearing the news, one of his high school teachers looked Johnny's parents straight in the face and said "You're putting me on"). The party was over and it was time to get a job (his lovely wife Susan had floated him for years with the expectation that upon graduation he would return the favor).

And so, he scraped together all of Susan's money and bought a round trip ticket to Hawaii where he planned to do some "job interviews" in between surf sessions. In a show of good faith, he left his surfboard with Susan (knowing that he could borrow one when he got there), put on a tie, and hopped on a plane. It was a hellacious five days of interviews with forty large Hawaiian firms who, he reasoned, may have some need for a clueless person such as himself with an impressive sounding degree. Fortunately, it was flat so he wasn't conflicted by the need to get serious and the need to go surfing.

Thirty-nine of these interviews were unsuccessful and could be described as somewhere between bad and disastrous. Johnny was forced to endure a series of unflattering comments such as:

"Who sent you? "
"Call Security."
"Are you kidding?"
"Leave immediately."

However, the 40th landed him a job at one of the largest corporations in Hawaii where he was shown to an office in the executive suite on the 20th floor of a brand-new office building overlooking the Ala Moana Bowl and several other great surf spots. Johnny had somehow arrived!

Actually, Johnny and Susan arrived early. Their belongings had been shipped to San Francisco where they were hidden away in a warehouse for several months before a longshoreman with a bad attitude and a twisted sense of humor finally fessed up to his little prank. In the mean time, Johnny and his bride slept on a hardwood floor, which made for very uncomfortable sleeping (among other things).

Johnny's stint at corporate headquarters was shortened by his inability to conform. A month into his new job he decided it might be a good idea to grow a mustache - not a regular one which is generally confined to the area under your nose, but one that falls off both sides of your upper lip and cascades down your chin, sort of a Hell's Angels on crank Foo Man Chew kind of look. This did not sit well with senior management and, when the elevator doors opened on the 20th floor and Johnny came face to face with the President (who he had never met and would never meet again), he was gone from the executive suite.

He would spend the next three years floundering around in corporate purgatory participating in something called a "management rotation program" which he later came to realize meant "ship Mr. Kung Foo to the subsidiaries (Siberia) cause he's a little far out there for the corporate office."

So, Johnny, honored by the opportunity to personally visit each of the fifty-two subsidiary companies, happily packed his bags and took the tour. He spent time in a pineapple cannery where he learned that the juices from this fruit can not only burn a hole in the soles of your shoes, but also in the concrete floor you're standing on. In a can plant he learned how razor sharp 6'x6' sheets of thin galvanized metal were formed into useful vessels, and nearly decapitated an innocent bystander when he slipped while climbing a large pallet of sheets and shot one across the room. At a crane and rigging company he learned how the boss got to pick his own secretary and that the criteria for selection was not a typing test but an elbow test (applicants clasped their hands behind their heads, then walked toward the wall – if their tits hit before their elbows, they were IN).

At a heavy equipment company, he got to see his first D-9. Oh, My Gawd! A D-9 is an amazing piece of equipment. At the time, it was the largest bulldozer in the world with 474 gross horsepower and an operating weight of forty-nine tons. It is propelled by hardened steel caterpillar tracks and its primary working tools are a huge metal blade affixed to the front and a huge metal spike (ripper) attached to the back. Thus configured, you can turn on a D-9 and blow straight through a redwood forest or the Grand Coulee Dam without slowing down. Later, D-9's would be used by the Israelis during the Al Aqsa Intifada to demolish terrorist's houses under fire since they could withstand massive 500 kg IED blasts, deflect RPG rounds with impunity, and were impervious to machine gun fire. Sitting in the driver's seat on one of these babies caused Big Joe to salute.

One weekend, while house sitting during a rainstorm, Johnny pulled a book off the shelf called "Fodor's Europe" – a travel guide. By the end of the second day and two ounces of

Maui Wowie, he and the wife had already mapped out their route through Europe, Africa, and Asia. On Monday Johnny marched in the door, unfolded the map, and allowed as how he would be resigning to pursue other interests. Surprisingly, his boss had done the same thing thirty years before, and wished him a genuine farewell.

The trip was astounding, and deserves its own chapter, which it may get as soon as the statute of limitations expires.

Upon returning to Hawaii, alas it was time to get another job. Since Johnny had spent a few semesters at the University of Hawaii to legitimize his surfing avocation, he was able to avail himself of the "student placement center" which was basically a guy in a room somewhere on campus cutting want ads out of newspapers and mailing them to ex-students.

Johnny opened the mailbox and found an envelope containing a want ad from the guy with the scissors concerning a position of some import at a company called Nail'em.

It was not actually called Nail'em. The real name cannot be mentioned here. There are two basic reasons for this. For one thing, if they found out that Johnny wrote about them, they would sue him. For another, if they found out that he spilled the beans about what actually went on there, he would be assassinated.

So, after a particularly long and exhilarating surf session, Johnny walked over to Nail'em headquarters, leaned his board up against the wall, patted down his salty hair, tucked his t-shirt into his trunks and walked in the door. The interview gave testament to the power of a diploma – they were so immersed in his resume they failed to pick up on the fact that the individual standing before them was decidedly different in appearance and demeanor from the norm of the group to which he was suggesting an affiliation.

He was ushered into the Chief Exec's office by two subordinates waiving copies of his resume. After completing his interview, and noting that Johnny had a seven-month gap between his previous employment and now (trip to Europe) he asked, "So, what have you been doing with your spare time?" Reasoning that the truth (smoking pot and surfing) might not be appropriate here, he straight up lied and said "Working on my golf game." The Chief Exec, a fanatic golfer, hired him on the spot, and thus began Johnny's thirty-year career at Nail'em.

Nail'em was a large Hawaiian company that leased the land it owned to unsuspecting lessees. Although it was great for a while because the rent was low, it was a bad deal in the end because upon rent renegotiation (thirty years later) you were reamed like a sheep stuck in a barbed wire fence ("honest, I was just helping that sheep over the fence"), and at lease expiration (fifty-five years out) ownership of your house reverted to Nail'em and your ass was on the street.

On his first day in the office, he met another new hire, Louie Kau (pronounced "cow"). Louie was deeply tanned with a ready smile and a quick wit, and they became instant friends. That afternoon they were sitting there listening to someone tell them what it was that they were expected to do. Johnny remembers thinking "This is a pretty unusual place – here's a Hawaiian organization hiring a white guy and a black guy to beat up lessees." Imagine Johnny's surprise when he found out later that not only was Louie a Hawaiian, but his last name was spelled K-a-u.

The first ten years were uneventful. The fifty or so people in the office would meet in the third floor "dining room" (actually a big empty space with windows all around, a kitchen on one side, and some cheap chairs and tables) where they would eat a free lunch (yes, free). Then Johnny, Louie, and Andy the janitor would retire to Mrs. Estimago's pool hall next door for a little noontime recreation. Andy, of Filipino extraction, had a hot temper and hated to lose. They heard one morning that he'd been arrested over the weekend for pulling a forty-four magnum and firing off several rounds at some poor fool who drove by and gave him "stink eye." This infraction, for which Andy was given a stern reprimand by the Chief Exec who did not want to get shot himself, did not go unnoticed by Johnny and Louie who, from then on, let Andy win. Years later, when they tallied up their losses, it became apparent that they had put all of Andy's kids through school.

Then it got crazy. Leases, which had been issued thirty years before, started coming up for "renegotiation" (rectal damage). The rents that had been $300/year for thirty years (when land was cheap) suddenly jumped to $6,000/year and more (after rock stars, movie icons, and Saudi Arabian sheiks discovered Hawaii and drove land values through the roof). People were screaming bloody murder, hiring attorneys, and circling the wagons. There were homicides and suicides, bills in the Senate, bills in the House, and lawsuits galore. And Johnny, whose job it was to renegotiate rents, was right in the middle of it.

In a private audience with one of the top executives, it was suggested to Johnny that he "nail 'em," hence the fictitious but appropriate company name.

And so, his days consisted of a continuous stream of hysterical lessees rotating through his office with tales of woe and threats of violence. His friends started to distance themselves, and when he went to cocktail parties, he'd get backed into a corner by an angry mob of screaming finger pointing wild-eyed lessees. Pretty soon he just holed up in his house, locked the doors, and hoped nobody would find him.

This, it turned out, was the easy part. Unlike most companies, which only have one CEO, Nail'em had a CEO and five Super CEO's. These Super CEO's, through some quirk in the law, were appointed by a government body (the name of which can not be revealed here because of the suit and assassination thing). So as the old Super CEO's died off (they had previously been appointed for life and held on to the gravy train like an Ethiopian grips a rice ball) new ones were appointed. This was all well and fine, except the new ones were part of the political establishment (dirty rotten politicians) and they brought their back-room deal making techniques to the board room in a dump truck.

So, they split up Nail'em into five parts, and each Super CEO became the lord and master of his own feudal domain. One of them was doing deals in the steam room at the YMCA where he would accept cash in exchange for arranging certain government promotions. One of them started sleeping with a female staff attorney and got busted in a men's room stall in a pose made famous by a president – she expired the next day from embarrassment and carbon monoxide. One of them would call Johnny into her office and swing those big tits up on the desk and leer at him. One of them would ask Johnny to arrange it so all the new computers for the office would be purchased from his son. And one of them was really cool, and only asked that he do the right thing. That guy became the enemy of the other four, for obvious reasons.

And then the newspapers started to pick up the scent. And one newspaperman in particular, the guy who sat next to Johnny in the locker room at the Y every morning Monday through Friday, started to write some really wild stuff. He dominated the headlines three out of five week days and almost every Sunday. He would ask Johnny every day what was going on. Johnny (who's office was thirty feet from the board room) was a survivor ever mindful of the probability of litigation and premature expiration - he accordingly did not rat. But somebody sure did, cause that guy had the goods and smeared it all over the front page.

Then a Federal agency (name withheld to protect Johnny) entered the scene to take a look at the books. It wasn't too long (in accounting years) until they figured out that something was seriously awry. The process of removing all five Super CEO's commenced, and one fine day the last of the five was wheeling a dolly full of boxes down the hall and stopped in front of Johnny's office. Johnny said "What now?" The Super CEO said, "I don't know" and disappeared into the mist.

The new bunch of Super CEO's came in, and although they were decent enough, they didn't really have a good grip on how to run what was by now a humongous company with thousands of employees and billions of dollars. They hired "experts" from everywhere and Johnny and the others had to sit through painful meetings where the "experts" would reinvent the wheel, or insist on going off on weird pointless tangents. They hired a new CEO who was available because his prior firm had been shut down by the government for gross improprieties. This new CEO immediately introduced a "revolutionary method" of calculating senior executive raises and bonus's which relied primarily on increases in land value due to appreciation and inflation (which had nothing to do with performance). He made a killing before he got canned.

Through all of this, Johnny tried to maintain his composure by surfing as much as possible. He hung a sign on his office door that said, "SURF ALERT, something came up, back in three hours." When he wasn't there, they didn't know if he was in a board meeting or a "board meeting" (i.e bobbing around out in the surf with a bunch of other guys on surfboards). He would go on frequent surf trips with his surfing buddies to far away lands. On one of these occasions, while floating in the pristine waters off the coast of Raiatea, one of his friends (Ron House, a good friend and a surfboard shaper from San Clemente) could tell he was stressing. He paddled over, looked him in the eye, and said "Do you really want to be the richest guy in the grave yard?"

That got him to thinking. Do you really want to endure this crap for several more years? If the answer to that is "no," how the hell are you going to get out of here with some money honey? You know too much and you've got too much underway. Up and quitting was an option, but this scenario would result in an empty bag and a place in line at the unemployment office.

After considerable thought, he concocted a scheme (some might say a brilliant scheme) to not do what was expected of him. When he got the call that "the bag" was ready for a certain

Senator or City Councilman, Johnny was "unexpectedly detained on other business" so somebody else had to be corralled to do the deed. When a particular "friend" of the Super CEO's happened to be the subject of a lease renegotiation, Johnny did not provide a drastically reduced rental rate but, instead nailed'em (ha ha). Strictly by the book baby! This greatly complicated matters in the executive suites.

As an added touch, Johnny began to fain computer ignorance. This was particularly frustrating for the rank and file who had been relying on Johnny to do the heavy lifting. A few, "Gee, I don't know – better let one of the guys in the computer room figure that one out" did the trick.

Since they couldn't fire him for doing the right thing, they were delighted to negotiate a generous severance package and his intention to retire early was announced. Jaws dropped and some staff members actually teared up. But it was time, it was over, and Johnny was getting out (thank you Ron).

The last day he road his Harley into the lobby, ate some cake, made some speeches, and posed for some pictures with the secretaries (who had dressed up in cop uniforms and chained him to his Harley). Then he fired her up and motored out of the building and through the courtyard lined with friends, palms outstretched for the last high five. He never looked back.

Chapter 22

Kilo Football

Brian and Ron were roommates at Cal Western. Johnny had passed the torch to them before his untimely departure from that institution of higher learning. Brian and Ron would later share a house in Mokuleia, a small beach community way out on the North Shore on the Island of Oahu. It was most likely a converted tool shed, or perhaps it had been intended as a domicile for very short people. But it kept the rain off and was across the street from the ocean, which made for a quick and easy surf check.

There was a huge "lawn" on one side, actually a barren spot the landlord had carved out of the surrounding sugar cane which sprouted some sort of vegetation that resembled grass when it was cut, which was often since the landlord just loved to get stoned and ride that lawn mower. When they weren't surfing or sucking on a hookah or staring at the sun, they whiled away the hours playing Frisbee on the "lawn."

They were the living embodiment of the ultimate surfer lifestyle. Pipeline was just down the road. It was the late-60's so the "Country," as they called the stretch of outrageous beaches and surf breaks that occupied the seven miles between Haliewa and Sunset, had not as yet been officially discovered, which is to say there were only a few thousand people there instead of a few hundred thousand.

Pipeline had been surfed for the first time only a few years earlier by Phil Edwards on a dare. Once the potential became known and the equipment caught up, Pipeline assumed its rightful position as one of the greatest waves in the world, and every good surfer aspired to challenge it. The gauntlet had been thrown down, and Brian and Ron eagerly picked it up. Ron got his ear ripped off and sowed back on, Brian got his wrist broken in numerous places – Pipeline is a dangerous place.

Their physical arrival in Hawaii coincided with a spiritual awakening of sorts. They diligently pursued Dr. Leary's advice to "turn on, tune in, and drop out" which they managed to do in spades.

They stumbled around for several months, dividing their time into two basic segments – surfing and drug induced comas. The drug of choice at that time was pakalolo, the Hawaiian word for herb. Those guys could smoke more pakalolo than just about anybody, and they never missed an opportunity to demonstrate their skills. Fortunately, this all went down before harder drugs came into vogue –

otherwise they would never have made it to the 70's.

So here they were, in the 60's, in the country, in a teeny little house just down the road from Pipeline, livin' it up. However, they gradually began to realize that it might be necessary to get a job in order to buy food and wax. This was both startling and depressing since they had been pretty sure they had left all that far behind in the cosmic dust.

Possessing no apparent marketable skills, they floundered around for an opening on the gravy train and, as luck would have it, found one. They had noticed that their/the demand for pot far exceeded the supply. Recalling the economics class they had pretty much slept through at Cal Western, they dimly reasoned that there might be a niche for a couple of enterprising young men if they could figure out a way to "supply the demand."

Bingo! Ya get on a plane, fly to San Diego, check in with Pedro, fill a few suit cases full of mud splattered Mexican, fly back to Hawaii and sell the stuff for ten times what you paid for it. Like a Julia Childs recipe, repeat often.

This plan was at once both brilliant and insane. On the one hand, they would be rolling in dough from the get go and would never have to worry about food and wax. On the other hand, they might (most definitely would) get caught, which would result in a host of complications, not the least of which could involve prison.

So, they hopped on United, disembarked in San Diego, dropped by Sears to pick up four suitcases, which they filled to the brim with smelly old kilos from Pedro's garage, and returned to Hawaii six hours later. Those suitcases were heavy and fragrant, but they cheerfully paid the excess weight fee and explained they had not had an opportunity to wash their cloths prior to packing. And they got away with it (for a while).

Gawd, life was grand for the next few months. They became very popular fellows indeed out there on the North Shore. In fact, everybody loved them. They were the Coast Guard coming to rescue the drowning masses, they were the bees bringing the honey back to the hive, they were working men who didn't have to sweat – all they had to do was casually inquire "Want some weed?"

Like any intelligent businessmen, when ya got a good thing going, ya wanna put the pedal to the metal. So, they made many runs and filled their little house with 2.2-pound bricks of pot. Now, to appreciate the grandeur of this situation, it is important to keep in mind that Johnny was lucky if he could beg or borrow a few grams of pakalolo, which he would, of necessity, ration over many weeks. Ron and Brian were sitting on thousands of pounds. And when this became known, Johnny (who was living in Honolulu and making a feeble attempt to go straight in the business world) picked up the frequency of his trips to the Country.

Ron and Brian got a big kick out of Johnny when he showed up with a tie around his neck. This would occur when he was able to combine a pot run with a site inspection to one of the enterprises in the area owned by the company he "worked" for.

And so, one glorious morning, on the way to a site inspection in the Country, Johnny showed up at Ron and Brian's front door in his blue and white polka dot tie. It was there that he would witness the largest pile of pot he had ever seen (until sometime later under decidedly different circumstances). The rooms were packed from floor to ceiling with cellophane wrapped kilo bricks of Mexican da kine. The place smelled like the inside of a pipe bowl.

In a demonstration of superb etiquette, Ron and Brian broke out the hookah and filled it to the brim with the good stuff. Realizing that the afternoon was probably shot, Johnny sucked with gusto on the gaily colored tube that led to the container that held the water through which the smoke from the bowl passed on its way to his lungs and, hence, his brain.

Five minutes later, they were so stoned it was not possible to rise from the floor. Fortunately, their vital signs were good, and within a half hour, they had regained some motion in their extremities, although it was more like involuntary spasms. By the time an hour had elapsed, they were able to formulate words and someone said "Frisbee." So, they stumbled out to the "lawn" but could not find the Frisbee.

It is not known whose brilliant idea it was, but somebody said, "OK then, how about a little kilo football?" 2.2 pounds of cellophane wrapped pakalolo was retrieved from the house and a three-man team was loosely formed. Upon the appropriate command, the "center" hiked the kilo to the "quarterback" who tossed the thing to the "wide receiver." Several passes were indeed completed that afternoon before the package hit the ground and exploded into a mound the size of a wagon wheel. Johnny stood there in shock, realizing that this was enough pot to get him through an entire year, maybe two, and now it was blowing away in the wind.

Brian looked at Johnny and said, "Don't worry, there's a lot more where that came from."

Chapter 23

Court

It did not turn out well for Brian and Ron.
Weekly first-class forays to San Diego piqued
the interest of the Drug Enforcement Agency,
which was just beginning to realize there
might be a drug problem on the North Shore.

The six-hour turn around time was a clue.
They also noticed that on the flight out, their
luggage consisted of a paper bag, while on the
way back it was four brand new super duty
suitcases with stainless steel locks and an
overpowering aroma. So, the DEA decided to
greet Ron and Brian at Honolulu International
Airport with leis and pleasant conversation.

This was back in the days before smoke
detectors were installed in aircraft restrooms,
so you could do pretty much anything in
there. Brian and Ron took full advantage of
this technological oversight, managing to get
quite high minutes after take-off. On the plus
side, the flight was quite enjoyable, even
funny, and those first-class meals were
especially tasty. On the negative side, when
you disembark and are met by a half dozen
gun toting DEA men with badges and serious
attitudes, it tends to promote paranoia and an
inability to clearly express yourself.

Brian and Ron were completely and utterly busted and they knew it. They pretty much just put up their hands in resignation and watched as one of the DEA guys pressed the button on his switchblade and cut into their brand-new Louie Viton luggage. It was almost, but not quite, amusing as the knife wielding DEA guy recoiled in surprise and disgust as pot spewed out onto the concourse.

It was a dark night in Mokuleia as the boys returned home, empty handed and preparing for jail. They were due the next evening at Johnny's for dinner, but were psychologically unable to show. Johnny was reading the newspaper when he noticed an article about two young men who had been detained at the Honolulu Airport the previous evening with an extraordinarily large quantity of marijuana. Their names were Brian and Ronald. Uh oh.

The next day Johnny jumped in his car (not wanting to use the phone) and drove out to Mokuleia. Brian and Ron were just lookin' at the floor, contemplating their future, which likely involved unwanted prison sex and possibly suicide.

It was pretty awkward. But just then the phone rang and a new attorney in town called and said he had heard of their misfortune and, although he would like to represent them himself, his position as a clerk to a Supreme Court Justice prevented him from doing so. However, he knew a guy – not a mobster, but another lawyer. Johnny pondered this – is there a difference? He wasn't really sure, but he did know that if he were trapped in an elevator with a lawyer, a mobster, and a pedophile with only two rounds left in his .45, he'd shoot the lawyer twice.

The guy was David Shutter, also new in town and lookin' to put a few notches in the handle of his brief case. Actually, he was amazing, and Ron and Brian had the good fortune of becoming one of his first clients (for a modest fee). Shutter would proceed immediately thereafter to cut a wide, nay, gaping swath through Honolulu's legal system, ripping, as it were, a new judicial asshole large enough to accommodate the exoneration of pretty much every member of the Hawaiian Mafia (including the guys who killed the Las Vegas thugs attempting to take over the China Town racquets, chopping them into little pieces and sending them back in a box with a note that read "Ummm, tastes good, send more") along with several hundred other absolutely guilty undesirables.

Lawyered up and ready to go, Brian got a haircut and Ron got a wig. Now, the physics of wig wearing, especially for a longhaired surfer/drug smuggler, is that the hair you have has to be stuffed under the hair you bought. This meant that Ron's wig (a tasteful dishwater blond affair) towered over the top of his head and anyone, even a blind man, could see that something was definitely wrong with this picture (the Cone Heads come to mind). But Ron convinced himself that he looked pretty good in the mirror, and off they went to the First Circuit Court for their initial appearance.

Not wanting to miss anything, Johnny ditched work and went on over to the court house to sit in the front row with his unjustly accused buds in their hour of need. He tried not to look at Ron's wig, but it was like trying not to stare at Brian's sister's tits – jeezus, that thing was bizarre. The judge was having the same problem and pretty much-fixated on Ron's bouffant but, in a display of unexpected mercy, neither mentioned it nor demanded that it be removed.

Shutter was unbelievable, strutting up and down, waving his hands in the air, and pounding the table to make a point. The judge, still looking at Ron, was not impressed, holding the boys over for trial.

Johnny went back to work while the others went back to Shutter's office to review their appearance. As soon as the door closed, Ron exploded, "What are you trying to pull,

Shutter? We can go to jail for FREE!" Shutter calmed them down, and arranged another court appearance a few weeks later.

This time around, Shutter was stupendous. He was in the zone. He could have gotten compensatory damages for OJ.

Shutter, "Was your luggage damaged?"

Ron, "No, it was new."

Shutter, "Then what is this incision down the side?"

Ron, "Uh, that's where the DEA guy cut it with a switch blade."

Shutter, pausing for a minute, then screamed, "CUT.... IT.... WITH... A..... **SSSWITCH BLADE?!**"

Ron, "Uh, yeh".

Shutter to Prosecuting Attorney, "And, did the DEA have a warrant to CUT MY CLIENT'S LUGGAGE WITH A......**SSSWITCH BLADE?!**".

"Well, no."

"Case dismissed!"

Brian and Ron waited almost a year before trying it again.

Chapter 24

The Tire Incident

Johnny is fortunate to live in a forest on top of a mountain overlooking Diamond Head and Waikiki. It is a toney address, and sometimes Johnny counts his lucky stars and remembers part of a song by the Talking Heads that goes "THIS is not my beautiful house, THIS is not my beautiful wife..."

It was pretty much serendipity that he would end up living here, instead of in some funky condo down there in the hot flat lands next to the freeway. To supplement his income early on, he had been doing "consulting work" for various small businesses on the brink of disaster. One such business was a health food store called Good Earth run by a consummate hippie husband and wife team, John and Lisa, who were long on exuberance but short on business savvy. They had been getting ripped off shamelessly and relentlessly by unscrupulous operators supplying them with just about everything they required and, as a result, found themselves in a very deep hole not entirely of their own making.

About ten minutes after walking in the door and glancing at the books, it was pretty clear that these guys were going down. Nevertheless, they were nice people who where earnestly trying to make a living selling healthy food, so Johnny resolved to try and help them out. He personally visited every rip off artist, dishonest service provider, and all the barnacles clinging to the bottom of the health food boat who uniformly promised violence and litigation. Surprisingly, they all folded, sending in generous refund checks and profuse apologies. Johnny became something of a celebrity in the health food field, and earned the owner's trust and friendship.

One day John, the owner, allowed as how he was going to build a house behind Lisa's folk's home at the top of a mountain, and asked Johnny if he'd like to help. Not having had the opportunity to build a house and wondering how it was done, Johnny accepted. "How ARE we gonna do this?" Johnny inquired. "Don't worry, I'm a carpenter" John not entirely correctly replied.

The day arrived, and they met on site, each with a hammer and a box of nails. Jeez, it was an amazing location tucked into the forest at an elevation of 1,100 feet with a remarkable panoramic view of Honolulu in the front and an awesome panoramic view of valleys and mountains in the back. John immediately produced a large dubie. Thus fortified, they began building a house out of the scrap lumber they had assembled from various demolition sites around town. (Look Ma, no plans!)

It turned out ol' John was not exactly a carpenter, but he had once been on the clean up crew at a hotel construction site on Maui so he was loosely familiar with the jargon and recognized several common tools, some by name (hammer). Beyond this, neither he nor Johnny had a clue.

They built a house, nonetheless, which they figured would be good for five years but which still stands (barely) today, more than fifty years later.

John and Lisa lived happily in their new home for several years, until an opportunity arose on Maui that was too good to pass up (pakalolo). Being that Johnny and his wife Susan were the squarest people they knew, and being also that it was important whoever occupied the place could get along with Lisa's parents Russ and Libby who lived in a large house in front, they asked them to move in, which they did.

It was delightful. Russ and Libby were way cool, the little house stood up well to the weather, and it only took ten minutes to get downtown. They lived blissfully here for many years and then their children came along. First Matt, then, in a failed attempt at zero population growth, identical twins Anna and Ingrid.

Matt was a handsome mischievous fellow and Anna and Ingrid were sweet little girls, although Johnny was never able to tell them apart and resorted out of necessity to calling them by generic names such as "Sweetie" or "Honey." To mistakenly call Anna Ingrid or vice versa caused considerable commotion.

A lot of things happened as the kids were growing up but we will skip here to the "tire incident" which pretty much sets the tone for everything else that preceded and followed.

There were two ways to get down the hill. You either took the direct route, which is a straight shot from top to bottom down Wilhelmina Rise, or you took the long way called Sierra Drive, which is a road that zig zags lazily down the hill from side to side, crossing over the direct route on each traverse.

If you took the direct route, you'd have to stop each time you came to a traverse route intersection. In practice, there was a lot of "rolling Honolulu stops" going on every morning on the way down, although on the way back up in the afternoon, some people would actually come to a halt before proceeding across the many intersections. If you were in a hurry, as most people seemed to be in the morning, you put your feet on the dashboard and headed straight down.

Traveling the direct route had certain disadvantages, chief among them being that the City, in its infinite wisdom, allowed street parking. Thus, this route was effectively a high-speed single lane thoroughfare on a 45-degree incline requiring great dexterity and lightening fast reflexes in order to avoid the parked cars going down and the on coming cars going up.

Johnny was a stone expert at this and it is believed he still holds the record for the fastest downhill run. However, his highly competitive niece beat him going up once by several minutes and pretended to be asleep when he arrived (in his defense he had stopped for a little old lady sporting a walker).

Several blocks below Johnny's house, perched at the top of the direct decent, was a small City Park. The kids from the neighborhood hung out there and got into whatever kind of trouble was available. A construction project was underway and the driver of a large backhoe suffered a flat. He had apparently asked whoever it is that stocks huge tractor tires to bring one up – then left for the day. The tire guy brought a new one up which was already mounted on a very heavy metal rim, leaned it against the tractor and left.

It did not take long for Matt and his circle of friends to find the tire and start messing with it. With every poke and prod it moved closer to the edge. One last nudge (administered by a party who shall remain nameless) and a thousand-pound tractor tire began rolling slowly and inexorably straight down Wilhelmina Rise.

It was late in the evening and, apparently, there were no witnesses, so no one actually saw what happened. However, the next morning when Johnny drove down the hill, it was clear that something really out of the ordinary (very bad) had occurred.

As he began his decent, he noticed squad cars, fire trucks and people everywhere along the route clustered around crushed automobiles, flattened mail boxes, broken street signs and the occasional downed telephone pole. The hill, previously pristine, was now strewn with twisted metal, busted glass and shattered timber (the termites had been set free). Some objects were completely unrecognizable. Others twisted in bizarre shapes and/or listing at peculiar angles, bore only a faint resemblance to their former selves.

At every stop, it was apparent that whatever had caused this carnage had rolled across each level intersection at high speed and then leaped into the air for a considerable distance before coming back to earth and another opportunity to flatten and/or mangle whatever might be unfortunate enough to lay it its path. Owing to the kinetic energy embodied in a thousand-pound tractor tire traveling close to terminal velocity, there was nothing that could or would stop it, and so it continued on it's merry way approximately a mile straight down to the bottom of the hill and quite some distance on flat land mowing down every perpendicular thing until it finally flopped over in the middle of the main intersection with Waialae Avenue.

We are not talking here about one or two cars; we're talking about dozens and dozens. Not just one or two mailboxes, a whole slew of them. Ditto hedges and street signs. A significant number of streetlights and quite a few telephone poles were also down (this would later send Hawaiian Electric and Hawaiian Telephone stock plummeting as the true magnitude of the repair job became known).

It looked as though an entire Nazi Panzer division had rolled through - twice. Miraculously, no humans or animals were hurt or killed, and this was the by line on the extensive newspaper article that appeared later that day. Matt was a little jumpy for a while, particularly when the subject came up, but Johnny figured it was too many Oreos and the incident was, in time, forgotten.

Twenty years later as they were driving down Wilhelmina Rise, Matt said, "Dad, do you remember that tractor tire that took out all those cars and mail boxes and hedges and street signs about twenty years ago?"

Chapter 25

Trifecta

Johnny worked hard at the office, and put in long hours too (no, really!). It sort of snuck up on him. The original idea was to do 9 to 5, then go home and roll out the hookah. This worked well for the first few years, but as responsibilities mounted, there was more to do than could be done in the standard time allotted. So pretty soon he was hoping to get home by six, then seven, then eight. In order to have a little quality time in the evenings with the wife and the kids as they came along, he cut back on the week day schedule and started going in on Saturdays when he pretty much was the only guy in the building and you could get a lot done without interruption. Also, you could surf the web and needn't fret about somebody coming up behind you in the middle of a hot poker hand. Toward the end, he was going in on Sundays too.

He noted with some alarm that several of his buddies doing similar work had begun to fray at the edges. One guy in particular, Paul, showed up one morning to ride up with Johnny in the elevator. He leaned in uncomfortably close and inquired "Ya wanna see my new tattoo?" Johnny responded "Oh sure" with about the same level of enthusiasm

Dustin Hoffman might have employed in responding to a question about plastic.

Paul unbuttoned the front of his shirt to reveal a grizzly looking bloody purple thing. It was an upside-down pyramid from chest to belly button consisting of a series of smaller upside-down pyramids, all of which were oozing some sort of multi-colored fluid. It looked like a herd of Samoans had been pounding on him with chisels and axes dipped in ink. This was no carnival tattoo – this one would not wash off and was so deep that even skin grafts could not erase it. Two days later, he was gone. This was somewhat of a wake-up call for Johnny, and it became clear that he needed to step up his extracurricular activities or end up in the Soilent Green scrap heap with the rest of the office burnouts.

Given that even early on he was working insanely long hours, he rationalized that he probably should take a little time off every so often for himself. So, he devised a plan with three components: racquetball, surfing and golf.

Racquetball –

He had observed some guys in an enclosed room at the Y beating the crap out of each other with sawed off tennis racquets and a small rubber ball. This looked like the kind of thing he might be able to get into. So, he started getting up an hour early and headed to the Y where he attempted to thrash whoever showed up (he was a legend in his own mind). Actually, there was a core group of guys who materialized around 6 am with pretty much the same expectation and mind-set.

If you've ever played racquetball, you know that one hour in a racquetball court can really poop you out. You can burn about 10,000 calories while you run yourself ragged chasing that little blue ball. It felt great afterwards to take a shower and head to work because the endorphins (a group of endogenous peptides found especially in the brain that bind chiefly to opiate receptors and produce certain pharmacological effects such as euphoria and delirium) were coursing through your veins and arteries in an attempt to mask the pain caused by the damage you had just inflicted on your body. At the office in this naturally induced state of grace, nothing and no one could faze you. You could always tell a racquetball player in a meeting – they were the one's who weren't screaming.

Of course, there were incidents and accidents. One guy refused to wear protective goggles and managed to implode his own eye on a shot to the back wall that rebounded perfectly into his retina – we called him Ace after that. Another guy stood up in the middle of a rally, grasped his chest, and fell over dead. He happened to be Johnny's secretary's husband. It was not a happy day. The racquetball brotherhood was later accorded the honor of being admitted to the inner sanctum of the Mormon Church for the funeral, (only actual Mormons are supposed to go in there) and found out a little more about the fundamentals of the religion than they needed to know (you had to be there). Suffice it to say the racquetball boys frequently looked at each other and said "WHAT?"

Racquetball enthusiasts get injured often. Contusions, dislocations, and torn ligaments are common along with the occasional fracture. Knees and ankles are the first to go. These problems arise principally from extreme starting/stopping and also from getting hit by the racquet or the ball, or from colliding with the wall. The ball was the worst. The pros are able to hit a racquetball 175 mph. In slow motion, such a ball traveling at that speed stretches out into a bullet shape until it hits an immovable object (like a wall or somebody's cheek) whereupon it collapses into a pancake and transmits all that kinetic energy to that one place. On a wall, you get a blue mark. On a cheek, you get what is referred to as "a wheel," which is basically a circular cluster of broken veins that radiate out in colorful yellows, purples, and reds. If you pull up at the McDonalds drive-thru with one of these, they will refuse to serve you.

But these minor annoyances were a small price to pay for the exercise and camaraderie derived by the participants. So, Johnny played racquetball every weekday for the next twenty-five years. Toward the end as his joints started to give out, he slowed down to three times a week and finally, after his fifth arthroscopic knee surgery, his doctor dropped a Soup Nazi bomb - "No more racquetball for YOU!" It was a hell of a run.

PS – Johnny just had a third hip replacement (on the same hip) and needs to get another one on the other hip when he recuperates. He's pretty sure racquetball is partly to blame.

Surfing –

This is the big one – the greatest sport there ever was and perhaps ever will be. Johnny was fortunate to have found it at an early age and, over the years, honed his skills to a high level. There is nothing, NOTHING, like hucking it over the ledge on a big one, dropping down the face through the spray, and pulling into a macking blue barrel with the sun diffusing through the water overhead. It is really not possible to describe this feeling. All the drugs in Cincinnati administered at once would still probably fall short.

So, it is no wonder that Johnny went surfing quite often. His favorite spot cannot be mentioned here (Threes) for fear of attracting a crowd. It is, with out a doubt, the finest wave on the South Shore of Oahu, and when it gets good, all other spots pale in comparison. Johnny had been introduced to this place in the early 60's by an adventurous fellow named Leonard who had the wherewithal to paddle beyond the Waikiki shore break to see what might be out there. It was a solid six-foot day and, as they paddled to the mystery break on the horizon, it became apparent they had arrived at the gates of Heaven – long blue barrels spinning down the line from way outside. That was it, Johnny was hooked, and that became his favorite sport and his favorite spot.

In the early days, the crowd was pretty mellow and everybody got along. Later, as the crowd swelled from a dozen to fifty to one hundred, things got tense and the brotherhood of surfers disassembled into a pack of wild animals. Guys were swingin' on each other, yelling and screaming, waiting on the beach with baseball bats – it was stone crazy. And then something happened. Critical mass had been achieved and then transcended (this later became known during the Covid slaughter as "herd immunity") and suddenly most of the guys got it – they were out there to have fun and so was everybody else. The vibes improved markedly and things settled down.

One of the great things about surfing is that "after surfing feeling" which are basically endorphins coursing through your veins and arteries in a heroic attempt to mask the pain from the damage you had just inflicted on your body (sound familiar?). So, in addition to racquetball, Johnny surfed a lot also.

Golf –

Johnny was introduced to golf at an early age (ten). His Dad insisted that he go down to the local golf course and take advantage of the free Saturday morning golf lessons, which consisted of several dozen ten-year olds standing in a line swatting balls. Every once in a while, a disinterested (and frequently inebriated) club pro (who would much rather be out there on the links taking people's money) would walk up and down the line dispensing pearls of wisdom which were poorly understood and poorly executed. By the time he was seventeen and had to go off to college, he could hit the ball reasonably well – but he was no champion.

It turned out that his Dad had been right to subject him to the anger and frustration that embodies the game of golf. It somehow moderated his temperament and enabled him to accept adversity a little better than, say, Happy Gilmore. It also came in handy as he rose in the executive ranks and was required to play golf to seal a deal. He could keep up with the other business guys out there on the course reasonably well, and appreciated a well-struck ball. His lowest score ever was a seventy-three but mostly he inhabited the eighty-five to ninety zone with the rest of the hackers. Pars and Birdies were fun but few and far between.

Trifecta –

One day it all came together. He got up at dawn, went down to the Y and played racquetball, made a cameo appearance at the office, then went off to play golf, and wrapped up the day with an evening surf session – a perfect trifecta.

Johnny went about establishing trifecta ground rules – it had to be a work day, you had to show up at the office, and you had to fake everybody into thinking that you were somewhere doing something important. His secretary Karla was in on the deal, and followed strict instructions to inform (with a straight face) whoever was looking for him that he was in a "board meeting" or "out in the field on business." These were not technically lies, as he would be bobbing around in a sea of boards while surfing, and would be on a field of sorts while golfing – racquetball happened before work officially commenced so it was not necessary to develop an elaborate ruse for that.

When the surf came up and the sun came out, Johnny would attempt another trifecta. Since he lived in Hawaii where the sun is almost always out and the surf is quite frequently up, he was on a trifecta roll. Johnny had refined his moves to the point where people admired the selfless dedication with which he threw himself into board meetings and field operations. When he waltzed down the hallway, making sure to say hi to anyone within earshot, his superiors approvingly nodded as he strolled by (on his way to the fire escape).

In this way, Johnny managed more trifectas than it is possible to count and maintained his sanity for thirty years.

Chapter 26

Road Rage

Johnny always thought of himself as calm and levelheaded. He respected his fellow man, was polite to his neighbors, good to his friends, and tried to get along with everybody else in an affable manner. Whenever there was a damsel in distress, he was there. Getting that little old lady across the street unscathed – no problem. Merging in heavy traffic – help yourself and throw a shaka sign with a smile.

It came as quite a shock, then, to learn that he had a deeply repressed dark side. Of course, when he slammed his thumb with a hammer, there was always an audible expletive (his favorite was "GAWD DAMMIT!") but he was usually able to shake it off and, in a few seconds, he was back in control. Even in very tense situations, say when somebody smashes a whiskey bottle on the bar and comes at you with the jagged leftovers, his usual response was to remain silent and calmly size up the situation, mentally calculating the distance to the front door and/or emergency room and the probable recovery period.

But there was this one time. Oops, a couple times. Oops, when Johnny turned seventy-five there was one more time. Please refer to the chapter entitled "Get Off the Bus Gus."

He had just been hired at a new job (which would end up being his only job for the rest of his working life). It was important that he make a good impression and fit in as best he could (a square surfer peg in a round corporate hole). Accordingly, he made great efforts to ingratiate himself to the most important people in the office – the secretaries. Chief among these was the Queen of all the secretaries, Shirley.

Shirley was the CEO's Personal Secretary and Confidant. This made her slightly more important than the Vice President of the United States, although she was not paid as well. However, this disparity in remuneration did not matter, owing to her marriage to Buddy, the wealthy owner of a thriving pool service business.

So, Johnny made a point of dropping by Shirley's desk on a reasonably frequent basis for idle chit chat, passing on or receiving the occasional juicy office gossip, and once in a while dropping off a cheap box of candy to enhance her day and his chances of advancement.

Things were going swimmingly and then, quite unexpectedly, an incident occurred which surprised even Johnny and stood out as a precursor of things to come.

There was this skinny Japanese guy named Ed, one of the worker bees. He was cursed with one of the most negative personalities imaginable – well south of Don Rickles. It was not a beautiful morning - "It stinks." It was not a good football game - "Those idiots suck." It was not a tasty plate lunch – "This shit makes me sick." It was like that, except worse.

The secretaries all hated this guy. On top of being a complete doofus, he loved to lord it over anyone he perceived as being below his station in life. This included secretaries and Johnny. Thus, the planets were aligned and Johnny and the secretaries shared a bond of mutual distain for this loathsome person.

As luck would have it, Johnny had watched a movie the night before called "Harry In Your Pocket." It had to do with this guy (James Colburn) who went around plucking the wallets out of people's back pockets with panache. Upon entering the office the next morning Johnny, perhaps a little too amped after that second cup of coffee, spied ol' Ed leaning over a drafting table with a big fat wallet hanging out of his trousers.

In a feeble attempt to mimic last night's movie, Johnny strolled by and grabbed that wallet right outta Ed's shorts. Unfortunately, Johnny fumbled and the wallet flopped to the ground, disgorging its contents all over the office floor (which included a couple naked lady playing cards and a wrinkled prophylactic). It was meant to be a good-natured prank, but was perceived by ol' Ed as a Caucasian effort to impugn his ancestors and achieve retribution for December 7th.

Ol' Ed came out swinging. Johnny, who was a foot taller and outweighed him by several stone, could not believe this guy could possibly be serious. He bobbed the first swing - Eddie spun around and nearly fell. Another haymaker came and went. Still Ed advanced. With each lunge, Johnny backed up just enough to avoid the thrust, ending up in front of Shirley's desk. Finally, it became apparent this guy just wasn't gonna quit. So, Johnny grabbed him by the throat, lifted him off the floor and slammed him to the ground with surprising force, knocking the wind outta ol' Ed and causing Shirley to soil her pants. The entire secretarial pool was thrilled, and Johnny's stature around the office was considerably enhanced.

This episode revealed the theoretical presence of a monster lurking within. It only took another week to find out how big the monster was.

Johnny's routine drive to the office involved getting off the H-1 Freeway at the Lunalilo Off Ramp. The Lunalilo Off Ramp is a study in

Department of Transportation ineptitude as it involves a quarter mile stretch of road that serves both as an "on" AND an "off" ramp. That is to say, cars decelerating from high speeds are trying to get off the friggin' freeway at the same time other cars accelerating to high speeds are trying to get on. Everybody's late for work and nobody's happy about it.

Johnny, ever a model of decorum and Aloha, let the first seven cars trying to merge onto the freeway pass in front of him. When the coast was clear, he began to slowly merge off. Looking dutifully into his passenger side mirror, he noticed a panel van in the distance accelerating at a rapid clip. A moment later it pulled next to him at sixty miles an hour with decided intent to blow by and merge. This might have passed without incident but for one thing. As they sped parallel to each other, neither one yielding, the driver of the panel van swerved into Johnny's lane and knocked his passenger side mirror flat.

They say when you lose it you see red. Johnny saw Magenta. They say your blood boils. It does. They say you want to kill. You do.

This guy floored it and narrowly missed getting T-boned on the pointed guardrail that separated the on/off ramp from the freeway (this was before they installed several hundred-gallon vats full of water that you could plow spectacularly into without getting seriously injured). He made it by inches, with Johnny inches behind. This guy was gonna die.

Johnny, driving a sluggish VW bus, mashed the pedal down and weaved through traffic picking up speed. A mile down the freeway he overtook the panel van and pulled in front of 'em. The driver attempted to swerve around, first left into the fast lane, then right into the slow lane. Johnny anticipated his moves as he watched the dashboard rear view mirror with blood in his eyes and a desire to do bad things.

Easing off the throttle, they began a kind of decelerating automotive waltz - fifty mph to the left, forty mph to the right, thirty mph center, twenty left ten right, dead stop bumper to bumper in the center lane of the H-1 freeway.

The drivers of the many other cars in the fast and slow lanes sensed there was something going down that involved testosterone and insanity, so they began to slow down and rubberneck. The middle lane was already backed up for a considerable distance.

Johnny disembarked from the VW bus and walked back to the panel van as the driver feverishly rolled up his windows, locked his doors, and started yelling, "Get out of here you asshole!" That was definitely the wrong thing to say.

Johnny was now beyond magenta in some unknown spectrum of light. His blood pressure spiked to 240 over 160. Violence was no longer an ethereal possibility - it was a stone-cold certainty. This was not going to be pretty.

Some shred of rational thought told him not to punch the guy through the window, as this may require stitches for BOTH parties. Instead, noticing the large flat panel with writing on it immediately behind the driver extending all the way to the back of the van, Johnny began to pound with his fist. Not a wimpy little thud thud, but a New York Philharmonic BAM BAM BAM. The driver looked startled as the side of his truck with the shiny logo slowly caved in.

Something in the BAM BAM BAM and the feel of the sheet metal deforming under his fist released just enough tension to rein in Mr. Death. Instead of rolling the van over and extracting this asshole through the floor boards for a good ol' Texas Freeway Woopin' (Well, ya gonna Cowboy up or ya just gonna lay there and bleed?). Fortunately, he got ahold of himself enough to peer into the window and say, "Don't ever do that again."

He stood there for a moment, waiting for the wise crack that would give him justification to do murder. There was nothing but silence and a look of stark terror, so Johnny walked back to his car and started slowly down the freeway. A few minutes later he watched as the van meekly rolled off the next exit.

Johnny pointed two fingers at his eyes, then one finger at the van's driver – "I'm watching you." As the van slowly left the freeway, Johnny noticed the crumpled lettering on the side – "Buddy's Pool Service."

Post Script

The incident was never mentioned around the office, but from the look on people's faces, it was clear to Johnny that the word was out. He did the best he could to put it behind him, and periodically gave Shirley a box of See's Candy instead of a crappy Whitmore. Actually, he was pretty embarrassed about the whole thing and very grateful that nobody died, although deep down he kind of felt like that guy deserved it.

About six months later the office Christmas Party was held, and Shirley (with the nicest house and biggest swimming pool) hosted the event. Johnny knocked on the door and Buddy answered. Instead of saying "Hello" he turned around and ran toward the pool, leaping high and disappearing head first into ....the shallow end.

He lay there for some time before Johnny jumped in and pulled him out. He was bleeding profusely from his forehead and babbled "Thank you, thank you."

There is a God.

Chapter 27

CLAY

In kindergarten, Johnny got high on two things – paste (the white stuff that came in a gallon jar and tasted pretty good but didn't really glue anything together very well) and clay. Clay is a naturally occurring substance composed primarily of fine-grained minerals with a plastic squishy feeling that hardens when dried and/or fired. It's great for making pots.

Later in life, Johnny developed an interest in clay pots, which he saw at craft fairs and in model homes. When the models really suck, developers had a tendency to load up on clay pots (which they called "ceramics") so as to make their houses look a little more stylish.

Driving home one day he passed a new neighbor who was in his yard building a peculiar little house. For some reason, he pulled over, walked back, and inquired, "What the heck are you doing?"

"I'm building a kiln and I'm gonna fire some pots." A few hours and a few beers later, they were finishing the kiln together and getting ready for dinner at Johnny's house.

When they walked in the door, their wives looked at each other and started to scream. They hadn't seen one another since high school. It was one hell of a dinner – lots of wine (have you ever felt like you've had too much wine? - me neither) and a pile of pakalolo that resembled a bale of hay.

The dye was cast and Johnny knew it was time to take a few ceramics classes and perhaps build a kiln of his own.

There was a neighborhood park where Johnny somehow got involved by virtue of his reluctant ascendency to the presidency of the Maunalani Park Improvement Association. On the bulletin board he noticed (during one of the interminably long and windy Association meetings) a flyer which read "Free pottery lessons."

Johnny was on it. The Park supplied all the clay you could use and a free electric kiln to fire it in. It wasn't too long before Johnny was burning through fifty pounds of clay a night and turning out some of the most gawd awful pottery ever seen.

But he kept at it, subscribing to all the magazines and going to all the craft fairs. Before long you could actually drink out of one of his cups.

The next step was to go to an advanced pottery class, which was sponsored by the University of Hawaii and located under an on ramp to the H-1 freeway. This was not "an" on ramp; it was "THE SHITTIEST" on ramp in the entire H-1 freeway system. What you got if you wanted to get on the freeway here was a sharply elevated ramp with a 180-degree turn at the top onto a ridiculously short merging lane. Here you are expected to accelerate to sixty miles per hour in fifty feet or stop dead before colliding with the freeway traffic whizzing by. Needless to say, there were many accidents and pottery class was constantly interrupted by the sounds of squealing tires, broken glass, and the occasional ambulance siren.

It was with this overhead music that Johnny sat for his first "advanced" pottery class where he consumed the entire monthly allotment of clay on his first night to the horror of the on looking housewives and dilettantes. A couple more classes and he realized it was time to strike out on his own.

So, he built his own wheel out of plywood and bricks (the lower part was a bunch of bricks sandwiched between two circular pieces of plywood which you were supposed to spin around with your feet. This lower wheel was connected by a shaft to an upper wheel where the clay sat waiting to become a pot).

When he had a room full of clay pots, it was time to go out in the front yard and build a kiln. The first one was a cone ten (2000 degree) high fire job made out of lite firebrick and insulating cloth (invented to keep returning space shuttles from burning up). It was a "sprung arch" affair where you build a plywood arch, lay the bricks against it, and when you got to the top, pull out the plywood (much like that parlor trick where you grab the table cloth and yank it out from under all the plates and glasses). Amazingly, the thing remained standing.

All he had to do now was hook up the gas and fire the thing up. There was a little problem, however. The burner ports were too tight to light, so he turned on the gas, leaned into the front of the kiln, and struck a match.

The resulting explosion and fireball pretty much burned all the hair off Johnny's body. This was awkward since when he returned to the office on Monday, he had no eyebrows and a singed scalp where his hair used to be. Jeez, it took weeks to grow his hair back. In the mean time, he was the subject of ridicule. But that's part of the price you pay if you're gonna work with clay.

The next kiln was a suspension drum "raku" deal which was basically a fifty-five gallon drum lined with space fiber and suspended from a beam. You'd put a pot on the base, lower the drum, fire the bugger to 1600 degrees, raise the drum, and remove the glowing pot with a pair of tongs and throw it into a pile of newspapers or wood shavings (very exciting at night after a few refers and a bottle of wine).

The apex of his kiln building career came when he salvaged a large load of firebrick from the Waialua sugar mill boilers, which were being dismantled as part of the demolition of the mill (because it cost $0.14 to produce a pound of Hawaiian sugar and $0.04 to produce a pound of sugar anywhere else on the planet). Johnny built a humungous walk-in salt kiln which resembled a brick house. It was the only one on the island for reasons that soon became apparent.

Salt kilns are used by Germans to glaze beer mugs. What happens is you fire the thing up to 2000 degrees, then open the door (being careful with your hair) and shovel in rock salt which volatizes into hydrochloric acid and chlorine gas, making a really nice (and cheap) glaze on the pots and spewing highly toxic fumes into the night air in a startlingly beautiful dense white cloud of death.

Johnny discovered not only did it curl the shingles on his neighbor's roof and measurably increase Honolulu's incidence of asthmatic emergency room visits, but also attracted the attention of the fire station at the bottom of the hill. They would dispatch a hook and ladder truck every time Johnny started shoveling salt. He quickly wised up and would call them in advance.

In this way, Johnny was able to throw and fire a serious quantity of pots, which were then stowed under the house. The ones that didn't turn out too well he'd throw over the side of the mountain and fantasize that 10,000 years from now archeologists would discover this pile of crap and reconstruct human civilization base on it.

One day his wife Susan suggested that he take some pots (which by now were spewing out onto the lawn) to the swap meet and see if he could get rid of them. So, he filled his VW bus and headed for Aloha Stadium. Much to his surprise, he was cleaned out in a few hours by an interior decorator in charge of model homes.

Johnny was able to move a tremendous amount of pottery in this way. He kept his best stuff. Over the years almost every one ended up exploding on the floor. Ironically, one of the few survivors was the first pot he ever threw – on the bottom it is signed, "FIRST POT 2-77."

Chapter 28

Mauna Kea 200

Johnny just loved to ride those motorcycles –
he and his son Matt and their friends down the
street, brothers Mark and Earl, would load up
their bikes every Sunday morning and head
for the hills. They could have gone Saturdays,
but Bruce Brown had made a film years before
called "On Any Sunday" which glorified dirt
biking and established Sundays as "the day."

Urban sprawl had taken a toll, and the number
of quality dirt bike areas on Oahu had shrunk
to only a few – they favored the mountains
behind Mililani Memorial Park, a cemetery
out in the boonies in the middle of the island.
Pretty much any place else you were likely to
get shot at or arrested.

Upon arrival they would unload the bikes – a
Honda, a Kawasaki, a Yamaha and, Johnny's
favorite, a Husquvarna (on a trip to Europe
years earlier he had actually visited the
Husquvarna plant but was side-tracked by a
clueless tour guide to the part of the factory
where they made matches, and missed the
whole other part where they made the bikes).

Most dirt bikes at that time had two-stroke
engines, meaning they would fire once every
revolution compared to a four-stroke engine

which fires every other revolution. Two-strokes had certain advantages. For one thing, these engines did not need valves, which simplified their construction and lowered their weight. Also, you mix oil with the fuel instead of putting oil separately into the crankcase. This was particularly advantageous since two-stroke engines will work just fine in any orientation, while a standard four-stroke engine would crap out fast if it were, say, upside down during an intentional or unintentional maneuver.

But the real benefit of two-stroke engines is that they pack twice the power into the same space because there are twice as many power strokes per revolution. The result is an insane power-to-weight ratio, which enables two-stroke dirt bikes to accelerate very rapidly.

Needless to say, all their bikes were two-stroke. And not the whussy 125 cc versions – these were the 250's and, in Johnny's case a 360 cubic centimeter fire-breathing mo' fo'.

Once unloaded, they would spend the next half hour suiting up. Dirt biking is fun but it's pretty dangerous. There are, therefore, literally hundreds of items of apparel designed to protect you from injury and death. A typical set of dirt bike duds consists of a colorful long sleeve shirt with built in elbow pads, pants made out of nearly indestructible material with padding everywhere, huge buckle up knee high boots with steel toes, separate plastic knee, shin, and elbow guards, thick gloves with protective inserts for each finger, a strap-on chest/back protector which made you look and feel like a Roman gladiator, goggles with a stack of removable plastic lenses that could be discarded one at a time when the outer ones became covered with mud, and sturdy helmets with built in jaw guards that are approved by the Department of Transportation to withstand terrific impacts. Then you strap on a "camel back" which is a pouch full of water with a tube running to your helmet, and a fanny pack full of tools and spare parts since you need to be self sufficient when you experience the inevitable break down in the middle of nowhere.

Once all this gear was on, they climbed on their bikes and headed out for the day. The hills and valleys were covered with trails that had been cut by dirt biking enthusiasts/maniacs over decades. They wound through beautiful uninhabited forests and jungles and up and down some pretty serious mountains. Every once in a while, you would come upon another group of dirt bikers, usually from opposite directions at high speeds, and collisions were a part of the deal. But it was a small elite crew that plied the hills on Sunday, and they considered themselves brothers. So, after a crash, you'd dust yourself off, pick up your bike, lean it against a tree, and sit down for a while to share the day. Sometimes they would lead you to a secret trail they knew, and sometimes you would do the same for them.

On one occasion, the crashees led the crashors up a riverbed to a previously unknown mountainside. They jumped out of the river onto a small flat clearing perhaps thirty yards wide. At the far side of the clearing, was a very steep mountain that resembled the Matterhorn. We are not talking twenty-five degrees, or thirty-five degrees, this mother was forty-five degrees which, when you're standing at the bottom, looks pretty steep. Surprisingly, there was a trail going up part way where some crazy person had actually tried to climb this thing. It was called "Widow Maker." Since they were there, they all took a stab at it, accelerating at top speed in second gear across the clearing, then straight up as far as they could go until the front end came up and over, and they tumbled bike over body back down the Widow Maker.

They would return to this place on many Sundays over many years, and although they would get higher and higher, they never made it to the top. Then, one day, a new guy showed up on a tricked-out Honda two-stroke 500 cc with a giant knobby back tire. He took a look, put on his helmet, cranked the throttle and, standing on the pegs with his entire body bent out over the front tire, sprinted nearly five hundred feet straight up to the top of the mountain, then disappeared. It was astonishing. They never saw him again. Who WAS that guy?

One day on an unfamiliar trail way back in the mountains, they came across a pack of wild pigs. They were scary looking things with curling tusks, long hairy snouts, and significant bulk – they looked to be about two hundred pounds apiece. The pigs just stood there and stared menacingly as the boys made a hasty retreat. Johnny had never seen one before and hoped he would never see one again. Little did he know.

When it rained, it became particularly dangerous. Sometimes they would just call it off. Other times they would go to the hardware store on Saturday and buy ten pounds of short machine screws with large heads. The preferred brand was the Slid Hex Washer Faced SXS Zinc Plated 10 x 5/8 manufactured by Curtis Industries. They would then jack up their bikes and spend an hour or more screwing these into the front and rear tires until they were completely covered. This made for exceptional traction, but also upped the ante since to get run down or run over by a bike modified in this way would result in painful and/or permanent injury (picture a chain saw five inches wide spinning at thirty miles an hour).

It was on a rainy Sunday, on bikes so equipped, that they came upon the person who would inadvertently provide the name for not only their future motorcycle racing team, but also for the macadamia nut orchard that Johnny would later create out of a jungle in Pahoa.

They came over a rise and, as they were preparing to accelerate down into the hollow, saw what looked like a pretty serious accident. Thanks to the studs in their tires they were able to stop just short of the victim who looked like he had been run over a couple times already.

It was ugly. This guy was lying in a pool of mud and blood and snot. His head was wedged up between the front tire and the frame; his right leg was wound up in the chain, his left leg and both arms splayed out in awkward and unnatural positions.

They dropped their bikes and ran to his aide. Leaning down, Johnny asked in a low and conciliatory voice, "Are you alright?" The guy, a local Hawaiian, still conscious, said "Gee, I don't know, I tink I wen huli maka flippa." They looked at each other and burst out laughing. The guy survived and became somewhat of a legend among the dirt bike community, and his refrain became famous - at every subsequent crash site you could hear somebody say, "I tink I wen huli maka flippa."

As the guys got better, they began to think they might be ready for the granddaddy dirt bike contest of them all, the Mauna Kea 200.

Local riders on the Big Island got to thinking that it would be pretty funny to send a couple hundred visiting dirt bikers out into the impossibly daunting jungle for a two-day race that would include climbing one of the world's largest volcanoes, Mauna Kea, not once, but twice. So, they actually went out into the vast interior of the Big Island (it isn't called "Big" for nothin'), and cut a trail one hundred miles long, which, when ridden both ways, would result in a two hundred mile race. Then they printed some flyers, got the word out in the dirt bike community, and invited anybody who was crazy enough to participate in the "Mauna Kea 200."

Surprisingly, dirt bikers came from all over the world to take part in this insanity. There were guys from the US Mainland, Europe, Australia, and South Africa, even Japan. But the bulk of the lunatics came from Oahu and this included Johnny, Matt, Bill, Mark and Earl.

The idea was to start and finish in the parking lot of the Naniloa Hotel on Hilo Bay (the only hotel willing to host crazy people). The first day would consist of a hundred-mile ride through the most punishing terrain imaginable, culminating in a high-speed climb up the 14,000-foot side of Mauna Kea and a high-speed descent down the other side to a base camp where the bikes would be stored over night and you would return to your hotel room to look forward with "enthusiasm" to the next day when you got to do it again in reverse.

The event was organized so there were three-man teams. In order to be in the hunt, each member of the team had to start and finish, and there were strict times that had to be met for each leg – no dilly-dallying. To compete effectively, each team also needed a ground crew to meet them at various waypoints with food, fuel, bandages, and spare parts.

Johnny, Matt, Bill, Mark and Earl got a hold of a beat up Econo Van, bondoed and painted it, filled it full of dirt bikes and related paraphernalia, and shipped the whole thing over to the Big Island.

Johnny, Mark and Earl would ride; Matt and Bill would drive the van and bind the wounds. There was no question about the name – they were Team Huli Maka Flippa.

This was back in the days when the focus on safety was, uh, minimal. Approximately three hundred riders started – it was carnage from the get go. There were broken bikes and bodies everywhere. Guys would miss a turn and go over a cliff, or fly over the handlebars at high speed going down a steep hill, or simply crash into a tree. And, for those lucky souls who made it through the first six or seven hours, there was Mauna Kea, in all her glory, waiting to rip you a new asshole.

That first year they, along with several hundred other riders, failed to complete the ride. However, in later years they finished several times, although they never won a trophy – but, hey, at least they tried.

Johnny knew that his dirt biking days were over on the second afternoon of the last Mauna Kea 200 he would ever ride. He had made it through the first day without too many mishaps, and although he was nearly unable to get out of bed on the morning of the second day, he forced himself to an upright position, swung a stiff leg over his bike, and took off up Mauna Kea as the sun rose.

It was cold as sin up there at 14,000 feet, the wind was blowing hard and you had to really inhale to get enough oxygen to keep going. But he made it to the top ahead of the others, and barreled down the other side thinking maybe this would be the year for a trophy. NOT!

Almost losing it several times on the steep gravelly descent, he made it back to 6,000 feet where he was flagged off the mountain onto the Saddle Road that connected Hilo and Kona and ran over the hump between the sister volcanoes Mauna Kea and Mauna Loa. The Saddle Road was paved and offered an excellent opportunity to make up time. He ducked down behind the handlebars, twisted the throttle wide open, and booked it at top speed.

All good things must come to an end. For Johnny, it was clearing a rise in the air to see a flagman one hundred yards below motioning him off the road and into the lava field.

There are two basic kinds of lava - Pahoehoe and A'a. Pahoehoe is a Hawaiian term for basaltic lava that has a smooth, ropy surface. It is easy to walk on and provides a smooth sure footing. `A`a (pronounced "ah-ah") is a Hawaiian term for lava flows that have a rough rubbly surface composed of broken lava blocks called clinkers (read "broken glass"). The incredibly spiny and razor-sharp surface of a solidified `a`a flow makes walking somewhere between very difficult and impossible. You do not, repeat, do NOT want to fall in an a'a lava field.

Unfortunately for Johnny, he was being flagged, at sixy miles an hour, into an a'a lava field. He hung on valiantly for a few hundred feet before his front tire washed out sideways and he executed what is known in the Alps as a "tip roll snow ball wipe out." He went over the handlebars and began to tumble, along with his bike, through the a'a. Although he was wearing very substantial protective gear, it was no match for the a'a, which shredded it and him.

It seemed like an eternity – he could not get away from his bike which would periodically land on top of him at the bottom of a roll, then fly up in the air again to hunt him down several rolls later. It also seemed to happen in slow motion, which prolonged the agony as well as the suspense, since he did not know when or if he would meet the occasional boulder that randomly stuck up out of the lava waiting to stop a freight train. Fortunately, his trajectory included no boulders, just a whole lot of razor-sharp a'a.

He finally came to rest approximately 170' from his initial point of impact, his bike on top of him (on a later trip over the mountains they had stopped to pace it off). He lay there for a few minutes, looking up at the sky and wondering how many bones he had broken and how long it would take for him to recover, if ever. He didn't know if he was going to be able to get up, and he didn't want to try because then he would know how bad it really was.

The flagman, horrified at the spectacle, dropped his flag and ran after him. It took quite a while for him to negotiate the surprisingly long distance through the a'a. He finally reached the scene of the crash and uttered those familiar words "Are you all right?" To which Johnny replied "Huli maka flippa."

It turned out that the bike was pretty broken up but Johnny miraculously escaped serious injury. The flagman helped him up and together they wheeled the smoking hulk of what was left of his bike out to the highway to wait for an ambulance. Johnny noticed that although everything else was bent or broken, the wheels continued to function. He was in shock but was able to stand. For some strange reason, the thing that popped into his head was a scene from the movie "Blues Brothers" where "Jake" (John Bulushi) is talking to "Elwood" (Dan Akroyd) and says something to the effect of "We've got a full tank of gas, 500 miles to go, and we're on a mission from God."

So, as the flagman frantically tried to slow down racers and passing cars, Johnny got on his bike and started coasting down the Saddle Road to Hilo twenty miles away. It was a little sketchy since he had only half a handle bar and no rear brake.

It took about an hour – the road had a fairly steep grade and he was able to coast almost all the way to Hilo Bay, walking the "bike" or what was left of it the last couple of miles.

Reasoning that there was nothing else to do, he took a shower, put on his Arnold Palmer outfit, and went across the street to the golf course to get in a round before dark. The starter put him with three other guys to form a foursome, and they headed for the first tee.

By this time, and unbeknownst to Johnny, blood from his crash had seeped into his clothing turning his shirt and pants bright red. Blood was also flowing down his legs on to his socks and shoes. He was standing there, leaning on this driver, when one of his playing partners approached him and said, somewhat hysterically, "You're bleeding, you're bleeding ALL OVER!"

This was the last time Johnny ever rode a dirt bike.

Chapter 29

Pigs

It was after one of the Mauna Kea 200 races that Johnny and his buddies drove the Huli Maka Flippa van out to Pahoa to scout a piece of land which might be good for macadamia. It was a forty-four acre jungle with trees ranging in height to one hundred feet and thick foliage covering every square inch. They decided to walk from one end to the other but found it nearly impossible. Normal people would have turned back but they had just finished a grueling two hundred mile dirt bike race and were not about to be defeated by a bunch of plants. It was slow going indeed, but they ultimately hacked their way to the other side.

The land had two redeeming qualities. It was relatively flat, so it could be worked mechanically once it was cleared (unlike most of the rest of the island which is steep and rocky and suited primarily for D-9's). And it was covered with big trees. This was a good sign since any tree, including a macadamia nut tree, should do well here. So, Johnny made a deal on the land without consideration for the fact that he had no money left and would, therefore, be unable to do anything with the jungle he was now responsible for. Fortunately, he met a papaya farmer who was looking for virgin land where papaya grows well. This guy was willing to not only clear and plant the land but ALSO to pay rent in an amount sufficient to cover Johnny's nut. Since papayas grow straight up for three years before flopping over and being abandoned, it was perfect. In this way, "Johnny" cleared the jungle.

Then came the real work. Johnny and Matt would hop a plane for the Big Island Friday night, pick, shovel and plant for two days, and fly back to Honolulu Sunday evening. It was very hard work and they could only do a few dozen trees at a time. Later they would wise up and dig holes with a rented back hoe and later a hydraulic auger. But, instead of having to plant a dozen trees they were looking at several hundred, and it wore them out. Sometimes in the evening they would go into Pahoa for dinner, but their abused bodies would reject nourishment and bedtime was occasionally preceded by projectile vomiting. In the night the pigs would come - in the morning the mess was gone.

This was the first tip off that pigs lived in the jungle. As the years went by, they would see many of them, but paid little attention since they weren't causing any problems. It was a blissful coexistence for about ten years. When the trees started bearing nuts, things got serious.

Macadamia trees take forever. A seed will grow in a pot to a graftable tree in eighteen months. Scion wood from the particular variety you want to grow is then grafted on, and six months later the grafted seedling is ready to plant. Six or seven years later, it will start to bare nuts and by the tenth year it will produce about one hundred pounds per tree per year. At $1.00 per pound, that's roughly $100 per tree per year. So, the trick is to grow a whole lotta trees. Johnny planted 3,000 over a period of years and sat around for a couple decades waiting for his ship to come in.

If he had known then what he knows now, he probably would have taken it all to Las Vegas and put it on red - one spin and it's all over. He could not have imagined what was in store. Needless to say, he encountered a few problems along the way.

(1) The Market - Demand for macadamia nuts was created by the pioneer nut growers (Mauna Loa was the first real player starting in the 1950's). They scored big by providing free bags of mac nuts on airplanes heading for Hawaii back in the day. People went crazy. By the time Johnny came along, Hawaii produced practically all the mac nuts in the world, and nut processors were paying nut farmers $0.25 a pound. By the time he had all his trees in and growing, it was $0.50. And when the first nuts hit the ground (when they're ripe

they fall), it was close to $0.70. The future was so bright he had to wear, uh, shades.

The Australians were a little miffed that fifty years earlier the Hawaiians had stolen a bunch of their macadamia nut trees, took them back to Hawaii and created a profitable industry. Noting the expanding market and the rising prices, the Aussies stole the new improved Hawaiian macadamia nut trees back (fair and square) and began to plant their own orchards. However, there was one huuuuuge difference. Hawaii is an island with limited land, whereas Australia is a continent with an enormous land mass.

The Aussies would get on a D-9 with a lunch bucket and a case of beer, drop the blade and drive off in one direction till the sun set. There they would camp and the next day turn around and drive back. They would repeat this for several weeks. Their orchards were measured in square miles, not acres, and ten years later the nuts from all those trees (along with the South Africans and many other nations who did the same thing) began to flood the market. Whereas fifteen years earlier 90% of all the macadamia nuts in the world were produced in Hawaii, they now produced only 33%.

As every economics teacher likes to say, "When supply goes up and demand stays flat, price goes down." For macadamia nuts, prices fell freely in the 1980's, going in two years from $0.70 to $0.50 and then to nothing, since the big processors had warehouses full of unsold nuts and would not take any more from the farmers they had previously courted. A bad situation indeed.

When Covid hit in 2020 the cycle repeated itself, going from $1.30 a pound to zero in the space of a few months when the five major processors sent their "Go fuck yourself" letters to the 500 or so growers on the Big Island.

(2) Diseases - It rains a lot in Hawaii. In Pahoa, it rains a whole lot, averaging 120 inches per year (an incredible ten feet each year). On the plus side, you don't have to irrigate. On the minus side, fungus and algae thrive on moisture.

Funguswise you've got Botrytis (bow-try-tis), which is the white fuzzy mold that makes strawberries rot. Algaewise you've got Phytopthera (Fi-top-thur-a), which caused Ireland's potato blight and more recently Sudden Oak Death, and Dutch Elm Disease. Both of these attack and kill the blossoms that would have later turned into nuts. Fungus and algae are everywhere all the time, but bloom with a vengeance during a prolonged rain – twenty days will do it. Also, phytopthera can kill whole trees in short order if it is able to hang around long enough during a bloom. Johnny had more than his fair share of both. Approximately twenty to thirty of Johnny's trees die each year from these diseases and must be replanted with new trees that take seven more years to yield a crop.

(3) Hurricanes – Hawaii has been pretty lucky for the last 100 years or so. Although four or five tropical cyclones appear each year, they rarely affect the Big Island where essentially all Hawaiian macadamia is grown. It is likely that the huge landmass of Mauna Kea and its sister Mauna Loa (the largest volcano in the world) divert cyclones and hurricanes south and north of the island chain. Two hurricanes (Iwa in 1982 and Iniki in 1992 were the most damaging – both followed a trajectory similar to a bowling ball streaking along the south edge of the island chain and then curving into Kauai. In 2018 Hurricane Lane hammered the Big Island with high winds and fifty plus inches of rain in one day. Macadamia and papaya orchards were severely affected. Johnny lost over 200 trees during this one event, which had to be removed, burned, and new trees planted. These new trees would not yield a substancial crop for approximately a decade.

(4) Volcanos – Kilauea, the youngest and most active volcano on the Big Island erupted almost continuously from 1983 to 2018. In 2019 enormous amounts of lava apparently escaped Kilauea via underground lava tubes and surfaced in the middle of Leilani Estate subdivision in what became known as Fissure 8. Lava from this Fissure spewed approximately 200 feet in the air and flowed all the way to the ocean destroying approximately 800 houses and many papaya and macadamia orchards. While the fumes from this eruption generally traveled south along the coastline of the Big Island (blown by the prevailing North Easterly winds) on several occasions when Kona winds blew in the opposite direction, the volcanic fumes travelled north. Since Johnny's orchard is only five miles North of Fissure 8, his orchard was heavily damaged by the fumes and essentially all of his 3,000 trees turned brown. Fortunately, the fumes and damage were short lived and most of the trees shed their brown leaves and grew new green ones.

(5) Pigs - All else pales in comparison to pigs. Wild pigs (called boar) are not native to North America. They were brought here from Europe by the Spanish explorers in the 1500's for food. They are NOT pink and cuddly with curly tails. They grow big (4'-5' long, 200-300 pounds, some exceeding 500 pounds) with

stiff black fur and straight tails. The males have tusks.

They are aggressive, particularly sows with piglets. In a typical attack, a male lowers its head, charges, and slashes upward with its tusks ripping its victim in half (or to shreds) while a female charges with its head up, mouth wide, and bites big chunks out of you. In addition to being aggressive, feral pigs pose a threat to human health from the thirteen diseases they are known to carry, including brucellosis, pseudorabies, tuberculosis, bubonic plague, tularemia, anthrax and trichinosis. You do not want to get ripped or bit by a wild pig.

They grow from a pound at birth to 200 pounds in six months. They start reproducing at four months. They have two litters a year averaging six (but sometimes as many as twelve) pigs per litter. Which is to say, with a steady food source, their numbers expand exponentially.

They live in groups called "sounders" which typically contain twenty but sometimes as many as fifty pigs. They are nocturnal, foraging from dusk until dawn. And they eat almost anything including roots, refuse, puke, insects, lizards, young live animals like deer, lambs, cats and puppies, the occasional small child, and just about any dead animal. But the one food they prize above all else is...macadamia nuts.

Johnny first noticed there might be a problem one evening when he had to stop his truck to let thirty or so pigs pass across the road from the jungle into the orchard. On another evening he noticed several dozen small furry objects running around in circles. Stopping to investigate, he reached down and picked one up – it was a small pig destined to become a monster. Johnny was lucky mom was not around.

The penny finally dropped when he was awakened one night by the sound of a hundred waiters working pepper grinders. It turned out to be the sound of hundreds of pigs lounging comfortably under his trees cracking shells (with their teeth) and eating his nuts.

And then it got crazy – pigs standing in front of his tractor or car refusing to move, pigs chasing him around, pigs parading by his lanai giving him the stink eye, pigs everywhere all the time.

Fortunately, Johnny happened to know a guy (not a mob guy – way better - a special forces guy). For purposes of anonymity, let's just call him The Spencinator. Johnny explained his problem and asked for advice. Shortly thereafter he was walking into a non-descript back street gun store where the Special Forces owner and all the Special Forces employees were hollering "Hooaaahhh" greetings to The Spencinator who said "My friend Johnny here has a little problem."

Johnny was led through a door (the kind you might find on a vault at Fort Knox) into a room where they kept the good stuff. Picture the movie Men In Black, the part where the wall of the apartment swings open and there's a hundred chrome plated space guns in there – it was like that. The owner gently removed a space gun from the wall and said, "This is what you need."

It was an AR-10 assault rifle.

The AR-10 is a wicked looking lightweight, air-cooled, magazine-fed, gas operated, large caliber rifle capable of burning through 700 rounds in sixty seconds and wreaking unimaginable havoc on the receiving end. At $1.00 per round, you do not want to hold the trigger down too long.

So, Johnny, ol' Peace and Love and Brotherhood Johnny, returned to the orchard with the machine gun from hell (it would only take a few of these to wipe out most of the Klingons in the known Universe). The pigs didn't suspect a thing. As the sun went down, Johnny fortified himself with an adult beverage (Jack Daniels out of a quart bottle), hopped on his quad, and drove out into the night with the AR-10 on his lap.

As luck would have it, quite a few sounders were at work that night, and when he turned on his two million-candle power spotlight, there appeared to be nearly a hundred pigs lounging around and looking annoyed as he drove into the middle of the herd. Safety off, auto on, Johnny aimed in a general direction and...damn near shot the handlebars off before regaining control and spraying anything that moved.

It was a grizzly sight, pigs splattered everywhere. For a moment he almost felt sorry until he realized that each one of these filthy bastards was capable of eating 10% of its body weight every night. If you figure an average weight of 200 pounds per pig, a crowd like this (or what used to be a crowd) could consume a ton of nuts (2,000 pounds) a night, every night, for the duration of the season, which is five months long.

The next morning, he got up and went to the scene of the crime where several dozen pig carcasses were scattered about. He got his front-end loader, picked them all up, and deposited them on the edge of the jungle. It made for a pretty large pile. By the next day they started to smell, the day after that they were gone - dragged by other pigs back into the jungle and consumed. Oh yes, on top of every thing else, pigs are cannibals.

But this suited Johnny just fine, for he reasoned, "As long as they're eating Uncle Bob, they're not eating Johnny's nuts."

Epilogue

The Spencinator came to visit a couple months ago. Johnny explained that even with advanced technology he was unable to control the mob that showed up every night to dine. The Spencinator said, "When they drop us into a hot zone, the first thing we do is string concertina wire to secure the fire base. Concertina wire will discourage anything with skin – you might want to try it."

Concertina wire (named after a musical instrument resembling an accordion and more commonly known as razor wire) is mean ass stuff. Imagine a slinky three feet in diameter with Gillette Blue Blades welded on every twelve inches. Imagine also that there are actually two slinkies wound together in opposite directions, so when you pull out the coil you get a 50-foot-long rigid tube of razor blade mother fuckin' hell fence.

Johnny quickly discovered there is no concertina wire in America (it may be illegal but he failed to check into this) – it is all in Iraq and Afghanistan and Cuba (Guantanamo). But the Internet is amazing – you can get ANYTHING. It turns out there's a place in China called Anping that prides itself for its razor wire. They actually have an annual razor wire festival, although they call it "wire netting" so as not to offend – they also have a razor wire queen and a razor wire museum. For a small fee, they will produce an enormous amount of razor wire, truck it 1,500 kilometers to the Yangzi River, and ship it on a Slow Boat directly to your door.

Johnny waits at the dock.

Chapter 30

Back Hoe

When he was little, Johnny prized miniature models of big machinery – bulldozers, front-end loaders, excavators, and particularly backhoes which seemed to incorporate all the best stuff. A back hoe had a front-end loader which was basically a big bucket you could use to dig, push, and carry stuff around in, and it had a smaller bucket in the back (a "back hoe") suspended by a giant arm that could bash down rock walls, gnaw trenches, and flip over cars if you wanted to. It had big tractor tires in the rear, way taller than a kid, and smaller ones in front that would come off the ground when a violent blow was struck.

Whenever he ran across a construction site, he was mesmerized by the sound and fury of these big machines as they tore away at the earth, blew down buildings, and otherwise wreaked havoc. He envisioned himself in the seat of one of these monsters, bouncing up and down as he pounded the living daylights out of some pile of rubble.

Thirty years later, Johnny scrapes together enough money to buy a lot on the top of a hill. Actually, it was a lot on the SIDE of the top of a hill and the average cross slope was close to forty-five degrees. That is to say, it was a steep mo' fo'. But it was all he could afford at the time and he thought that maybe he would be able to level it out in the distant future.

Before Craig's List, there was sort of a newspaper called Buy & Sell, which had a picture of each item for sale along with a little blurb about it and a price. Johnny picked one up and came across an ad that said, "Case 580 Back Hoe for sale - $5,000."

He was intrigued. He knew that back hoes, even shitty old ones, sold for $20,000 or more - new ones for approximately $100,000. He also knew that no matter how bad it might look, if the hydraulics worked and the engine ran, it could do a lot of damage. You might even be able to level a hillside with the thing. Johnny was able to scrap together five grand by nefarious means and immediately drove to the address on the ad.

It was dark by the time he got there. Johnny pulled up just ahead of several other people who were coming for the same thing – a ridiculously cheap backhoe. But Johnny got there first by a few minutes, and that was all it took to look at the tractor in the moonlight and hand over a check. Jeez, it was big. It probably weighed 20,000 pounds and, with the rear arm extended, must have been at least thirty feet long. You could probably get $5,000 for it at a scrap metal yard. It looked like it had been well used, but the engine sounded good and the hydraulics worked. If you squinted, you could almost see a shiny new miniature backhoe in a cellophane box under the Christmas tree. So, Johnny realized one of his fondest boyhood dreams and became the proud owner of a life size Case 580 Back Hoe.

He found an equipment hauler who was willing to drag the thing to the top of his mountain for a reasonable fee. The next morning, he wandered out with a cup of coffee to marvel at this enormous piece of machinery, which he now owned. In the light of day, he could see that it was really trashed – we're talkin' deplorable.

It was caked in mud with bald tires and a rusty paint job. The hydraulic lines were cracked and frayed. There were gnarly welds all over the frame where the metal had torn from abuse and been repaired by some guy with a shaky hand and a very large welder. But, by gawd, when you turned the key the thing started right up, and when you pulled a lever, something would go up and down or back and forth. Sitting there in the ripped-up tractor seat, his hands on the levers, the motor purring, he was in heaven.

It took several hours just to pressure wash the mud off and several months to get the thing back into shape. It is difficult to comprehend the amount of surface area a piece of equipment like that has until you commence to grind down every square inch to bare metal. It's a bit like taking that first step into the Gobi dessert – it's a long way to the other side. But in time all the rust and chipped paint were gone. The company that makes Bondo would have been proud to see so many holes filled with their product. And then a friend with a reputation as a "hoser" (one who paints cars with a garden hose) came over and sprayed several gallons of bright yellow paint over, under, and around. New tires, hoses and a seat completed the transformation. It looked brand new – it was, in the immortal words of surfer Miki Dora, "Bitchin.'"

So, Johnny began scratching away at the hillside. It was impressive indeed to see the amount of earth that could be displaced in a day. Fortunately, it was not necessary to rent a fleet of dump trucks to cart away the excavated material. Living on the top of a mountain has its advantages – one of these is you can dump everything over the side and watch it disappear into the valley.

In time, it became clear that there were two kinds of earth – the dirt kind, and the rock kind. The dirt was great because it would slide down the hillside and build up on an angle so after a while you could move out a couple feet and keep dumping until you had both widened the cut AND created a newly expanded flat area. In this way, the useable area of Johnny's hillside lot expanded by a third.

Rocks are a different matter all together. They can be as small as a marble or as big as Jupiter's moons which are called Galilean satellites after Italian astronomer Galileo Galilei who observed them in 1610 – the largest of these (similar to what was lodged in Johnny's hillside) are Io, Europa, Ganymede, and Callisto. The smaller rocks would roll through the brush, bounce a few times, and disappear. The moon size ones were not only truly exciting to discard, but demonstrated clearly and unambiguously the immutable laws of gravity.

When a truly large boulder goes over the edge, it starts off very slowly and seems to continue rolling very slowly. You know in your mind that it is blazing down the hillside at incredible speed with massive amounts of unspent kinetic energy just waiting for something to get in the way. It bounces off precipices in slow motion, reaching surprisingly high altitudes before crashing back to earth with a reverberating thud that can be heard for miles on a calm day. Trees and other boulders in its path are pulverized. And, depending on the distance from the top of the mountain to the bottom of the valley (in

Johnny's case, over a thousand feet), you can hear it for a minute or more crashing all the way down until it rolls to a stop.

On a really steep valley hillside such as Johnny's, sounds are amplified and come back as an echo, so you get to hear the mayhem twice. Watching a really big one go over is morbidly fascinating – you're kind of waiting for the train to hit the trailer. It is also somewhat disconcerting to know that once the thing starts rolling, there's no way to stop it. Fortunately, the valley at the base of Johnny's mountain was an uninhabited natural wilderness area.

After a whole day of slamming away at the hillside you forget important details. One of these has to do with the fact that every action creates an equal and opposite reaction. On a backhoe, when you slam the hillside, the tractor jumps backwards a fraction of an inch. If you're slammin' all day, you can move several yards without knowing it.

It was in this way that Johnny found himself in a bit of a bind. As the sun went down, he banged one last time and dislodged a monster, which fell against the back of the tractor. He turned around in his seat and prepared to drive forward to a safe location to park for the night. To his horror, he realized that the left front tire was suspended in space several feet beyond the edge of the cliff, and the right front tire was part way over the edge. It was impossible to go forward or backward. A wrong move would send Johnny and the backhoe over. This was particularly topical since a few weeks earlier a friend of his with a similar backhoe went over the side on Haleakala (it was a closed casket funeral). He turned off the engine and gingerly disembarked so as not to upset the delicate balance. Jeez, that was close.

He did not sleep well. The next morning Johnny was up before dawn, still unsure how to extricate himself from this awkward situation. The sun was still below the horizon when he climbed back into the driver's seat and turned on the engine. He reasoned that his best chance would be to use the backhoe to pull himself backwards, but this did not work because a huge boulder was lodged tightly against the rear back hoe. Fortunately, there are foot pedals, which swing the boom left and right. He was able to get the bucket on the side of the boulder and press the foot peddle just enough to nudge the monster rock, although the tractor moved sideways in the opposite direction. This disrupted equilibrium, and the tractor gently teetered. Johnny prepared to jump but things settled down so he tried it again. And again. And again. Miraculously, he was able to get the boulder far enough to one side that he could claw backwards from the cliff edge and finally, after a tense hour, got all four wheels back on solid ground. Holy shit.

It was at this moment that his neighbor, a screaming asshole if ever there was one, happened out on to a rock promontory below and to the right with a perfect view of Johnny, the backhoe, and the cliff all the way down to the valley floor. Mr. Asshole was sipping his coffee and enjoying the sunrise when the mother of all boulders went over the side. He was totally unprepared both mentally and physically for what happened next.

His composure evaporated, he dropped his mug and his mouth flopped open as he watched Johnny's Jupiter moon boulder roar down the hillside. He remained transfixed for quite some time.

Johnny saw him out of the corner of his eye, but did not let on. The neighbor from hell slowly backed away, then turned around and ran. A few months later he sold his house and moved to Nebraska (it is apparently flat there).

When Johnny finished the job, he parked his tractor in the back of the newly flattened lot where it stayed unused for a decade rusting in the rain. He finally put an ad in Craig's list and sold it for $1,000 to a guy who is undoubtedly still working on it. Good luck brudda!

Chapter 31

Krakatoa

Johnny was eight before his parents were flush enough to afford a gardener, but their financial situation did not permit them to get a really good one, or to employ him for more than one day a week. What they got was Albert, a spry eighty-eight year old retired sailor with a penchant for blarney and a propensity for drink. Although he came with rather feeble credentials, his presence enabled the folks to participate when cocktail conversations turned to landscaping.

Albert knew very little about gardening, but took pride in his ability to keep the weeds from overtaking the back yard. Nobody really knew what he was doing out there, but he would periodically make a great show of pushing a wheelbarrow full of dead vegetation from here to there. Johnny suspected it was the same pile every time, but he did not let on. The yard always looked just a little bit better when he left, so the folks figured they were getting their money's worth.

He was an engaging fellow with a ready smile who loved to talk on into the afternoon. He did not like to sweat so these conversations generally took place in the shade. He enjoyed company, and since Johnny was pretty much the only one around, he was "it."

Albert told of a life spent on the high seas, of places and things far away and mysterious. Johnny had no idea if all or any of this was true, but it was interesting and kept both of them out of the sun and away from their chores.

One day, however, Albert showed up sober, and carried with him a wrinkled paper bag. When they got together for their weekly conversation, he solemnly pulled a book out of the bag and said he had something very important to share about his life. The book was called <u>Krakatoa</u>.

He began by saying that at the age of eighteen he had shipped out on the first of many vessels and had traveled the world for the next half century. During that time, he had seen and done many things. But of all those things, the most amazing, remarkable, and death defying had occurred on his very first voyage.

He had secured a berth on the Governor General Loudon, a mail steamer and excursion vessel captained by Johan Lindemann and operated by the Netherlands Indies Steamship Company. They toured the world, delivering mail and hauling passengers on sight seeing tours. They had heard of a "smoking island" off the coast of Indonesia and, inbetween mail deliveries, they would take tourists out to this island which the locals called Krakatau but which the English called Krakatoa, where they would disembark and spend the day walking around in the smog. Surprisingly, there were lots of people who wanted to do this, and they made the trip several times.

Albert was there for the last one.   On the morning of August 26, 1883, they pulled into the Bay of Lampong, a small anchorage on the southern end of Sumatra, to load tourists for a Sunday trip to Krakatoa, a mere twenty-five miles away.   They heard explosions and noticed churning clouds of ash and pumice, so it promised to be an interesting trip.   The mood on shore was festive. The sea, however, was rough and the winds, already strong, had picked up.   They stood off from the pier, unable to dock.

Fifty-three minutes passed high noon Krakatoa delivered the opening salvo to a climactic eruption that would last for two days.   The initial blast generated an ear-shattering fusillade and a cloud of volcanic debris that quickly rose ten miles above the island. All Albert could do was put his fingers in his ears and look up.

The intensity of the eruptions increased throughout the afternoon. The cloud now rose twenty miles high and fanned out, the explosions got louder and more frequent, and a series of small tsunamis battered the coastline. Captain Lindemann didn't like the looks of it and, leaving the other ships in the harbor, headed out to sea where they spent the night bobbing and spinning around in the unusual currents.

At 5:30 a.m. on Monday, August 27, 1883, Albert and the rest of the crew and passengers were awakened by the first in a series of four stupendous eruptions, climaxing in a one hundred megaton blast (Hiroshima was twenty) that blew Krakatoa to smithereens. Because they had sailed out to sea, they were now less than twenty miles from the epicenter. Imagine standing on the pier at Huntington Beach and watching Catalina vaporize in a nuclear blast. The final explosion, which was heard 2,200 miles away in Madagascar on the other side of the Indian Ocean, created a horrific shock wave and a tsunami exceeding 130 feet in height.

Albert was at the railing, holding on for dear life, blood streaming from his ears, as the horizon began to rise. Captain Lindemann reacted immediately, turning the bow of the ship into the on coming wave. Imagine the movie Perfect Storm where the fishing boat goes up the face of the one hundred foot wave. Now add thirty feet and a hundred more people. The ship accelerated up the face to vertical, shooting up over the crest and slowly cartwheeling 180 degrees stern over bow before crashing steeply down the backside of the wave. Albert watched as the wave continued toward land and consumed it, all of it - 163 towns, 36,000 people, and all the ships at sea for a hundred miles in every direction.

But it wasn't over yet – not by a long shot. When a really big volcano goes off (and this was the biggest volcanic eruption in recorded history), it creates something called a pyroclastic flow. This is a fluidized mixture of hot rock fragments, hot gases, and entrapped air that moves at high speed in thick, gray-to-black, turbulent clouds that hug the surface. Pyroclastic flows move especially well over water because the heat turns the surface to steam making for a fast and slippery ride. As the cloud of hot ash and gas roared down on the Louden, everyone sought cover within the ship, and although they were scorched, remarkably no one was burned alive.

But it still was not over. Large volcanic explosions (and this was the grand daddy of them all) also produce something called tephra. This is basically rocks and other solid material ejected into the air during an eruption. The amount of tephra generated by

Krakatoa is thought to have exceeded twenty cubic kilometers, which is a lot of material, especially when falling from a height of several miles.

So, when Albert went back out on deck (after surviving a blast and shock wave that dwarfed Hiroshima, one of the largest tsunamis in recorded history, and a pyroclastic flow that could cook a turkey in twenty seconds) he looked up and was greeted with the specter of thousands of tons of rock and ash falling out of the sky. It bashed and blanketed the ship in a few minutes, and in a few minutes more had accumulated to a height of nearly six feet. The ship started to list under the weight, and it became clear to Albert they were going to capsize – he was getting ready for a swim. But Captain Lindemann once again saved the day, calling every crewman and passenger on deck to scoop up the hot material with their bare hands and throw it overboard. Many blisters and an hour later the ship had been righted and saved.

Albert's job for the next several days was to pull bodies from the huge fields of floating debris that transformed the Sunda Straits into something akin to solid ground. Every once in a while, they would rescue someone or something still alive, but this was rare.

The one redeeming feature of all this was the sunsets – they were unbelievable. While tephra from the eruption continued to fall as far as 1,500 miles away, the finest fragments were propelled into the stratosphere, spreading outward across the entire equatorial belt (where they would remain suspended for many years). This stratospheric dust cloud also contained large volumes of sulfur dioxide gas, which rapidly combined with water vapor to generate sulfuric acid droplets. The resulting veil of acid aerosols and volcanic dust created a type of atmospheric shield that reflected enough sunlight to reduce the Earth's temperature by several degrees. It also produced an optical phenomenon the likes of which had never been seen before by man, creating halos around the sun and moon and the most outrageous sunrises and sunsets imaginable. The afterglow from these vivid red sunsets was so intense that fire engines were called out in New York, Poughkeepsie, and New Haven to quench the apparent conflagration. These sunsets continued for three years.

Albert closed the book and sat silently for a while. Remembering that he had forgotten to show Johnny something important, he opened the book again, and in the back found a list of the crew of the Loudon. With great pride he pointed to the last entry and said, "This is me."

Post Script

In September of 1998, Johnny, now fifty-two, would take a surf trip with his pal Brian and a bunch of their aging surf buddies to the Mentawai Islands off the coast of Sumatra where some of the most excellent waves in the world can be found. They were on the Indies Trader for the last voyage of the season. Over dinner, Captain Martin Daly allowed as how he would be sailing down the coast of Sumatra back to Jakarta on the island of Java, and if the guys wouldn't mind extending their trip, they could come along and explore new surf breaks. There was instant and unanimous consensus, and they spent a pleasant week wandering down the coast, stopping here and there at likely breaks, some of them pretty good and one or two of them raw sucking dry reef death traps.

The final leg of the voyage took them through the Sunda Straits between Sumatra and Java, and as they steamed along, Captain Daly asked if anybody wanted to see Krakatoa. Johnny instantly developed an acute case of what Hawaiians call "chicken skin."

They pulled into what was left of Krakatoa on the afternoon of October 7, 1998, 115 years after the most powerful volcanic explosion in the history of the world. All that was left was a sheer volcanic wall that stuck straight up approximately a hundred feet. There was a small sandy beach at the foot of this wall.

Johnny paddled in and sat there for some time, silently reflecting on that conversation in the shade with Albert all those many years ago.

Chapter 32

Pakalolo

It would be correct (but not completely accurate) to say that Johnny's first "experience" with pakalolo (Hawaiian for herb) occurred in the Summer of '61 between his sophomore and junior years at Riverside Polytechnic High School. He had gotten a phone call from a representative of the Poly High Booster Club who excitedly advised that "the wheels have been greased" and he would be "hired immediately." All he had to do was show up at the gas station on 14th Street and he was "in for the summer."

This struck Johnny as odd since he was not looking for a job and had planned to slide through the next three months surfing and carousing. But he knew that Standard Oil paid well and even provided clothing (white pants and shirt, black bow tie, and a little white hat like the ones ice cream vendors and milk men wear). You looked like a penguin but the money was good. Also, he had never had any kind of interaction with the Sports Booster Club since they pretty much boosted football exclusively (football was a big deal in this small town - Johnny was on the wrestling team, but they had to fend for themselves as it was not much of a spectator sport).

So, he went down to 14th street and presented himself anyway. The station manager was rather curt – "Who the hell are you?"

Johnny, "Uh, I was told to come down here. I'm Johnny."

Station manager, "JOHNNY?! Oh, man, I've seen every one of your games – you are terrific! I've been waiting for you. We need a good guy like you to man the pumps. You're HIRED!"

Needless to say, there was another guy with the same name at Poly High. He was a senior, quite large, captain of the football team and a real stand out. How they could ever mistake Johnny for the *real* Johnny was beyond comprehension. Apparently there had been some confusion down there at the Booster Club and they had called the wrong guy. But it was too late now. Johnny put on his bow tie and started pumping gas. It took several weeks for them to realize they had hired an imposter, but by then they were too deeply immersed in an unethical bind and were kind enough to allow him to finish out the summer on the Standard Oil gravy train (the other Johnny got a new Corvette – some guys have all the luck).

The Riverside Police had all their squad cars serviced at the 14th Street station. Johnny loved this. After a fast lube and oil, he got to hot-rod around town without having to worry about getting arrested ("Road test, officer"). Those cop cars could really fly – you could burn rubber for nearly a block and it handled really well (cop engine, cop shocks).

Part of the deal was to clean and vacuum the inside. It was there, wedged under the back seat, that johnny found a couple huge joints left by the Chicanos who had been hauled in the night before under what they said were false pretenses.

In those days, finding a joint was pretty much the same as running across a syringe full of heroin. Still, Johnny wrestled with the idea of maybe just one puff. But he was a pretty straight kid (in those days) and in the end he went to the office and said, "Look what I found."

Pandemonium ensued, this being perhaps the biggest thing to ever happen at the 14th Street station (until later that summer when Johnny forgot to remove the nozzle from the gas tank of a '59 Desoto which drove away, stretching the hose quite a long way before it burst, sending several thousand gallons of highly flammable Standard Oil gasoline spewing all over 14th street during rush hour).

Johnny's first bona fide pakalolo "experience" came on his way out to the Makaha World Surf Championships in '65. It was late evening. The plan was to sleep on the beach and be ready for the first heat. He'd given a ride to one of the other competitors who produced a fat one as they rounded the curve to Maile. They proceeded to smoke it down to where blisters began to appear on their fingers.

Johnny's mind understandably began to wander and his reflexes faded. When he regained consciousness somewhere in Waianae, he noticed two things" (1) he was going ten miles an hour in a twenty-five zone and (2) there was a cop car on his bumper. This was also his second experience with paranoia (the first one was precipitated by that really scary movie "The Blob" back in the 50's). The cop apparently laughed it off and wagged his finger as he sped by.

They pulled into the Makaha Drive Inn (which is now a Long's Drug Store) and ordered the lunch plate special. There appeared to be veins and bone shards sticking out here and there, but they'd been smothered in some kind of gravy so you couldn't really tell for sure what the heck was in there. He started in on the thing and realized this was perhaps the best plate lunch he had ever had or would ever have. He went back for a second plate (much to the surprise of the people behind the counter who had never experienced such a request for reasons known only to them).

He had now become acquainted with the first axiom of pot smoking – things (everything) taste great when you're stoned.

The next morning, Johnny prepared to paddle out for his heat. He noticed a familiar face in the crowd standing on the beach waiting for the horn to blow. He had recently seen a totally bitchin' movie called "Endless Summer" which was filmed by a talented photographer named Bruce Brown. It was about two surfers who travelled around the world surfing. The surfers were Mike Hynson and Robert August. They were generally considered to be two of the best surfers in the world at that time. The guy standing next to Johnny was Mike Hynson.

Needless to say, that kind of popped Johnny's balloon. The thought of coming in last and slinking out of the water to avoid the crowds that would be surrounding Mr. Hynson (movie star and super surfer) was, uh, debilitating. Johnny nevertheless jumped on his board and paddled out. The surf was pretty solid that day, maybe 6' to 8' Hawaiian. It was a little scary. Fortunately, Makaha is a gentler wave than, say, Pipeline (which could grind you up and spit you out with impunity and regularity). At Makaha, you could usually make the drop and navigate fairly confidently from way outside to almost onto the beach (although the wave exploding up the beach and sloshing back down at you could throw you up into the air a considerable distance).

Fortunately for Johnny, Mr. Hynson had apparently just discovered pakalolo (and perhaps other drugs as well although this is just a supposition). Johnny noticed that every time a big one would jack up over the outside reef his eyes appeared to roll back and he'd paddle for the horizon (which is the wrong way to go if you're trying to win a surf contest). In fairness to Mr. Hynson, he might have seen a bigger wave further out, but, again, this is just a supposition. Johnny was fully prepared to surrender every wave to Mr. Hynson but when he noticed him paddling out to sea, he took off and did his best not to fall or run somebody over.

The heats were thirty minutes long. Johnny got approximately five waves. It is not known how many waves Mr. Hynson got, but it may have been somewhere close to zero. Johnny would, however, like to apologize to Mr. Hynson if his recollection is incorrect.

When Johnny finally got to the beach, he was surrounded by a small group of photographers, reporters, groupies and little kids seeking autographs. Johnny had surprisingly and against all odds won the heat. One of the groupies slapped three joints into Johnny's palm, a very nice gesture.

It should be noted that several days later Mr. Hynson pulled up to the parking lot exit in Waikiki where Johnny was working, and handed him his ticket. Before waiving him through and in a disgraceful effort to ingratiate himself, Johnny blurted out "It was a pleasure and a privilege to surf with you at Makaha the other day." Mr. Hynson looked directly at Johnny and muttered something that sounded a lot like "Go fuck yourself" before speeding off into the night.

Chapter 33

Marrakech Express

By the time he was in graduate school, Johnny and Susan were good for approximately a kilo a month (to relieve the stress of academic life), which was graciously provided by a surfer/drug dealer friend who shall remain nameless (Brian Kennelly). A hookah full of mud splattered Mexican in front of the TV on Saturday night watching the Smothers Brothers Comedy Hour was the highlight of the week (those guys were *hilarious*). Second axiom – things are really funny when you're wasted.

He matriculated in '69 and got shipped back to Hawaii by a company that sought somebody with his skills (which were actually pretty meager). He accepted his fate and went to work in an office.

Several years later Johnny and Susan found themselves house sitting a beach cottage one rainy day in Kaneohe. Browsing through some books in the midst of an electrical blackout, Johnny came across a fat one titled "Fodor's Europe '72." It had large type and colorful pictures and was therefore a candidate for a quick read by candlelight.

As he leafed through the pages, he envisioned the two of them cruising through Europe in a Volkswagen Camper (he had always wanted one of those), stopping here and there for a glass of wine, a skinny dip, or a bull fight (he was relieved to discover that in Portugal they don't kill the bull). By daybreak he had read the whole damn thing and was inspired. By the next evening, Susan had read it too, and it was a foregone conclusion – they were going.

They found a map of Europe folded up to the size of a regular street map. But when you unfolded this baby, it covered most of the kitchen floor. With a pencil and later a yellow marks-a-lot, they traced a journey that would get them close to or in the middle of just about every famous landmark in Europe as well as parts of Africa and Asia (when you're on the moon, you might as well see what's on the other side of that ridge). When they stepped back to admire their work, they noted that just about every major road in the upper part of the globe was colored yellow. There's a lot of stuff out there to see.

It took several more days to pare it down to the bare essentials, and what they ended up with was a loop that started in Wiedenbruck, Germany (where they turn new Volkswagen buses into campers), meandered north to the Arctic Circle and South to the Equator, encompassing forty countries give or take. It was, admittedly, an ambitious plan.

What they had was a $100,000 plan and a $10,000 bank account. Now what? This was the question Johnny posed as he chatted with his friends, several of whom actually knew people who had made similar trips.

Johnny had always thought these people were independently wealthy. One day he asked a surfer/drug dealer buddy whose name cannot be revealed (Brian Kennelly) how it was that he knew so many idly rich surfers. He allowed as how all these guys were paupers who were out there on a mission to bring home the "bacon," so to speak. The light went on.

Johnny reasoned that he could buy a VW Camper with 10% down through a local dealer, take delivery in Germany, drive the thing as far as he could with as much as they had, then throw a little weed "in the trunk" for the trip home, thereby actually making a few dollars on the whole deal.

Susan was, uh, dubious. So was Johnny. But the thought of returning from a short vacation with no money and no prospects did not appeal.

The concept had been glorified to a certain extent by songs like "Marrakech Express" where Crosby Stills Nash and Young harmonized sweetly about a train ride through Morocco. Also, Woodstock "happened" in August of '69 and as long as you weren't one of the unfortunate few who doubled up on the purple acid, it was by most accounts pretty entertaining.

Johnny and Susan were on the outer fringes of the drug scene, but did enjoy a dubie now and then (every night and twice on Sunday). They had responsible jobs, college educations, and adequate vocabularies. They looked like they belonged at Oxford, which made them perfect for the task at hand since NOBODY would ever suspect what they were up to.

Johnny reasoned that the key to not having a problem was to not share your plans. They'd seen movies where one guy blabs to another guy and pretty soon everybody's in jail. So, it was their little secret.

There were many times when Johnny figured maybe this was not his brightest idea. In the back of his mind he thought, "What if something goes wrong and we end up in the slammer in some seedy foreign country?" (Susan would never forgive him for that). Of course, they could end up in the slammer right here in Honolulu. The true potential of this concern hit home when the son of one of the guys at work was arrested when he took delivery of a box full of pot after the postal inspector grew suspicious of the overpowering aroma and the Thailand return address. That put a lump in Johnny's throat.

But, with the optimism of the Great Wallenda as he stepped out on the high wire for the last time, a can-do attitude, and a lust for adventure, Johnny trudged blindly onward (dragging Susan all the way) and the trip took shape.

If you ask a pot grower how he got into the business, he will most likely tell you "Well, I just planted one for my personal use, then three, then a thousand." It's a little bit like that when you think about going half way around the world to bring back some herb. You've got the same problems whether you bring back one, three, or a thousand, so you may as well go for it. And that's what Johnny did.

Now, with the benefit of hindsight, it is important to note that this was, without a doubt, the **stupidest thing Johnny ever did**. He would sincerely advise anyone else thinking along similar lines to "get a grip." If you prefer to remain "young and foolish" in the classic sense, the odds of success are definitely against you and the consequences of failure are serious and long lasting. Johnny will never, ever, do this again. You shouldn't either (you know who Johnny's talking to).

The ol' profit incentive caused Johnny to further refine his plans. Instead of pot (which sold for a few hundred a pound) why not hashish (which sold for several thousand a pound)? Hummmm, what to do?

Hashish is a hallucinogenic derived from resin in the flowers of hemp plants. Marijuana, a product of the same plant, is far less potent. The active ingredient is tetra hydra cannabinol (THC). The content in good hash is up there around 15% compared to mud splattered Mexican which is down there around 1%. Given a choice, the connoisseur will go with hash every time. Due to the strong demand and limited supply, a slab of Moroccan hash will fetch quite a tidy sum on the retail market. The profit incentive inherent in capitalist enterprise often induces people to do really stupid things. Alas, Johnny was a Stupid Capitalist (capital S, capital C).

Johnny noticed there were two types of VW campers – one had a pop-up tent top, the other had a solid metal roof. It occurred to him that if you built a solid sheet metal superstructure on the inside of the van that mimicked the curvature of the roof above, you would end up with a vacant cavity about 2" deep covering the entire roof. You could probably cram a substantial quantity of hash in there if ya really packed 'er tight. So, they ordered a hard top.

Now, where to get the hash? In those days, the two hashish epicenters of the world were Afghanistan and Morocco (Mexico was a distant runner up since the quality of their "product" was abysmal and they mostly sold pot because it was too hard to make hash). Afghanistan was really heavy since they also grew 98% of the world's heroin and the place was swarming with crooked cops, narcs, and mafia types (this was way before the Taliban and Al Qaeda). So, the trip got considerably shorter by erasing the lines that went all the way down to Kabul and back. That left sunny Morocco as the most likely candidate, and they penciled in a little trip across the Straight of Gibraltar to Tangiers.

Johnny realized that he had everything covered except for the cost of the "petunias." Coincidentally, there was this guy at work who was always bugging him about pyramid schemes and Amway parties. So, Johnny came up with his own little investment opportunity, which promised to double your money in six months or your money back. This last part was a straight out lie since Johnny would probably be in jail somewhere but they didn't need to know the particulars.

It got a little weird when Johnny found himself giving a presentation to a poolside gathering of engineers and accountants, explaining that this short-term investment opportunity was not only exciting and devoid of risk, but in fact a sure thing (Gawd, what a liar). Precise details could not be revealed in order to preserve the element of surprise that generally accompanies insider trading, er, investments of this type.

Johnny lied like a Moroccan rug merchant but his story was plausible since the company he worked for had been mentioned extensively in a recent newspaper article concerning illegal stock manipulation. He left an open brief case on the coffee table. At the end of the evening, it contained a little more than $10,000 in hundred-dollar bills and a list of investors/co-conspirators.

Armed with $10,000 in traveler's checks, another $10,000 in hundreds, and a receipt for a new hard top camper from Ala Moana Volkswagen, they waved good-bye and boarded the plane for Europe.

In those days passenger planes could not make it all the way to Europe in one flight, so they had to stop in Iceland to refuel. The problem with that is (1) you're most likely landing at night (2) there's most likely high winds and rain, and (3) the pilot is probably pretty tired. All three of these problems converged as they sped down through the darkness, rocking back and forth and up and down in high winds and rain, then violently jerked back up at a steep angle into the blackness at the last minute. They did this two more times. By then, everyone on the plane had a real bad case of anxiety (in operating rooms they call it "White Coat Syndrome", in airplanes they call it "We're Gonna Die"). On the fourth attempt they hit the run way hard, fish tailed left and right, and finally stopped just short of the end of the pavement. Johnny never really got over this episode and remains to this day a little leery about flying.

Who was it that said, "The crown lies heavy?" Well, when you're trying to enjoy yourself while tooling around Europe with the knowledge that at the end, you're gonna do something really outrageous, it kind of weighs you down.

Nevertheless, they were up beat as the taxi pulled into the VW Camper Factory. As luck would have it, they were just starting to work on the camper conversion for Johnny's van, so he was able to watch as they fabricated and installed the false interior plywood roof panels. It was pretty ingenious. There were metal gutters on both sides of the interior into which the edges of each panel were placed, then the whole thing was pushed up and popped in. The tension of the curved surface held it in place.

This had been a weak point in his otherwise hair brained scheme – how to modify the ride to take the load so that an innocent VW Camper could become a nondescript "loader." That morning in the camper factory this particular problem was solved. All he had to do was remove the wood panels, make sheet metal panels with the same dimensions, sandwich the two together and pop 'em back into place. Voila!

Two days later they were at a sheet metal factory in Hamburg getting panels cut to size for an "art project." That afternoon the loader was ready.

Noting that the Army and NASA often make test runs when they are contemplating something risky, Johnny blazed a trail through Europe that included a trip down to Yugoslavia, Greece, and into Turkey, then back out by way of Bulgaria. Since this was a major route for heroin traffickers, and since those Russian border guards were known to be pretty thorough, he figured this would be a good test run on an "empty tank" ("Hey, vot iss diss empty false compartment?!" "Oh that? I think they fucked up at the factory").

Bulgaria turned out to be a shit hole controlled by very unfriendly military types. At a campground they had pulled out a Frisbee and were throwing it back and forth to the amazement of the other Bulgarian campers who had never seen such a thing. To blow their minds, Johnny would occasionally throw the Frisbee to one of the onlookers. Pretty soon it was a love fest and several dozen Bulgarians enthusiastically whiled away the afternoon throwing a Frisbee at each other.

The next morning Johnny and Susan were perp walked by a squad of Bulgarian military personnel into the "office" (lots of prison cells in there) where several soldiers frisked them thoroughly (especially Susan) and took away their passports. They were detained for two more days until they were able to convince the authorities that they were not spies. General Bonislava Lyubova Tsvetanka finally, reluctantly, handed back their passports and kicked them out of the campground.

The Bulgarian border was anti-climatic. When they pulled up, a fat Bulgarian guard came lumbering out with a large screwdriver. He flipped it over and smashed the roof with the plastic handle, which produced a noise like a truck crashing into an airplane hanger. He stamped their visas and waived them through. Johnny wondered what it might sound like with a few hundred pounds of hash in there, but tried to push this out of his mind.

Six months into the trip, they made it to the Rock of Gibraltar and "Showtime." They drove onto the ferry and landed in Tangiers where they found a remote section of a campground overlooking the ocean. This would be their base of operations.

Johnny went into town and rented a car. The guy at the counter was a little suspicious, but ultimately handed over the keys. Johnny immediately cut all the springs out of the back seat (turns out the counter guy had good instincts).

And then it was time to make it happen. So, Johnny grabbed $10,000 in hundred-dollar bills and headed for the hills.

Tangiers is separated from the Sahara Desert by the Er Rif Mountain Range. It is here that approximately half the world's supply of hashish is grown by the Berber tribes that inhabit this area. It was here that Johnny was headed in his springless rental car (a shitty little Fiat). It had Moroccan plates and Johnny wore a djellaba (a long flowing garment with full sleeves and a hood popular with Arabs – the sort of thing Obi Wan Kenobi would wear to a cocktail party) in a vein attempt to blend in.

You can't just pull up to a store and get some hash. You have to know where to find it. Unfortunately, Johnny didn't have a clue. So, he cruised for hours higher and deeper into the deserted Er Rif Mountains. At a curve in the road near the top, he saw two things: (1) the great Sahara Desert spread out before him and (2) a little kid waving and shouting "Hashish? Hashish?" Johnny pulled over. The kid jumped in and pointed down a dirt road, which they stayed on for a half hour until they came to a few mud huts in the middle of nowhere.

A dozen bearded men in long robes and turbans greeted Johnny. They all had guns (mostly ancient rifles that looked like muskets but which could probably blow a hole in a boulder) and nobody was smiling. Johnny thought to himself "This must be where the rubber meets the road."

There is a language barrier between American smugglers and Moroccan drug lords. The true meaning of "awkward" manifested itself as Johnny sat down in a room full of smelly gun toting Muslim pot farmers for a little "discussion." They just looked at him. He had seen that look before down on the farm when he was trying to communicate with a cow – it can't be done. The only word they shared in common was "hashish" and that wasn't even

English for Pete's sake. But then one of them said "Como esta?" BINGO!

It turns out that the second language in Morocco is Spanish owing to their close proximity to Spain. And, as it happened, Johnny had taken three years of Spanish in high school. Unfortunately, he had been a very poor student, and barely passed his third-year final exam with his famous one sentence mountain speech "Pues, aqui esta en la montana" ("Well, here I am on the mountain") while standing on a chair in front of the class which garnered a C-. Oh man, he wished he had paid more attention.

Strange things happen to people when they are under pressure – sometimes they fall completely apart, sometimes they do better. Fortunately, Johnny did better as he launched into an intricate negotiation in Spanish with a room full of Berber drug lords. It turned out that the going price for a kilo of hash (2.2 pounds) was about $100 US. Johnny thought he might be able to negotiate this down, but then he thought about the enormous amount of labor required to produce 2.2 pounds of the stuff, the horrendous amount of money he would get for it in America, and the tenuous nature of his negotiating position. So, he said "Ole!!" The drug lords loved that, and started to smile. Johnny could not remember how to count past ten so he just said, "I need a hundred kilos". The room went silent. Then the guy with the grey beard and the multi colored turban said "A **HUNDRED** KILOS?"

Apparently, they were used to one or two kilo transactions. One hundred kilos had stunned them. It turned out they needed to contact several other farmers from across the mountain range to assemble that much dope, but agreed that they could do it by tomorrow night. So, Johnny gave them a hundred-dollar bill to validate his intent, shook hands and drove away. As he bumped back up the dirt road, he watched the rear-view mirror as they danced around and fired into the air.

Johnny returned the next day at dusk and was greeted by the same bearded farmers in turbans and djellabas with their rusty old guns slung over their shoulders, which Johnny took as a good sign. There was sweet tea, pleasant conversation, and a procession of farm workers who brought in one hundred kilos of you know what.

And then things got serious. Someone came running in yelling "Policia! Policia!" The room erupted as the farmers grabbed the product of their hard work and stuffed it into what looked like potato sacks. They pushed Johnny into a closet. It was sketchy.

But ten minutes later they let Johnny out, said the coast was clear, and advised him to follow several vans that had just arrived back up the dirt road to a "safer place" to consummate the transaction. The occupants of these vans were younger looking Moroccans. They wore street cloths, not djellabas. They were clean-shaven. There were no turbans. And their guns looked more like Kalashnikovs than blunder busts. They were also very serious.

And so, with considerable reservation (what was he gonna do, make a run for it and get shot to pieces?), Johnny followed them to a barren hilltop where they stopped under a full moon and piled out.

They produced a mound of hash, which looked roughly like a hundred kilos (Johnny was not going to run the risk of offending them by counting). He handed over a satchel containing $10,000, which they counted carefully. Then, while Johnny was stuffing the dope into the springless back seat, they went through his car and his pockets to see what else they might be able to include in the transaction.

Johnny had nothing else of value. They looked at each other for a long moment and whispered something that sounded a lot like "muerto" which he remembered from his

Spanish classes meant "dead, lifeless" as an adjective and "corpse, cadaver" as a noun. Uh oh.

Then they looked at Johnny. Johnny just smiled and said "Muchas Gracias Amigos" and they let him go.

This was as close as Johnny came and hopefully would ever come to being murdered in the night.

This kind of situation has a tendency to drain you, so Johnny was not real perky as he drove back down through the mountains and took the last turn before heading down to the main intersection back to Tangier (left is Morocco, right is Algeria). It was two in the morning and the intersection was lit up like a serious crime scene. This was not good, what with a hundred kilos of hash in the back seat and all.

Johnny stopped behind a large boulder, turned off the headlights and engine, and waited. Around 3 am he realized that although the intersection was lit up with klieg lights and a generator, there apparently were no cars or people down there. He didn't know if they were home sleeping or just hiding in the bushes waiting for him, but he wasn't going to miss this opportunity. So, he rolled down the last three miles before turning on the engine and lights, pulled up to the deserted intersection, turned left and continued on with both eyes on the rear-view mirror.

Susan was very glad to see him, and he was very glad to see her. The sun was just about to come up, so they still had a little time to transfer the load from the back seat of the rental car to the floor of the camper. In the process, Johnny dropped several slabs, which broke into pieces on the ground. He picked up most of it but it was dark and he didn't get it all.

They slept until noon when another camper full of Aussies pulled up next to them. They got out, looked at the pile of hash next to Johnny's camper, and quietly got back in and drove away.

Now it was time to pack the loader. Johnny removed the wood panels and unscrewed the cover on the square holes he had cut into the center of the sheet metal. They got out a dozen cans of deodorizer and several boxes of zip lock baggies. Each slab of hash was sprayed with deodorizer, bagged, sprayed again, bagged again, sprayed again, and bagged once more. These pleasantly smelling baggies were then stuffed one by one into the space above the false roof and below the real one. As luck would have it, one hundred kilos of hashish fits perfectly into the roof of a hard top Volkswagen Camper – ya gotta love those Germans.

The next morning, they headed for the ferry. Customs on the Moroccan side was perfunctory, but when they got to Gibraltar it got serious. As they drove off the boat, they were flagged into a separate lane from the other cars. Susan looked at Johnny and said, "WHAT'S THIS?!" Johnny, anticipating a possibly tense situation, had consumed four Valium, which he had carried all over Europe for this occasion (two of them were supposed to be for Susan but somehow ended up with Johnny as he sincerely felt he might need them more –he was right).

He was cool as a cucumber and his Spanish was impeccable. Gawd, his Spanish teacher (who had refused to sign off as a reference on his college application) would have been proud. He made some small talk, told some jokes; the Customs officer laughed, put his screwdriver away, and waived them through. Whew!

The rest of the trip was delightful, except when they went over large bumps the ceiling would sag and there was some concern that the whole thing would cave in. They slowed way down for bumps after that, and the roof held. They made it all the way to Bremen, Germany where they rolled 'er on a cargo ship bound for America and ultimately Hawaii by way of the Panama Canal. The trip would take six weeks. It was the longest six weeks of Johnny's life.

They flew home and tried to distract themselves until the camper finally arrived. Johnny got the call "Your car is in – you can come down and pick it up today if you like." It sounded a lot like a narc on a tape recorder, but there wasn't really too much he could do about it now (ya can't just leave the thing sitting on the dock).

So, he kissed Susan goodbye, told her he would call her "either way" and headed down to the pier. They showed him into the warehouse and there in the corner was his camper with the sliding side door open. It smelled like somebody had emptied a dozen cans of deodorizer in there. The warehouse foreman said, "We get this all the time – these new cars smell like shit so we have to air 'em out." Johnny thought this was humorous but did not laugh – in the back of his mind he was fairly certain this guy was a DEA agent just fucking with him.

He was pretty sure by now that he would be arrested at the gate, but he pulled up anyway and gamely produced his bill of lading. The cop looked at the paper work, then looked at Johnny and said.............

"Have a nice day".

Chapter 34

Matt's Wedding

The news came in the form of a phone call. The exact words (which are indelibly etched on Johnny's brain) were, "Hey Dad, guess what, I'm getting married – on Halloween, in Las Vegas, by Elvis."

This was not surprising, since Matt (the apple) did not fall far from Johnny (the tree). His full name is Matthew Makani Ma La'au ("wind through the trees") Peterson, and although he kind of likes the idea of a Hawaiian middle name, he curses the day he got it every time he has to fill out a form requiring more than a middle initial.

The idea came during a drug-induced moment of clarity while his mother and father lay in a forest listening to the wind blow through the ironwood trees. His mother, although reluctant, ultimately submitted, and also agreed to the name. Johnny's penchant for peculiar names extended later to his twin daughters Anna Pukana la "Sunrise" and Ingrid Pa'ana a ka 'la "Sunshine" (they were born at dawn) and even to his e-mail address.

He tried to sign up for a new g-mail account and every single permutation of his name and initials had been taken. He had just finished a book about a surfer who lived under the Malibu Pier and worked across the street at Tube's Steak and Seafood Restaurant. He would answer the phone "Tube's Steak" and he accordingly became known as Tube Steak. So, in desperation, Johnny typed it in and it was instantly accepted. Johnny's son Matt was appalled as were many people over the years on the other end of g-mail, but he's not giving it up.

Life with Matt growing up was interesting. At the age of one he developed a fondness for sand and every time he found himself at the beach (which was often), he'd consume huge quantities of it and crapped silica for days. At two, he discovered hammers and the damage they could inflict on just about anything, especially tile floors and counter tops. At three he discovered electricity (two nails deftly inserted into the socket of an extension cord – he danced around for some time before Johnny could climb down off the ladder and pry him loose). This may have had something to do with his straight hair, which, up to that point, had been curly.

Every year it was something new and exciting. At five he discovered girls and was sent home from kindergarten with a terse note. At eight he discovered Johnny's wallet and cleaned him out. By ten he had discovered freedom and stayed at his friend's house for three days ("won't your parents be worried?") before returning home to his hysterical mother and pissed off father. Coincidentally he also discovered that it was possible for your butt to turn blue after a spanking. At fourteen he discovered that he could drive a car unaided, and periodically "borrowed" the family vehicle. At sixteen he discovered weed and booze (a chip off the ol' block). At seventeen he dropped out of high school with a semester to go. He later got a GED and "enrolled" in college on three separate occasions – then immediately dropped out (keeping the tuition and book money).

But he had many fine qualities. He was kind, considerate, loving, and surprisingly intelligent. Johnny was thankful for this. So, when the subject of his wedding came up, Johnny was ready to embrace his new daughter-in-law (in a non-biblical sense) and welcome her to the family. Her name was April.

He got a phone message one day saying, "Hi, this is Kristy, I'm in town – let's get together for a drink." Not knowing who Kristy was but anxious to share a drink and the prospect of unsolicited sex, he discovered that she was the bride's mother come to check him out. She was a very nice person and held her tequila quite well. Thus integrated into the impending family circle, he looked forward to Las Vegas.

Johnny did not actually get to meet the bride-to-be until he arrived in Las Vegas and they rendezvoused at Denny's for breakfast the day of the wedding. Since they had driven from Oregon all night to get there, Johnny expected Matt and April would be pretty thrashed. Matt was surprisingly chipper. April, on the other hand, was totally cooked (stick a fork in her, she's done).

Although a beautiful girl, she came with some baggage – she had been a heroin addict for quite some time, but with the help of modern medical science she was able to shuck the monkey and was now a methadone addict. Coincidentally, the first order of business upon arriving in Las Vegas was to get a "treatment" prior to wobbling into Denny's for breakfast. She had a hard time keeping her head up, and every so often would drool on her pancakes. It was difficult to engage in conversation since she was only good for one syllable at a time – "Huuuuhh?" and "Whaaaah?" Her previous husband had apparently been an aspiring tattoo artist and had used her for practice - she was covered head to foot with prison tattoos that would not wash off. And she had a bit of a bad attitude and a hard edge. Aside from that, she was lovely.

So, Johnny sucked it up and waited for the wedding. While passing idle time, he found himself in "the world's largest souvenir store" and, in perusing the goods, came across a pile of Elvis wigs. He tried one on, looked in the mirror (not bad), then noticed the Elvis sunglasses with side burns attached. When he put these on and snuck a peek at the mirror, he realized that not only did he look like Elvis, he WAS Elvis. And so thought many of the people that day on the strip who were honking and waiving as he made his way to the chapel.

Fortunately, Matt and April (now resplendent in a white gown with lots of lace and vacant space so the tats could show through) enjoyed the idea of TWO Elvis's at their wedding. They waited their turn (one couple every ten minutes 24/7). When the "real" Elvis made his entrance, he came over to Johnny and exclaimed "DAD!?" The wedding was actually quite enjoyable with Elvis interspersing solemn words of matrimony with "Hound Dog" and other inappropriate songs. When it was over, the wedding party adjourned to the bar, which was conveniently attached to the Chapel, and everybody got smoked.

That evening, Johnny threw a gala dinner for the wedding party, and everybody got smoked (again). Tipping the waiter heavily to make up for the broken glass and food fight, he wandered down to the casino floor. Inasmuch as he was alone and it was not yet midnight, he saddled up to the crap table for a little game.

And there, looking up at him over an ample bosom, was cute little Kim with a question - "Can you teach me how to do dice?" Needless to say, Johnny was very attentive, and this was not lost on Kim's two girlfriends who had been standing nearby all night fending off every drunken sailor and pervert who dared to make a pass at their inebriated friend. Johnny innocently turned around and said, "How about a group hug?" It did not go well. But Kim hung in there. Johnny would occasionally spin around to catch the two girlfriends making hysterical gestures, which seemed to connote variously "cut his throat" or "let's get outta here."

But still Kim stayed, now rubbing up and down his arm as he tried to concentrate on the game. Johnny ended up losing north of $1,000 but Kim, with a little help, won $500 on a $10 stake. So, she took Johnny to the bar for a few Bloody Marys and then asked if he would be so kind as to help her to her room. Why, yes!

The Luxor, where they were, is a pointy shaped building that looks sort of like a modern-day pyramid topped with a fifty million-candle power searchlight aiming straight up into a whirling column of flying insects. Planes are not allowed to fly anywhere near this thing. Surprisingly, there are no elevators. Instead, they have "inclinators." This can be very confusing at three in the morning if you're totally gone and want to find your room. You press the button and off you go diagonally up the inside of this very strange building.

They eventually got to the room and Johnny, ever the gentleman, was admiring the view when sweet little Kim jumped him from behind and took total advantage. Johnny did not put up much of a fight. It would be indelicate to go into the details here. Let's just say they made it half way through the Kama Sutra before dawn.

The next morning, Johnny was awakened by sweet little Kim who was now half dressed, looking in the mirror, and asking herself over and over again, "Oh my Gawd, what have I done?"

It was one of the best weddings ever.

Chapter 35

Geezer Golf

There had been talk of a Geezer golf trip. It
was basically idle conversation among a
bunch of old guys in an old guys golf group
(inappropriately named the Men's Club). It
started out innocently but soon escalated into
a testosterone-fueled war of words "Yeah, well
if you go, **I'm** going." It was pretty funny to
hear these guys pledge their intent to go on a
month-long Mainland golf tour without first
having checked with the misses.

Inasmuch as Johnny was not married (having
been divorced years earlier for reasons still
not clearly understood but probably valid),
there was no higher power with whom he
needed to check, so his response was "I'm in."
This precipitated an awkward moment since
the other guys had been careful (up to this
point) to couch their intentions in theoretical
terms. "I'm in" had thrown a load of feathers
into the fan. It got really quiet as it became
clear that the gauntlet had been thrown down
hard – you were either in or out (a stud or a
wuss). There was a lot of hemming and
hawing.

Ultimately, eight blood brothers pledged their
allegiance to one another and prepared for the
golf trip of a lifetime. The original idea was to

start on the West Coast and roam the United States for a month in a couple of drop top Cadillacs (which they would buy in San Diego and sell in New York) playing exclusive courses, consuming expensive scotch, and reveling in deluxe accommodations along the way. When reality set in, the concept was pared back somewhat. In the end, the idea was to drive a nondescript econovan rental from San Diego to San Francisco in a week or so, playing whatever courses would have them, drinking beer, and staying in Motel 6's (or Super 8's in a pinch).

One by one, the wusses began to fold – the excuses proffered were ingenious. One guy said he had to have his gall bladder removed (while technically true, he neglected to mention this had happened in the 5th grade). Another "forgot" that he had booked himself and the wife on a Mediterranean cruise "to save our marriage." Another said "demands at home" precluded him from spending more than a couple days away. Another said, "Yeh, I got that too." And one guy just quit the club. In the end there were three whole brothers (Gerrit, Ellis, and Johnny) and two halves (Jim for the first week, Arnie for the second). Then it occurred to them - who's gonna plan this thing?

Fortunately, Gerrit was absent from that conversation, having been temporarily kicked out of the Men's Club (for the third time) for bad behavior. Punishing Gerrit with expulsion was particularly hilarious since the Men's Club is made up of guys who thrive on bad behavior. Gerrit's sins, however, were egregious and unforgivable (leaving at the turn after a miserable first nine – twice!). So, it fell to Johnny to talk Gerrit into assuming responsibility for the trip. Gerrit made it easy, advising everyone the next day that since he possessed the requisite skills and a hopped-up computer (along with a burning desire to be readmitted to the club and an ego as big as all outdoors) he would take command.

It was January. Gerrit informed his "squadron" (since he was a retired fighter pilot anybody standing in the immediate vicinity was considered a member of his "squadron") that the trip would commence May 1 in San Diego and terminate May 20 in San Francisco. Over the next four months he arranged airline tickets, car rentals, accommodations, tee times, routes, maps, suggested suitcase contents, and a host of other things. The guys were receiving an email daily from Gerrit advising of progress. And, by gawd, on May 1 it actually happened.

Overlooking for a moment Gerrit's bad attitude, he had an uncanny knack for stretching a dollar and, to his credit; he pulled it off in spades. Ol' Gerrit got free round trips on a military plane (the pilot baked cookies for the passengers on the way) and produced a monstrous Ford Explorer at the airport (you could fit twenty illegal aliens in there and, in fact, Johnny saw on the news where they actually had, but they missed a turn at high speed and ended up scattered all over the desert outside of Phoenix). He'd gotten some kind of discount and in the end, it cost about as much as a taxi from Honolulu International Airport to Waikiki.

Then he lined up military housing. This was not your standard barracks; we're talking beachfront hotels on Coronado Island, the General's quarters on the golf course at Marshallia Ranch, etc. They were living large and it cost way less than Motel 6. Finally, he had lined up a slew of really nice courses including a few high-end venues. Even there, he'd arranged to join the Northern California Golf Association, which entitled him and several of his guests to play the toney $500 courses in Carmel for a hundred bucks. They were set - thanks Gerrit (you son of a bitch).

All went well for two days. By the third, Johnny's snoring had caused his roommate Gerrit (nobody else would share a room with this miserable bastard) to miss a substantial amount of needed sleep. He became even more edgy and disoriented than usual. He began having a hard time discerning the difference between an earnest comment and a joke. The vessels in his eyes filled with blood. He got snippy. He started messing with the wrong guys.

The day started out on an interesting note. Johnny had risen at dawn after a good night's sleep (he left Gerrit whimpering in the death throws of some kind of terrible nightmare). Grabbing a cup of Joe, he walked across the broad white sand beach to the waterline. Noting an extreme low tide, he turned right toward Point Loma and splashed along the water's edge looking for shells. Now, he had been collecting sand dollars for fifty years and had a collection of six, which is about one per decade. As he shuffled along, he found a big one just lying there. It was in perfect condition. Wow! He picked it up and kept walking. He found another one. And then another. He was all by himself on a pristine beach loaded with sand dollars! He could not believe his good fortune. He noticed that even the birds were friendly (as opposed to the usual run-of-the-mill shore birds who take delight in dive bombing unsuspecting beach goers with surprisingly accurate payloads).

As he neared the end of the island, he noticed a coast guard cutter laying close off the beach with guys on the rail waiving in a peculiar fashion – sort of like the wave at a football stadium except from side to side instead of up and down. Figuring that this was a boat full of friendly sailors, Johnny gave the wave right back at 'em. Then they started honking the horn. Really a fun bunch. Then a truckload of MP's came roaring over the dunes and surrounded him.

They said "What in the hell are you doing here?" (Wow, so much for friendly). "You are standing in the middle of a live fire range – thank God we got a message from the Coast Guard – you could have been killed – didn't you see the razor wire fence and the sign?"

Johnny replied, "Uh, no, I was just collecting sand dollars."

As they escorted him back down the beach in the Hummer, he noticed the fence with the razor wire, which stopped just below the high-water line, maybe fifteen feet from the low tide water's edge. He also noted the 12' x 20' sign, which read "Extreme Danger – Live Fire Range – Keep Away."

Whew, what a way to start the day. But he had a dozen sand dollars rolled up in his shirt and had tripled the size of his lifetime collection.

The first nine holes that day were delightful. At the turn, Ellis and Gerrit (Jim had a hang over and failed to make muster) went to the car to refill the "water bottle," so Johnny proceeded to the 10ᵗʰ tee and sat for a while enjoying the view of the ocean. A single came up from behind and engaged in pleasant conversation. Johnny invited him to join up and finish the round. When the boys got back from the car, Johnny introduced the new player. Gerrit, by now completely frazzled, said "Well, you should have talked to me before inviting a complete stranger to play with us" to which Johnny replied "Fuck you, you blithering idiot." In retrospect, he (Johnny) probably could have employed less offensive language, but at the time that's all he could come up with. Also, in retrospect, this was the beginning of the end.

It was an uneventful round, followed by steaks and scotch on the beach – Gerrit was somewhat withdrawn and seemed to be having a hard time holding on to his glass, having developed periodic episodes of uncontrollable shaking. Johnny snored extra hard that night, which may have pushed the proverbial car off the cliff.

The next morning, they drove north to a surprisingly nice course at Camp Pendleton Marine Base. Johnny had been here many times in the distant past to retrieve his surfboards, which had been occasionally confiscated by the Marines when he tried to sneak into Trestles and was apprehended. It felt extremely weird to be welcomed there, but he got used to it immediately.

The round was about to start, and on the tee Gerrit announced "Today I'm not gonna let Johnny get under my skin." Quietly, Johnny said to himself, "Oh yeah?" They played a game that day called Poker. It involved a sack of poker chips, which were distributed amongst the players depending on whether you did something good (say, a birdie) or something bad (say hitting a tree or sand trap). There were rewards and penalties associated with these chips. If, at the end of eighteen holes, you possessed a good chip you collected a dollar from each of the other players. If you possessed a bad chip, you had to pay a dollar to each of the other players.

The worst chip in the pouch, and the one you really did not want to be holding at the end of the game, was the Fugly Chip. This was a very bad chip, so bad that it required both a nomination and a unanimous vote to bestow it upon a player. It was only to be used in the event of an extremely bad shot (FUcking uGLY). It cost the owner $60 ($20 for each of the other members of the foursome). You did not want this chip.

Gerrit was having a particularly bad day (four days without sleep had taken a toll). Chips were passed good naturedly back and forth –

Gerrit would not accept his and it became necessary to place his in a separate bag for presentation at the 17th hole (so if you were down, you had the opportunity to go double or nothing on eighteen). Poor guy, he reeled around for sixteen holes with triple boogies and a smoldering sense of self-loathing. On the 17th, he stubbed a tee shot, hit a tree, hit another tree, hit a third tree, then, in desperation, swung wildly at a buried lie and chunked it three feet sideways into a sand trap.

Johnny gathered the boys for a Fugly caucus. The other guys said, "Oh man, he's gonna blow - we don't want any part in the nomination, but if he is nominated, we'll cast affirmative votes." So, Johnny nominated Gerrit for the dreaded Fugly chip and the vote was unanimous. Ellis was tasked with the responsibility of placing a towering stack of really bad chips next to Gerrit's ball when it ultimately arrived on the green. When Ol' Gerrit realized what had happened, he lapsed into something resembling an epileptic seizure.

On the 18th tee, Gerrit was preparing (in a Joe Cocker sort of way) to tee off when Johnny, who was responsible for the score card, asked "What'd you get on the last hole?" to which Gerrit, momentarily emerging from his psychosis, screamed "WHAT DO YOU

313

CARE??!!" to which Johnny replied "Gerrit, your golf score is the most important thing in my life." The pin had been pulled; the grenade would be exploding shortly.

Gerrit wandered off into the desert and made some phone calls. On the trip to Newport Beach, he remained silent, even when Johnny twisted the knife, "Hey, you owe me $30." At the hotel, Johnny attempted to defuse the situation, grabbing Gerrit in a bear hug and saying, "We were just kidding – we love ya man – are we allright?" to which he responded "No."

Ellis and Jim came over from the other room just in time for the explosion. Gerrit wheeled around and said, "I hate you guys! I'm never going to play golf with you again and I'm going back to Hawaii in the morning." He probably regretted this outburst, but it was too late.

Johnny lost it. "You better step outside cause I'm going to fuck you up." Jim and Ellis impeded Johnny's forward progress or there would have been a body at the bottom of the pool. Gerrit jumped through the window and escaped, sneaking back around midnight to get some sleep.

After the shock of what went down, Jim, Ellis, and Johnny jumped in the hot tub with a bottle of Jack Daniels to sooth those jangled nerves. Several hours later, Johnny had to go back to the hotel room he shared with Gerrit and try to sleep. Have you ever tried to sleep with one eye open waiting for some guy to stab you with a fork? No? Well, it's hard to snooze under those conditions. Gerrit got up at 4 am, banged around the room for a few minutes and was gone. He had planned for four months and lasted four days.

The show must go on. So, the remaining three guys wandered up the coast, shooting holes and blowing minds (Dylan would have loved it). They dropped Jim off at his house on a hill overlooking Palmdale and Edwards Air Force Base in the high desert about fifty miles north of Los Angeles. Once in a great while there's a sonic boom and the space shuttle comes screaming in for a landing when the other ports of call are socked in. It can get to 130 degrees in the summer. Fortunately, it was the middle of May so it was only 115. Unfortunately, golf is not played in the shade.

There was a lot of reckless eating and drinking. Johnny could feel the seat belt getting tighter. In the morning it was getting harder to zip up his pants. He knew it was getting serious when he chanced to put his finger on his belly button and felt it pooching out. It's a good thing there were no scales readily accessible. They had to make a special stop so Johnny could get a pair of fat boy trunks. He chalked it up to the perverse influence of his compatriots. However, not wanting to spoil the party, he continued to participate in the gluttony.

They met up with Arnie north of Santa Barbara in a weird little town called Solvang. There were windmills and tulips everywhere (Trump has avoided Solvang because he apparently thinks windmills cause cancer). People were walking around in wooden shoes. Apparently, there were a lot of illegal European immigrants there – but the food was good. After lunch they drove to Lompoc (famous for its federal prison where a few of Johnny's high school friends had passed some time) and then on to Marshallia Ranch where they stayed at an outrageous lodge overlooking a spectacular golf course and the ocean.

It had belonged to Mr. Marshall who had owned a 7,000-acre ranch, which he called Marshallia until the military bought it and built a missile base called Vandenberg. If that friggin North Korean midget-retard-bastard-dictator ever tries to lob one on Hollywood, this is where the wrath of God will be dispensed – first ya shoot down the incoming missile, then ya turn North Korea into glass – the ol' one-two. The generals apparently deduced that the Marshallia lodge would be the perfect place to view the show, and so claimed it as their own and built a very nice golf course instead of a lawn.

The trip up Highway 1 from San Louis Obispo was both amazing and eventful. It was a sunny day, the sea was calm, and there were thousands of walruses lying on the beaches making crazy noises. The scenery was stunning all along the winding road, which went up and down many times (along with the temperature which varied between fifty-five at sea level and seventy-five at several thousand feet). It's a good thing they had electric windows or they would have gotten tennis elbows.

They stopped for a cup of Joe in a place called Ragged Point. The proprietor didn't speak, he whistled – actually, he was a damn good whistler but it was difficult to carry on a conversation.

"I'll have a latte please."

"Tweet tweet."

"You live around here?"

"Tweeeeettt tweet de tweet." And so forth.

He must have slipped (most decidedly did slip) something in the coffee because things got really intense there for the remainder of the afternoon and it was necessary for them to pull over frequently to admire the view and get their bearings, although there was really only one way to go.

They pulled into Carmel with a raging case of the munchies, and the Garmin GPS took them directly to Clint Eastwood. Actually, it took them to a restaurant that everybody thought Clint owned – the Hog's Breath Inn. When they walked in, they found the place covered with pictures - Dirty Harry, the Good the Bad and the Ugly, celebrities of every make and kind – it looked like a talent agent's office with burgers. They later found out that Clint had sold the place years before, but allowed the new owners to keep the pictures and pretend it was still his. It worked – the place was packed with tourists. Also, a lot of locals (you could tell by the way they sagged under the weight of their jewelry) with dogs – lots of dogs - which seemed strange but apparently, they have lax health codes in Carmel.

Ah, Pebble Beach – the ultimate golf course. It costs $540 to play a round (that's $30 per hole, but who's counting). You're supposed to make tee times several months in advance, but they apparently have fallen on hard times and are willing to let you out as a single on stand-by if you don't mind playing with Saudi Princes and Japanese tycoons. The only trouble with that is Saudi Princes and

Japanese tycoons are notoriously poor golfers. OK, let's tell it like it is – they are freaking horrible. Every once in a while, you'll see what looks like a rugby scrum with burnooses followed closely by a course marshal in a cart with a bucket of balls. Every time somebody would chunk one into the sea or through somebody's window, the marshal would just throw down another ball and they'd flail away at it. The marshal looked a lot like that Sergeant in Mash who was assigned to drive the jeep for Hawkeye and Pierce – "God damn Army." They brilliantly passed on Pebble Beach but played several other courses in the area (Poppy Hills was so nice they played it twice) and still had money left over.

As suddenly as it had started, it was over. They made the run to San Francisco, and ended up at Travis Air Force Base where the free airplane rides are. Johnny bid adieu, rented another car, and headed out alone to attend his Nephew's wedding half way across the US. The rest of the guys, as far as Johnny knows, are still there, waiting for that space available seat back to Hawaii.

Chapter 36

Napa Valley to Winnemucca

Next stop Napa Valley (they have wine there). Johnny played a delightful round at the Chardonnay Course with two out of work investment bankers who managed to pound a case of Budweiser before the turn. Johnny remarkably abstained (it was 9 o'clock in the morning for Christ sake) or there would have been golf cart bumper cars for sure. These two guys (who noted in passing that they had invented something called "credit default swaps" and had made godzillions of dollars before everybody else in the world caught on to their little scheme) actually made it through all eighteen holes, but it wasn't pretty. The last two holes were "air guitar" holes – that's where you've run out of balls and have broken or lost most of your clubs, so you take a swipe at an imaginary ball with an imaginary club. These were some of the finest shots of the day.

Next was a visit to his nephew David in Oakville. He and his girlfriend Lisa live on Money Road (really). There is only one other street that comes off this one, and it's called Penny Lane (honest). They live in a barn surrounded by wine barrels in the middle of a vineyard that was featured in a movie called Bottle Shock about the time in 1976 that a

California Chardonnay won a wine tasting in France. This nearly precipitated a war but France surrendered, as usual.

Driving north to St. Helena was like commuting to LA – there were freekin' tourists lined up for miles, all trying to get to the winery of choice. Every once in a while, the Wine Train would roll by – on the way up the passengers were waving hankies and eating cheese – on the way back they were puking and screaming obscenities (Johnny's kind of train).

At the top of the valley, the Garmin GPS said turn right to go north. The map Johnny was looking at seemed to indicate a reasonably adequate and potentially picturesque northbound road accessible by turning left. Relying upon his exceptional seat of the pants navigational skills, Johnny turned left. This proved to be not only unwise but unhealthy as well. That road had more curves than a snake on acid. It turned to dust ten miles in. Stuck behind a slow-moving logging truck, Johnny inhaled dirt and fumes for approximately a hundred miles. Several hours later, with mud filled lungs and a serious case of motion sickness, Johnny merged back on to the main highway fifty miles from his brilliant left turn (when in doubt, go right). The next 2,500 miles were driven strictly in accordance with Mr. Garmin's suggestions.

Grant's Pass Oregon is a picturesque little town with a sign over the main street that says, "It's the Climate" (they left out "Stupid"). Johnny never quite understood this (in the winter it's freezing, in the summer it's blazing). He arrived on "Boat Day" which is actually an excuse for a weekend of drunken debauchery and drag boat racing (a volatile combination) in the river, which runs through the middle of the town.

This river (the Rogue) starts 200 miles away in the Cascade Mountains at an elevation of 5,300 feet and barrels through Grant's Pass on the way to the ocean. It's really cold and runs really fast. Every once in a while, you'll see somebody, or something blow by on the way to the end of the line. You do not want to fall in here.

He gathered his son Matt, his girlfriend Michelle (having divorced his first wife shortly after their Las Vegas wedding), and a host of other people for cocktails on the riverbank immediately adjacent to the drag boat starting line. Holy smokes, those boats were amazing. They started out with the 100mph barges and ended up with the 200mph+ fire breathing monsters. When they dropped the flag, your beer would foam, and your ears would bleed. Now and then a piston or a flywheel would sail through the air as an engine exploded in flames – pretty exciting (no wonder these guys were so fond of alcohol). You'd have to be out of your mind to get in one of those things.

The way they express love and friendship in Grant's Pass is food. If you go into a restaurant, you're gonna get a large pile of stuff on your plate. If you go into a restaurant operated by your son and his girlfriend, you are gonna get the Matterhorn special. The way you express love and friendship back is to eat what they give you. Those were some of the largest breakfasts, lunches, and dinners Johnny had ever eaten all of. He was rapidly catching up to Jaba the Hut.

It was now time to turn East and head across the great plains of the United States to get to his other nephew's wedding in Omaha, Nebraska. Dwight D. (Ike) Eisenhower declared in 1950 that there should be good roads across America linking all the states. Interstate 80 was one of the many that were built in that era. It goes from California to New York along a northern trajectory that takes you through Nevada, Utah, Wyoming, Nebraska, etc. So, this is the road Johnny took.

In Hawaii, the equivalent to Interstate 80 is Interstate 1 (top speed limit 55). "Interstate 1" is a ridiculous misnomer since there are no other adjacent states to which you can drive (the nearest one is 2,100 miles away on the other side of the Pacific Ocean), nor can you drive to 98% of the land area within the state (which is spread out over many islands). Somebody obviously pulled a fast one on the Federal Government in order to get them to finance the thing. And, get this; they pulled it off TWO MORE TIMES by extending it to Wahiawa (which they called "Interstate 2") and to Kaneohe ("Interstate 3"). If the Feds ever catch on, Hawaii is gonna have some explaining to do.

Unlike Hawaii, the speed limit on Interstate 80 is 75mph but if you don't want to get run down from behind, you better be doin' 100 plus. Johnny now knew what it must be like to drive a dump truck on the Autobahn.

It was kind of controlled mayhem out there. Johnny clutched the wheel of his red convertible Ford Mustang GT rental until the blood ran out of his fingers and managed to push 'er over the 100 mark and stay there. It occurred to him that he would never make it at Talladega and that Richard Petty, if he were still alive, would have nothing to worry about in terms of Johnny suddenly appearing in his rear-view mirror. Every once in a while, he'd pass a tractor trailer and noticed that at speeds approaching 100mph the eighteen large wheels on these beasts appeared to elongate to where the top front part of each tire leans forward and the bottom rear part sags back. If you hit the brakes on one of these babies at these speeds, there's no tellin' what might happen, but it'd probably be all bad and would most likely last for several minutes/miles. Johnny made a mental note to cross truck driver off his list of potential future occupations.

The police were helpless. Thousands of cars were hurtling down the freeway at 100 mph+ and there was nothing they could do about it. At least that is what Johnny thought. But the police had developed a novel way of dealing with their apparent impotency. They would turn on their sirens and flashing lights, get 'er up to 150 and blaze by (cop cars with cop engines, cop shocks and cop aftermarket parts can do this easily - ask the Blues Brothers). Naturally, everyone thought they were being pulled over for a juicy ticket (Johnny wondered what the fine would be for 30 over in a 75 zone) so they'd slow way down until the cop was outta sight, then speed back up. The brilliance of the police mind would not manifest itself for another 50 miles.

At 150 mph, a police car will gain fifty miles in one hour on all other cars going merely 100. The police (who probably excelled at those high school problems where two trains left the station at the same time) took full advantage of this mathematical certainty, selecting a blind curve on a down-hill stretch to apply the binders, throw it sideways and screech to a halt essentially blocking all three lanes of East bound traffic. This, in effect, created a fifty-mile-long traffic jam wherein a thousand cars travelling at 100 miles per hour needed to come to a horrifyingly abrupt stop in the middle of the desert (Johnny had seen this many times before on the Harbor freeway in LA where bent fenders and broken teeth protruding from random steering wheels were common sights). Out here in the desert, generally accepted etiquette appeared to involve the officer exiting his vehicle, leaning on the hood, index finger up waving slowly side to side, and eyeballing all 1,000 drivers as they filed by at 5 mph. Brilliant!

Towards the middle of the afternoon, Johnny chanced upon a town in the middle of nowhere (Northern Nevada) called Winnemucca (for some reason he repeatedly referred to it as Winnebago, much to the consternation of the local inhabitants). Most of Winnebago's 7,000 residents are employed directly by mining companies or casinos. Much to Johnny's surprise, Winnebago is famous for its many legal brothels (more on this later).

One of the great features of a Garmin GPS is that you can press a button called "golf" and it will display all the golf courses within a fifty-mile radius. Johnny got hip to this right away, and it became a daily routine to hit the golf button around three, pick a course with a nice name and follow Mr. Garmin there. On this particular afternoon, he ended up at a course which, unbeknownst to him, was in the middle of a heated local tournament. The pro shop just gave him a key to a golf cart and sent him out to the first tee which also turned out to be the tenth tee since the course suprisingly had only nine holes.

Johnny felt like a poodle on the freeway as a procession of serious foursomes spun around from the ninth green to the first/tenth tee. He asked several groups if they would mind him tagging along but the typical response was "Jeezus H. Christ we're in the middle of a tournament here." This pretty much set the tone for the ensuing round. During a brief lull, Johnny teed off, then waited for the green ahead to clear as the foursome behind bombed him with tee shots. The third green down was adjacent to the fourth tee coming back. Realizing that it was going to be a slow round, Johnny decided to play two balls off the fourth tee. After hitting the second ball, a player on the adjacent third green said "Hey, idiot, if you're going to practice, take it to the range." This did not sit well with Johnny who began to ponder his options ranging between forgiveness and fisticuffs. Arriving at the fourth green he noticed a twosome preparing to tee off on the third and asked if they would mind him joining up. Thankfully, they agreed.

His two new golf partners, Jake and Elwood (really) completely changed Johnny's view of Winnebago's inhabitants. Elwood managed a casino; Jake managed a gold mine. Neither had ever been outside of Nevada, and both were way cool. As they proceeded back down the third fairway Johnny related what had happened.

Coincidentally, the gentleman who had yelled at him was coming up the fourth fairway and was now only thirty yards away. In a moment of clarity, Johnny asked his new friends "Where's the nearest hospital?" to which they responded, "Right over there – why?" to which Johnny replied, "That guy may need it." as he wheeled around and headed for Mr. Asshole. As he pulled to a stop, he took off his hat and removed his sunglasses, then proceeded to within an inch of Mr. Asshole's nose and said, "Are you from around here? Because if you are, I want to know if this is the way you treat visitors to your town. I do not feel the Aloha Spirit here. I am from Hawaii, and if anyone there where to say what you said to me, they would be picking their fucking teeth up off the grass." Mr. Asshole began to ponder HIS options, ranging between apology and a dental appointment. He wisely picked apology, and in the end, they shook hands. Johnny noticed, however, that his palms were rather sweaty. His three playing partners seemed somehow amused. He found out later that they were Mr. Asshole's bodyguards.

They finished the round and headed toward the clubhouse. As they approached, the tournament participants spilled out onto the lawn toward Johnny. It looked pretty sketchy, and Johnny concluded his best chance was to jump the fence and lock himself in the rental car. But they caught up to him and started shaking his hand, patting his back, and laughing loudly (man, what a relief). It turned out that Mr. Asshole was the mayor of Winnebago whom everybody hated because he was such a bombastic blowhard idiot, and Johnny was something of a hero for staring him down on the fourth fairway. Drinks were proffered, and later his golf buddies invited him to dinner.

Chapter 37

"Dining" and "Dancing"

Johnny and his Winnebago golf buddies ended up in a Basque restaurant. There are many Basque restaurants in Winnebago owing to the fact that many Basque sheep herders were imported there before the turn of the century to "mind the sheep" of which there were several million. They were later displaced by cattle ranchers and moved into town to open restaurants. Their favorite joke is "What were you doing with that sheep?" "Honest, I was just helping her over the fence."

They have a drink there called Patxaran (pronounced pacharan). If you go there, DO NOT ORDER A PATXARAN! By way of introduction, this vile liquid was invented in the Middle Ages by a Basque tribe on the slopes of the Spanish Pyrenees. It is made by soaking fruit, coffee beans and a cinnamon pod in anisette for half a year (something similar goes on in prison toilets). This process results in an electric-red liquid around 30% in alcohol content by volume. If you soak it longer, the alcohol content can go through the roof. Although for most of history it has been a home brew, they started selling it commercially in 1956 and today seven million liters of the stuff is produced annually. In Winnebago, they make their own and they soak it for a long time.

Patxaran is the beverage that is consumed by young Spanish men in Pamplona just before they release the bulls. It produces a feeling similar to that which one might experience if you got your penis and/or vagina stuck in an electric socket. The help in this particular restaurant wore tee shirts with bold lettering "ASK ME FOR A PATXARAN".

Johnny called the waitress over and asked, "What's the house record?" She said, "Fifteen but he died." Johnny ordered a beer.

Basque food is, ah, different. The three big things on the menu are sweetbreads, tongue, and tripe. Johnny, having grown up in a California fish/steak/burger culture had not encountered these foods and had no idea what they were.

His hosts patiently explained that sweetbreads are cow's brains (really), tongue is actually a cow's tongue (really) and tripe, real tripe, is the four chambers of a cow's stomach - the rumen (blanket, flat or smooth type), reticulum (honeycomb or pocket type), omasum (book, bible or leaf type), and for real connoisseurs, the abomasum (reed type) which is rarely consumed outside Winnebago owing to is glandular tissue content.

For some reason Johnny's appetite was practically non-existent, although he did force down a small fork full of each delicacy which was way more than he needed or wanted. But the conversation was pleasant and interesting.

Jake and Elwood had gone to high school together. Jake married Elwood's sister and they had twins (Jake and Elwood - really). Elwood married Jake's sister and they had a son (Jakewood). It is impossible to make something like this up.

Elwood had run a small casino for the past thirty years and talked about all the various scams professional gamblers and swindlers had attempted. Jake talked about his thirty years looking for gold.

Johnny was particularly intrigued about the gold. After a couple beers and a couple Patxarans, Jake extended two invitations – "You can visit my mine tomorrow but tonight you're gonna go "dancing" with us at the Pussy Cat Ranch." Oh boy.

The Pussy Cat Ranch is perhaps the most famous of the brothels in Winnebago owing to the dozens of enormous and exotic roadside billboards strung out across several hundred miles of Northern Nevada. It is a non-descript one-story building with a really big parking lot (those eighteen wheelers take up a lot of room). Once you've parked, there's no place to hide. As you step out of the car several young ladies immediately greet you in various stages of undress waving and yelling "Yooo Hoooo."

As they got closer, the girls instantly recognized Jake and Elwood. At that point Johnny knew he was gonna get in some trouble tonight.

There's a small bar in there and the first thing you do is order a Patxaran. Ms. Bazooms (the "den mother") takes you into a separate room and lays it out for you. One girl for 30 minutes is $200. Two is $400. If you want a midget in there too its $700.

Johnny opted for the Platinum Experience. This was followed by a rather embarrassing few minutes as Ms. Bazooms thoroughly inspected Big Joe for any signs of unusual wear and tear. Then you have another Patxaran and are lead down a long corridor into what looks like a hospital ward but is referred to as a "bedroom."

Modesty prohibits further graphic description of the experience. Suffice it to say, the one thing that stood out and is remembered vividly even today was the midget saying, "You're so big!"

Chapter 38

Jake's Gold Mine

The next morning was very difficult. Why mince words – it was brutal. Johnny was reminded of that dawn in his college dorm room following an all-nighter during which he and his roommate had consumed nearly a gallon of wine (each). His roomy was heard to inquire, "Where is that dog?" "What dog?" "The dog that crapped in my mouth?"

The Platinum Experience augmented by Patxaran and Winnebago style tripe had taken a near lethal toll. Johnny frightened the innkeeper when he stumbled into the office to return the keys and was reminded of Richard Pryor's famous line "When you're on fire, people get out of your way."

He sat behind the steering wheel for several minutes trying futilely to collect himself. It was no use – he was gonna reap the rewards of extremely irresponsible behavior and there was nothing he could do about it. He figured his best bet was to find a supermarket where he could buy medicine but had to settle for a cup of coffee and a croissant.

It did not help any that the sun came up in the East exactly in the direction he was heading. Fortunately, his sunglasses and the film on the windshield from the guts of a thousand dead insects (you know how you tell a happy Hell's Angel? – count the bugs in his teeth) reduced the glare to a manageable level. It was the splitting headache, the upset stomach, and the broken blood vessels in his eyes that were of more concern.

He had the directions to the mine on the back of a Pussy Cat Ranch bar napkin. He seriously doubted that Jake would even be there given that he had consumed much larger portions of everything Johnny had the night before– plus it was a holiday. Although Johnny desperately wanted to check into a hospital, he gamely pushed on, pulling to a halt at the bottom of a freeway off ramp in a patch of barren desert near a town called Battle Mountain.

Battle Mountain is perhaps best known as having been designated "the armpit of America" in a 2001 Washington Post article. The good citizens of that community attempted to capitalize on the notoriety by staging an "Old Spice Armpit Festival" but due to lack of enthusiasm and only one float, it was cancelled.

Battle Mountain has one thing going for it – this is where gold comes from. If Nevada were a country, it would be the world's third largest gold producing nation. Most of that gold comes from the empty windy hills overlooking the Battle Mountain off ramp.

Johnny's concept of a gold mine was a hole in the side of a mountain into which you could walk with a pick and a shovel and get some gold. When he pulled up to Jake's mine, he realized he was completely and utterly mistaken. It turned out it was not Jake's mine in the possessory sense, it was a mine owned by a large gold mining conglomerate for which Jake worked as the Manager. Jake was miraculously there, and for the next three hours drove Johnny over man made mountains and down into man made canyons explaining how gold is mined.

Modern gold mining is practiced on a gargantuan scale. A mining company first stakes a claim to many square miles of rough terrain. Geologists are sent in to take core samples. These are analyzed to determine where and at what depth gold appears. Then the earth is moved to get at the gold by a fleet of the largest bulldozers and transporters known to man.

Jake's mine has a dozen Komatsu D-575-A bulldozers. Each one of these weighs in at 288,000 pounds and has a ninety cubic yard blade capable of moving 480,000 pounds of mass in a single pass. It is estimated that one of these machines could push all of downtown

Honolulu into the sea in a couple days.

To move all this rock and mud from one place to another, Jake's mine has a fleet of sixty Liebherr T 282 B mining trucks. Each one of these weights 448,000 pounds, has a 3,650-horsepower diesel engine and is capable of moving 800,000 pounds of earth in a single load. When you stand next to one of these, you know how a mouse feels standing next to a bus.

If core samples indicate that gold appears in a certain location at a certain depth (say 100 feet), an open pit many acres in size is dug to that depth. All of the "waste material" is transported somewhere else where a mound (in this case 100 feet high) is created. They simultaneously dig many other pits and transfer that waste material to the same mound, which over time becomes a mountain.

In the meantime, they locate a large valley (or create one) with a "V" shaped bottom, which is covered with a heavy rubber tarp. It looks like Napa Valley in a raincoat. On top of the tarp at the bottom of the "V" they lay a huge pipe full of holes, which follows the slope of the new valley down to what will become a lake.

Then they send the dozers and transporters back into the pit where the gold is. If the gold containing earth is 100 feet thick, they remove those 100 feet and haul it to the upper end of the valley where they dump it in a big pile. The contents of many other gold pits are also dumped on the same pile, which ultimately becomes a gold mountain. When they get to the top, they finish it off with a concave surface resembling a huge shallow swimming pool. Then they run hundreds of large capacity waterlines up the side of the mountain and into the "swimming pool."

Then, and here's the trick, they mix cyanide with water and pump it up the hillside into the pool at thousands of gallons per minute. This witch's brew leaches down through the mound, attaching to the gold particles, which end up sliding down the tarp into the pipe and down to the newly formed lake.

This lake is full of gold. There are massive vertical filters through which the water, cyanide, and gold are forced and separated. At the end of the process, there's gold over here, cyanide over there, and a monstrous lake of reusable water (Jake said you could drink it but that's what he said about Patxaran so Johnny wasn't takin' any chances).

In this way a mine can produce between a few thousand to 300,000 ounces of gold per year. At today's spot price of $1,800 per ounce a gold mine can generate a couple million to half a billion dollars a year – not bad, but remember, those trucks and tractors ain't cheap.

Although Johnny inquired, gold mines do not give free samples.

Chapter 39

Cannon Ball to Columbus

Back on I-80 for a cannon ball run to Columbus, Nebraska and Tyler's wedding.

As Johnny passed through Nevada into Utah at 110mph, he blazed past the Bonneville Salt Flats where essentially all of the world's land speed records for the last seventy-five years have been set.

The salt here is six feet deep and flat as a pancake. There is no vegetation, and the rain erases any little scuffmarks leaving a 150 square mile virgin drag strip. In 1935 Malcolm Campbell made this place famous when he became the first person to travel faster than 300mph. Today, poorly tuned dragsters routinely exceed 300mph (in a quarter mile) – today's Bonneville cars routinely exceed 600mph.

One fellow, who was somehow able to get his hands on a solid fuel rocket booster and modify his car to receive it, *substantially* exceeded 600mph. His feat, however, was not officially recognized by the sanctioning body for two reasons: (1) he left the surface of the ground before finishing the run and (2) he crashed into an adjacent mountain range and failed to survive. Speed has consequences.

A little past Salt Lake City (a great place to get away with having more than one wife if you are insane enough to go in for that sort of thing), Johnny entered Wyoming and traveled 500 miles through high grassland along what was known in the mid-1800's as the Overland Trail. During that time it was the only route explicitly approved by the US Government to get from the East to the West because everywhere else Indians, who were understandably upset with the influx of foreigners, slaughtered anything that moved.

Looking out the window at 110mph Johnny thought about the tens of thousands of people on foot and in covered wagons who had passed through this area 150 years before (at approximately two miles per hour).

Every once in a while, he'd look up at the sky and see the contrails of passenger jets passing overhead at 500mph. The really high ones were military jets travelling at Mach 3 or more. The speed of sound (Mach 1) is 1,100 feet per second, so Mach 3 is 3,300 feet per second or 2,250mph. Although this is pretty fast, these planes are slow travellers compared to the X-43.

The X-43 is an unmanned vehicle designed to test an experimental engine called a scramjet (supersonic combustion ramjet) at hypersonic speeds. Carried aloft by a modified B-52 bomber, the twelve-foot-long wedge-shaped craft is propelled to an altitude of 110,000 feet by a Pegasus space booster where the engine is fired and the X-43 cruises at 6,600mph (almost ten times the speed of sound).

The X-43 was recently overtaken by the Falcon Hypersonic Technology Vehicle 2 (HTV-2). It is now billed as the fastest aircraft ever built. It is part of an advanced weapons program called Conventional Prompt Global Strike, which is working to develop systems to reach a target anywhere in the world in less than an hour. It cruises at 13,000mph (nearly twenty times the speed of sound). At these speeds, an early pioneer could have traveled 2,451 miles from New York City to Los Angeles in less than twelve minutes. You would definitely need to hold on to your hat.

Johnny knew he was getting deep into the heart land of America when he crossed the border into Nebraska. It was hard to believe that the western part of this state was once owned by Mexico and, if it weren't for his ornery forbearers, he'd be reading road signs in Spanish.

The early American settlers apparently believed they had both a right and a duty to expand the country's borders with impunity. This belief (referred to as "Manifest Destiny") would eventually inconvenience a lot of Mexicans (and quite a few Indians as well) who already lived there. Mexico was persuaded to cede this part of Nebraska along with the balance of the western half of the continent to the US in 1848 as the result of an unfortunate (for Mexico) incident called the Mexican-American War. Adios Amigos.

The eastern part of Nebraska was earlier acquired fair and square as part of the $15 million Louisiana Purchase in 1803 (did the French get screwed on that deal or WHAT?).

Notwithstanding the visitor brochures, there are no mountains in Nebraska. There really aren't any what you might call hills either. That sucker is FLAT. The one thing they have going for them, geologically speaking, is a 150-foot-tall boulder called Chimney Rock just outside of North Platte. When the early pioneers heading west made it to this rock, they are reported to have exclaimed, "The hard part is over." They didn't know that (a) they were only halfway, and (b) the hard part was just beginning.

Nebraska is geologically challenged. There are no ski resorts, mountain climbing clubs, or zip lines. It does, however, hold the distinction of having been bombed on June 22, 2003 by the largest hailstone ever recovered in the United States (seven inches in diameter with a nineteen inch circumference – about the size and weight of a bowling ball). These days, very few people walk around Nebraska in a hailstorm.

The corn just happened. Nebraska, known as the "Cornhusker State," is the third largest producer in the US. It used to be that people, chickens and cattle ate all the corn. Now, courtesy of the wonders of modern science, there are more than 3,500 different uses for corn including aspirin, shaving cream, paint, and diapers. The new one, the really big one, and the one that has really screwed things up, is ethanol.

Forty-three percent of Nebraska's corn is diverted away from the dinner table and into the gas tank. While this may have initially seemed like a good idea ('green' as well as a way to stick it to the Arabs under whose sand most of "our" oil currently resides), this diversion has caused the price of food to skyrocket since just about everything we eat contains corn.

The other thing is it makes no sense economically. Scientists generally refer to the making of ethanol as "unsustainable, subsidized food burning." About seventy percent more energy is required to produce ethanol than the energy that actually is in

ethanol. This helps explain why fossil fuels --
not ethanol -- are used to produce ethanol.

And on top of all this bad news, the US
government currently provides
approximately $1 billion a year in federal and
state subsidies primarily to large corporations
who produce ethanol (your taxes). Is this
crazy or WHAT?

This is what was going through Johnny's head
as he drove mile after monotonous mile across
the practically infinite flat cornfield plains of
Nebraska. Fortunately, he was able to snap
out of it when he came upon a 7-11 that sold
beer (and from which he was not banned for
life like the one in Pahoa).

The trains happened in 1865 when The Union
Pacific began its transcontinental railroad at
Omaha. Nebraska is now loaded with train
tracks going off in every direction (no tunnels
or bridges required, just lay them tracks and
roll them trains). There is a railroad yard
there (the longest in the US) that handles
10,000 cars *a day*.

Johnny realized he was in train country when
he pulled up on a caboose and drove fifty miles
before catching up to the engine. He was so
impressed with the size of this train (which
contained a hundred plus hopper cars loaded
with coal) that he raced ahead a few more

miles, screeched to a halt, and ran with his camera over to the tracks in time to take a picture of the conductor frantically waiving and blowing his horn.

Just for the hell of it, he snapped another picture every fifteen seconds. Forty frames later the caboose whizzed by. He turned for one final shot in time to pick up another train coming the other way on the opposite track, which was good for another thirty-five frames. Fortunately, digital had supplanted film or this would have been a very expensive photo shoot.

When he pulled into Lincoln he realized (a) he'd taken a wrong turn and (b) he was driving down a very long main street. It turns out that O Street is fifty-nine miles long making it the longest Main Street in the US.

Back tracking through the corn, he finally reached his destination – Columbus. The "main event" (wedding) was right around the corner.

Chapter 40

Tyler's Wedding

Johnny made it to Columbus. As he disembarked, unshaven and disheveled after 3,000 miles of sight seeing, several empty beer cans hit the pavement. He looked around and realized he was in another place and time. He figured Neil Armstrong experienced a similar sensation stepping out onto the moon.

Everyone within a quarter mile stopped and stared at the guy in the Aloha shirt and flip-flops who had just "landed." The circus had come to town.

When he shuffled up to the front desk there was a definite undercurrent of "Jeezus Christ, how can we get out of having to give this guy a room?" When he introduced himself as an attorney on his way to the Supreme Court and signed in as "Esquire," all was forgiven, and a key was promptly proffered.

It was a pretty big room as hotel rooms go. This was not some cheesy chain motel where you sleep with one leg in the bathroom and the other on the windowsill. This thing was HUGE. In California they have Cal-Kings. In Nebraska they have Corn Kings, which are at least 25% larger. Johnny got winded just walking from the door to the window. The view was spectacular if you like corn. The AC worked and the refrigerator was full of booze, so he had something to do until the rest of the wedding entourage arrived. Since he had maintained an average speed of 105mph over the past week, he was early.

They showed up the next morning – sisters and brothers, aunts and uncles, cousins and total strangers – about a hundred of 'em. There was to be a "rehearsal" and a "wedding." They climbed into several dozen cars and caravanned through the cornfields to a hundred-year-old church in its final stages of decay where they met the bride (Amy) and the groom (Tyler).

Tyler had met Amy at Big Bear Lake where he was hiding out from the police while attempting to dry out from a little problem with alcohol (he was good for a handle a day).

For the uninitiated, a "handle" is street parlance for those large 1.75-liter glass jugs of whisky with a built-in glass handle they sell at Costco. He was a brilliant guy and blazed a trail through Berkley with dual majors (mathematics and aerospace engineering) while simultaneously captaining the Berkley racquetball team. However, he discovered alcohol near the end of his junior year and failed to appear for nearly all of his senior classes. On the strength of his academic record, Berkley gave him a diploma anyway. He was also hired sight unseen by a large aerospace firm, but he did not show up there either.

Left for dead in his rented apartment, he was later found, resuscitated, and brought back home by his parents (Johnny's sister Jackie and her husband Jim from whom Tyler may have acquired the gene that tweaked him) where he was slowly nurtured back to life.

There were hiccups along the way. Every once in a while, the folks liquor cabinet would be discovered strangely empty, and Tyler would reel around mumbling about "a bad reaction" from his medication.

So, the liquor cabinet was locked and the word went out to all the liquor stores in the area. With no booze available to buy or purloin, Tyler turned to Red Bull. On random evenings, he would down a case and run screaming naked through the avocado groves, scaring the shit out of the wolves and the illegal Mexican laborers who camped there. The police began to look for him.

As a last resort, Tyler's Uncle Tom gallantly offered to take him up to his isolated cabin in Big Bear (similar to the Unibomber's place, but nicer). There is nothing, absolutely nothing, to do there in the winter except stare out the window at the snow. And this is where, miraculously, Tyler pulled out of his nosedive and met Amy.

Amy came from a religious Nebraska background and aspired to be a minister. She was coincidentally in Big Bear at minister school when she met Tyler. Her religious views appeared to be mainstream, so Tyler didn't have to worry about her jumping around and speaking in tongues.

Apparently, religion and a puritanical upbringing prevented the pigskin bus from pulling into tuna town prior to the wedding, much to Tyler's dismay. So, there was, understandably, a host of suppressed emotions bubbling mightily just beneath the surface as they met there in the hundred-year-old church for the rehearsal.

Tyler was shaking like a leaf in a hurricane while Amy was some how able to suppress the cosmic vibrations and remain reasonably poised, although the whole place felt it.

Johnny suavely introduced himself to the bride by saying, "Hi, I'm Tyler's Uncle, where's the bride?" Fortunately, Amy had a great sense of humor and gaily replied that she was it. They rode the rehearsal out well, and when it was over the wedding train headed back to Columbus for a non-alcoholic dinner party (not that there weren't any alcoholics there, just no booze).

Johnny, Jackie, Jim and a few of their West Coast friends with superb foresight expertly anticipated this and accordingly loaded up at the the pub next door prior to making their entrance which was somewhat less dignified than the locals were used to. Johnny, having built up a significant tolerance, breezed through dinner while occasionally and nonchalantly lifting his sister's head out of her salad plate, explaining that's how they eat vegetables in California.

The wedding was everything a wedding should be. There were a hundred people all packed into a little white church in the middle of an endless sea of corn (Amy's grandmother and mother had been married here – there used to be a surrounding town but the whole thing burned down except for the church which was badly singed but remained standing).

A 100' extension cord was plugged into the only functioning electric outlet, somebody with skills fired up the organ, and the wedding was on.

The bride and groom were resplendent in their wedding attire. Johnny tried his best to fit in, having dragged a suitcase full of marginally appropriate clothing halfway across the Pacific Ocean and then halfway across the United States.

There were, however, some problems. For one thing, he had gained thirty pounds on the trip and now resembled the Pillsbury doughboy. For another, he was too cheap to buy a new rig, so his suitcase was full of "outdated attire." He gamely slipped on a blue blazer he had won twenty years earlier in a golf tournament. He attempted to compliment this with a blue-checkered long sleeve dress shirt he found on sale at Banana Republic about the same time as the tournament. Then came the white linen slacks, which were now several sizes too small and had to remain partially unzipped to accommodate his newfound girth. A woven pair of zapatas he had picked up in Tijuana in 1963 on a college bender pathetically substituted for a pair of shiny wing tips. The piece de resistance (since he did not own a tie – nobody wears ties in Hawaii) was a white cravat that resembled a dish rag. As they might say around the still at midnight in Alabama, "He looked as sharp as a mosquiter's wiener."

The overall impact of this ensemble, which he later understood upon reviewing the wedding photographs, was that of a fat boat captain with peculiar shoes. As it turned out, Johnny, in comparison to just about every other male in the room, looked like a mannequin in the window of Bob's Bridal Shop. The unspoken Nebraska dress code applicable to this particular ceremony apparently did not prohibit bib overalls, which are quite popular in this neck of the woods.

Vows were spoken, rice was thrown, and it was over.

At the celebration dinner, Johnny, who was very inebriated, was asked to say a few words – "We must save the Earth since it is the only planet in the Universe with wine and chocolate – Amen."

Chapter 41

Chopper

Never, ever, go to a motorcycle store drunk and/or stoned.

Johnny was by now a divorced bachelor living alone so Friday nights were nothing special and there was no one around to restrain him. He was lazing about with the usual assortment of intoxicants close at hand when, for some inexplicable reason, he decided to hop on his Harley and ride down to the local motorcycle shop.

Now, his Harley was a pretty good bike. It was called a Fat Boy. It had been given to him by a friend who had several. It was a gift he did not deserve (but did not decline). To get the full details you'll have to talk to Wolf Man when he gets out of rehab (returning home on one of his bikes from Haliewa Joe's in an advanced state of inebriation, he managed to hit the car he'd been following square in the rear bumper at high speed, catapulting himself over the handle bars and also over the car, whereupon he was brutally run down (surfers on the North Shore generally refer to this as "a twofer"). This maneuver is a testament to the fact that motorcycles are dangerous.

Johnny's bike was a factory custom motorcycle with visual impact. But in the end it was basically a stock Harley with a few do-dads. Easy Rider had come out a while back and Johnny was enamored with Peter Fonda's chopper. He started looking into what it would take to drop it, extend the forks, stretch the frame, hop up the engine, put on a monstrous rear tire, and chrome that mother out. When he tallied everything up it came out to just over a hundred thousand dollars.

So, Johnny mounted his stock Fat Boy and toodled on down to the motorcycle store on Nimitz out by the airport. He walked in and BAM fell instantly in love with a glorious bike sitting in the middle of the show room floor. It was a "one off" made by a company called UMC (Ultimate Motorcycle Company). Basically, a bunch of guys out of Glendale, Arizona (who were rumored to look a lot like ZZ Top) stood around in a shop and built the baddest motorcycle they could imagine.

When they were through, they put it in a box and shipped it out, then started in on another one. No two were exactly the same, and each one was totally bitchin'. Those UMC boys kicked it up a notch when they produced a new heavy weight V-Twin cruiser powered by a very large engine. This new bike was called a Fat Pounder Rigid and was referred to on the street as "one mean mother fucker." It was totally decked out and roared down the road powered by the newly released S&S 113 cubic inch engine (a monster compared to the 88 cubic inch Harleys).

Johnny had walked in on the first Fat Pounder Rigid to reach Hawaii's shores – he had to have it. Unfortunately, the dealer was thinking $20,000 cash and Johnny was thinking trade in. It took an hour or so to finally reach an agreement (the dealer was also hammered so the negotiations were fluid). In the end, Johnny turned over the keys to his Harley, wrote a check for a few grand, and rode out the door on a really amazing bike.

The first thing he came to understand was the true meaning of the word "rigid." A normal motorcycle has a rear suspension system consisting primarily of springs and shock absorbers for a smooth ride. A rigid (hard tail) has no rear suspension. Every bump no matter how small is felt straight up through the tire and frame into your spine. A rigid on a long ride will help you realize that your body has several internal parts that you didn't even know where there. Johnny became simultaneously and intimately acquainted with his liver, spleen, vertebrae, colon, and both kidneys.

The next thing that occurred to him was that a fire breathing 113 cubic inch motorcycle engine has HUGE balls. Twist that throttle back and the front wheel comes off the ground (it is very hard to steer when the front wheel is not in contact with the pavement). Johnny began to picture Evel Knivel rolling down the ramp at Caesar's Palace just before his unfortunate landing. The police took note but could not accelerate fast enough to catch him.

Another thing that came up was the ride height. This baby was slammed several inches lower than a normal motorcycle. While this is all good and fine (and very cool) a problem occurs when negotiating turns at speed. Under these circumstances the motorcycle frame has a tendency to scrape the pavement and lift the rear tire off the ground. This loss of traction can be both unsettling and hazardous to your health. On the plus side, all those sparks look really great at night!

And finally, with a rear tire almost as big as those on an eighteen-wheeler there's a considerable amount of traction which, when paired with a very large engine results in astounding wheelies. You do not normally see somebody on a 700-pound motorcycle pointing the front wheel at the moon, but Johnny managed this unintentional maneuver several times down Kalakaua Avenue, horrifying both himself and quite a few tourists. Other than that, it was one hell of a bike.

Returning home, Johnny decided that instead of leaving his new bike in the garage he would drive it up the brick foot path to his house and enshrine it in the front room (there was nobody home to tell him not to). The bricks had come from the Waialua Sugar Mill which had shut down years before, affording Johnny the opportunity to strip the boilers of all their fire brick (good for sidewalks and pottery kilns). The resulting footpath was nice to look at but a little uneven. Johnny gunned it and made the ascent on the rear tire but failed in his efforts to bring 'er down square. This resulted in a sharp right turn into an adjacent tree. So much for Friday night.

The bike was fine but several bones in his right foot were broken, necessitating crutches for several weeks. Also, his face bounced off the tree trunk and he ended up with quite a shiner. When asked at work what happened, he replied, "I kissed a tree."

Johnny's advice is to buy a car and use your seat belt.

Chapter 42

Golf at Punaluu

Rick had been thrashing Johnny regularly for years at his home course in Kona. There were many reasons for this, some of them to do with skill, flexibility, and course knowledge, others with equipment and cunning, but Johnny was certain that the main reason was because he had to get up at four in the morning (he was not a morning person) and drive several hours over two of the worlds largest mountains to get there, swilling coffee and trying desperately to stay awake.

One of those, Mauna Loa, sores 13,796 feet above sea level and at it's underwater base is over 2,000 miles wide. It is the third largest mountain by volume in our solar system. If it weren't for that one on Mars and the other on one of Jupiter's moons, it would be the biggest bastard circling the sun, which is saying something. The other one, Mauna Kea, is higher (13,803 feet above sea level), but with lesser volume.

So, by the time Johnny got to Kona, he was tired and wired. Fortunately, they can't arrest you for coffee. Drugs of every kind and nature were plentiful in his hometown of Pahoa, and kids by the score with something to sell would accost him as he walked down the main street there. His standard reply was "I'm trying to quit." This really threw cold water on the party, and, after a while, they would let him pass by unmolested since they knew he was, in their view, a loser.

It came as no surprise when Rick called to lure him back to Kona for a game (Johnny was a secondary profit center and Rick was running low). Winding up and hurling a perfect split fingered fastball, Johnny suggested that they meet halfway at a golf course in Punaluu called Sea Mountain (let HIM drive a few hours down the Kona coast with the morning sun in HIS face and nothing on the radio but static).

Sea Mountain in Punaluu (there's an ocean in front and a mountain behind) is the southernmost golf course in the United States by virtue of the fact that it resides on the south flank of the third largest mountain in our solar system, which protrudes below the latitude of the Florida Keys. Rick, not wanting to ruin a sure thing, suggested that Johnny drive to Kona "as usual." Johnny held firm, pointing out that the change of venue would do them both good. Besides, in Kona ya gotta buy $8 beers from the lady in the beer cart – in Punaluu (Johnny lied since he had never been there and really didn't know), you can bring a bottle of whiskey and get shit faced for practically nothing. Rick, seeing the logic in this, accepted the invitation (swinging wildly as Johnny's perfect pitch blazed by).

Rick, by the way, is 6'3" with short arms, so he looks really weird hunched over a golf club, sort of bent at the waist (in prison, they call this posture "picking up the soap"). His height had determined his destiny, since the Coast Guard, in charge of Hawaii's shallow coastal waters, was looking for sailors over six feet tall so in the event the boat sank they could wade to shore without drowning. Rick had spent many years plying the Leeward coast searching for drug smugglers and crashing into porpoises and whales.

On shore leave he met his future wife Claire, the slender good-looking daughter in a large family of large Hawaiians who lived in Nanakuli. Nanakuli is the third most dangerous town in the world, right behind Detroit and Kabul. It is a tightly knit community, and when word spread of the impending wedding of the loveliest daughter of the Humu'humu'nuku'nuku'apuap'a family, the whole town turned out for the party.

Rick, a straight up Caucasian, was completely oblivious to the fact that he was about to perform a maneuver known in the Air Force as "kissing the propeller." Preceded by his lovely bride, he walked into the party in a white button-down long sleeve dress shirt carrying a four pack of lemon spritzers and a bag of Fritos. The music stopped. The wind died. Several dozen blahlas stood in unison, and the knarliest one of 'em all stepped forward with clenched fists and said "Watchu want haole?" Rick, ever the bon vivant, cheerily remarked that he was following a hot lookin' teetah to the bar. The lights went out.

Modern medicine is truly remarkable. A few pints of O negative, a plastic wedge under his left eye socket, and two large titanium screws in his jaw were all that was required to restore Rick pretty much back to normal, although he was neither able to consummate his marriage nor return to sea for several weeks.

Mindful of the likely crowd of tourists that would be swarming over the Punaluu resort course, Rick attempted to reserve a coveted 9 am tee time. To his surprise, his request was granted without complaint or demand for gratuity.

At the appointed hour, Johnny pulled up to the resort entrance from the north and Rick from the south. As they drove down the main road toward the golf course, it was eerily silent. There were no cars, no people, no stray cats, no nothing. When they got to the clubhouse, they found a jar on a card table with a note that said, "Put your money in here and take any cart." They were utterly alone except for the sound of the waves pounding on the lava beach and the occasional coconut falling from above.

The sun was out, the sky was blue, and Johnny, ever mindful of the need to establish an early edge, cracked the seal on a quart of Jack Daniels and offered Rick a sip.

And then, without ceremony or fanfare, one of the greatest unrecorded rounds in the history of golf commenced. At least that's how Johnny would remember it. Rick, on the other hand, would flash back to Nanakuli on every hole. We are not talking here about winning and losing; we are talking about the Titanic meeting the iceburg thirty-six times in one day (incredulous at his misfortune, Rick insisted they play a second round so he could, as they say in Las Vegas, "win my money back").

It was as if Johnny had been touched by the Holy Ghost. The Mormon Tabernacle Choir could be heard in the background as almost every tee shot rose crisply and at high velocity, piercing the wind and soaring through the morning sky, later touching down in the center of the fairway with a forward roll. Not a single tee shot that day stopped less than 300 yards from point of departure. Not one approach shot missed the green, not a single putt failed to fall. The only bad tee shot of the day hit a rock 320 yards out, ricocheted another 100 yards onto the green, and found the cup for an albatross. It was ridiculous. It was unbelievable. It was glorious. Johnny had delivered a bitch slap of monumental proportions.

Rick is still recovering. It has been several months. He left a phone message yesterday. He wants to go bowling.

Chapter 43

Banned for Life

Johnny had surfed through life inside the tube and under the radar with reasonable success and a blissfully low profile. Private, public, and governmental institutions have, for the most part, taken little interest in his trajectory or whereabouts. Except for the IRS, which had audited him three years in a row for what they termed "aggressive assumptions on taxable income." And also, the DEA, which was undoubtedly still looking for him as a result of the hundreds of letters he had written to them over the past fifty years concerning the absurd proposition that marijuana should be considered a Schedule 1 drug. The DEA divides drugs into five "schedules," the worst of which are those "with no currently accepted medical use and a high potential for abuse." Notwithstanding the remarkable medical benefits of CBD and THC, marijuana is lumped in with heroin, LSD, ecstasy, meth, and peyote (Johnny thinks peyote might be mislabeled also, but that's just his own personal opinion).

Christopher Williams is somewhat famous for receiving the harshest penalty for pot in recent history. As a Montana medical marijuana provider, he initially faced eighty-two years behind bars (his sentence was later shortened a bit). Patricia Spottedcrow bought a small sandwich bag of pot for $31 and served twelve years behind bars during which she was only allowed to see her four children twice. Jonathan Magbie, paralyzed from the neck down after being hit by a drunk driver at the age of four, was charged with possession of marijuana in 2004 when police found a joint in a vehicle in which he was a passenger. He was given a ten-day sentence in a DC jail but died there four days later because the jail had no ventilator to sustain his breathing. There are literally hundreds of stories nearly as ridiculous as these. Fortunately, Johnny's story is not among them.

However, the next rung down from jail for a specific period for a ridiculous offense is being banned for life for no offense at all. Notwithstanding his exemplary lifestyle, Johnny has been banned for life – TWICE.

The first involved the 7-11 in Pahoa on the Big Island of Hawaii. It started out innocently enough. Johnny and his son Matt worked hard all day in the macadamia nut orchard, then decided to drive into Hilo for dinner and a movie. On the way, Johnny had the brilliant idea of stopping at the local 7-11 for a six-pack to tide them over on the long drive in.

Matt, a lovely son, volunteered to pop for the beer and suggested that Johnny wait in the car while he procured the groceries. Unfortunately for us all, Matt's license had been suspended several months earlier when he crashed into one of those large stop light rigs that hang out over really busy intersections. At the time he was marginally inebriated with a blood alcohol level somewhere north of .08 x 3 and his driver's license was accordingly confiscated. However, he did have a valid passport left over from a surf trip several years earlier, and with a flourish and a twelve pack of Bud, he presented his credentials to the 7-11 clerk who was most likely not the sharpest tool in the shed. Having never seen a passport, she advised that driver's licenses where the only acceptable form of identification and age verification. Matt attempted to explain the subtleties of government issued documents, but she was offended and told him to put the beer down and get out. Words were spoken and, in the heat of the moment, Matt was thrown out of 7-11 by the security guard.

So poor ol' Matt dragged himself back to the car and advised that he'd been turned down for lack of proper identification. Johnny said, "Don't worry son, I'll take care of it," whereupon he entered the store, retrieved the Budweiser, and proceeded to the front desk.

The clerk, clearly upset and marginally incoherent, said "You wid dat haole out der?" pointing to the parking lot. Johnny replied proudly, "Why yes, that's my son," to which she replied "Get otta here you bastard, you is band for life too." Twenty years have passed and Johnny has still not returned to the Pahoa 7-11, even during dire beer emergencies.

They say history repeats itself. Unfortunately, history recently got the best of Johnny and his status snowballed in the banned for life club.

It started innocently enough (again). Wanting to show their friends who were visiting from the Big Island a good time, Johnny and his lovely wife Terry took them to a resort area called Ko Olina, which has four public beaches and several nice restaurants. Each beach has a hotel, which is basically a front for a time-share scam (if you are reading this and think it would be a good idea to invest in a time-share, DON'T DO IT). The developers of the Ko Olina decided early on that they wanted to keep the local riff raff out, so they slowly reduced the number of available parking stalls to the point where the only viable alternative for visiting the beach after 7 am (when the tiny little parking lots were full and long lines formed down the street waiting for the next available stall) is to valet your car at one of the hotels.

So, since Johnny and Terry liked the Longboard Restaurant, which was part of the last hotel, they pulled in there (to avoid downstream litigation for slander etc., Johnny will not reveal the name of this hotel – suffice it to say it rhymes with "Chariot").

The Marriott (oops, Chariot) hotel has a policy that allows you to park free for three hours (in lieu of the normal $35 charge) provided you return with a receipt from the Longboard Restaurant attesting to the fact that you spent at least $40 there. Since dinner and drinks for four would run several hundred dollars, Johnny felt confident in their decision. They had a good time and returned to the valet desk three hours and ten minutes later. While Terry took care of the details, Johnny summoned the car and tipped the valet $10.

This is where it got sticky. The desk clerk advised that because Johnny's party was ten minutes over the three-hour limit, they would have to pay the full $35 fee. Terry suggested that seemed unfair, to which the clerk responded, "Well, I see you are wearing a bathing suit – did you go to the beach?" Terry allowed as how they had, and the clerk said, "Well then, we'll just charge you a $20 'beach fee.'" Terry forked over a twenty and hopped in the car.

Upon hearing what had happened, Johnny felt compelled to further explore the issue. He walked back to the desk and attempted to reason with the clerk – it went something like this:

Johnny, "We stuck to our agreement for three hours of free parking in return for dinner at your restaurant – here's the receipt for $200. Shouldn't we just be required to pay for the extra ten minutes?"

Clerk, "Uh, no – you must pay the full amount."

Johnny, "Does that sound reasonable to you?"

Clerk, "Uh, it's our policy."

Johnny, "Didn't you abandon your policy in exchange for the payment of a 'beach fee'?"

Clerk, "Yes, we cut you some slack."

Johnny, "But aren't the beaches public?"

Clerk, "Uh, yes."

Johnny, "Well how can you charge a fee to use the beach if it is public?"

Clerk, "Uh, it's our policy."

Johnny, "Well, how about this - I'll file a class action lawsuit on Monday naming Marriott (oops, Chariot) and you as defendants and we'll get a definitive answer as to the appropriateness of your policies and procedures?"

The Clerk paused for a moment, said "You've got a point," and gave back the $20.

Upon returning to the car, the valet began swearing profusely at Johnny "for what he did at the front desk" and advised that he was "a god damn haole" and was "banned for life" from the Marriott (yikes, Chariot) and would be required to wait until the police arrived. This guy was barely five feet tall with crooked teeth, a buzz cut, and obvious mental issues. Fortunately for him, Johnny was attempting mightily to pursue the basic tenants of anger management so with an exemplary display of patience he let it slide (just barely).

The valet then stood in front of the car to block a hasty exit (oh boy, this guy was living dangerously). Johnny, having driven himself out of many tight situations, backed up and started to turn. The valet ran around to the driver's side door and proceeded to tippy toe backwards screaming as Johnny completed the turn. On the way out a hotel security guy on a moped screamed "halt!" Johnny slowed down just long enough to roll down his window and say "Riiiiiiight."

It was a rather unsettling experience, so Johnny wrote a letter. It was addressed to the

State of Hawaii Department of the Attorney General, the City and County of Honolulu Department of Planning and Permitting, the CEO of Marriott (uh, Chariot) International, the Resort Manager of Marriott (oh dear, Chariot) Ko Olina Beach Club, the President of the Ko Olina Resort Association, a reporter for Hawaii News Now TV, and the president of the Free Access Coalition.

There was quite an uproar. Johnny declined repeated invitations to appear on TV to "discuss this travesty of justice." The president of Marriott (for Pete's sake, Chariot) responded with a glowing letter of love and apology and his personal cell phone number if Johnny ever encountered any future difficulties involving his hotel. The State of Hawaii and the City and County of Honolulu confirmed that the beach is, in fact, public but disclaimed authority to become involved in Marriott's (oh, for Christ sake, Chariot's) policies. The Free Access Coalition said, "You da Man!" It's been several years now - the dust has still not settled.

Word got around and a band at Duke's Bar and Grill in Waikiki began frequently singing a song whenever Johnny showed up that goes something like "He never returned, no he never returned, and his fate is still unlearned...."

Chapter 44

Lanipo Trail

Johnny lives on top of a mountain overlooking Diamond Head called Wilhelmina Rise. It was originally covered in sandalwood, then with pineapple, and finally with hundreds of houses developed in the 1930's by Matson Navigation, a shipping and transportation giant that also built Waikiki's iconic pink Royal Hawaiian Hotel. Several streets in the neighborhood were named after Matson ships including Lurline, Matsonia, Monterey, and Mariposa – the mountain itself was named after a Matson ship built in 1920 called Wilhelmina.

Johnny had lucked out and got his hands on an acre of mountain top land and built a house. The way surfers build houses is to go to a demolition site, load up on used wood, locate an abandoned toilet and a bag of nails, and go for it (plans and permits not required). The original all in cost was a little less than $2,500, which pretty much cleaned Johnny out. He thought it would be good for about five years. Fifty years later it still stands. It is occupied by a good buddy, Jack Shipley, who was the first surf judge on the North Shore in the early 60's, cofounder of Lightning Bolt Surfboards in the early 1970's, and head judge at over ninety Pipeline events. He never complains about the leaks.

There is a trail next to Johnny's house - it leads from the top of Wilhelmina Rise to the much higher top of the Koolau Mountain Range (when you get up there, you're looking straight down on Kailua – you do not want to fall off of there). It was incorrectly named the Lanipo Trail by old timers who were so lost and winded by the time they got to the top they guessed they were sitting on the Lanipo Summit, which actually was several summits to the right. The newcomers refer to it as the Mau'umae Trail because it goes up the Mau'umae Ridge. The hiking cognoscenti refer to it as Mau'umae Ridge Trail to Kainawa'aunui Summit (the correct one).

Since it's what he's used to and easier to pronounce, Johnny calls it the Lanipo Trail. It is one of approximately 250 trails scattered all over Oahu. These trails are graded to reflect their degree of difficulty. Green is easy, Yellow is moderately difficult, Red is difficult, and Black is beyondo. There are four black trails on the island – the one running next to Johnny's is close to the top of the black list.

It is peculiar in the sense that ownership is unclear. While most of the other trails are owned and maintained by the State

Department of Land and Natural Resources, Lanipo is a red-haired stepchild since no one claims ownership or responsibility (although it runs through the Board of Water Supply's reservoir lot, the BWS staff is curiously uninformed and totally in denial). Fortunately, the Hawaiian Trail and Mountain Club (HTMC) periodically clears and maintains the trail – if it weren't for them, it would be just about impossible to use it. Also, every time a tree falls on Johnny's driveway, house, or car, he gets out a ladder and a chain saw and takes care of the disaster zone as a kind of public service. The next time one goes over, he's hiring some Samoans. He gets along very well with the Samoan community, particularly when he mentions the name bestowed upon him by Samoan royalty on one of his surf trips – "Fella Felloffa Sofa."

The Lanipo Trail was most likely created by the earliest Hawaiians to walk the land. Dead Chiefs were buried secretly so no one could disturb their bones. It is thought that the Lanipo trail was originally used to access some of these secret sites.

The trail had one other thing going for it – it led to the mountains immediately behind Honolulu, which were covered with iliahi – Hawaiian for sandalwood. In the late 1790's, somebody took some Sandalwood to China and somebody in China made incense out of it. The

Chinese went crazy. Except for the War of 1812 when the British blockaded Hawaii for two years, there was an intense sandalwood trade. This trade was so important to the Chinese that they called Hawaii "Tahn Heung Sahn," or Sandalwood Mountains."

The wood was sold by weight using a measure called a picul (133 1/3 pounds or about what a strong man could carry on his back down the Lanipo Trail to the Honolulu Harbor). Traders made a profit of three to four dollars on each picul, which, in those days, was good money, and King Kamehameha shared handsomely in the proceeds. The Native laborers "got nothing and liked it." At the King's "request," his workers pillaged the forests to the point where sandalwood stands were hard to find so they set fires to detect the trees by their sweet scent. While mature trees could withstand the fire, the flames wiped out new seedlings. By 1830 all the sandalwood was gone. Between 1800 and 1830 the Lanipo trail was the original "highway to hell."

Now the Lanipo trail has a different reputation. The guidebooks kind of mince around a little, but it's easy to translate their flatulent prose to mean "one tough mother." One common hiker observation is "I underestimated the ruggedness of the trail and overestimated my ability to traverse it."

Another is "This god-damn thing is one of the most hellish trails on the island."

There are several valid reasons for this very bad reputation. Although it is merely an eight-mile round trip (for those who actually make it back), the ridge goes steeply up and down many times, so just when you think you've made it to the summit, you realize you're going back down another cliff. Since the sandalwood trees are all gone there is no shade and the intense heat creates the illusion that you're hiking in an oven on high with sun lamps.

The trail in parts is very narrow (about a foot and a half wide if you're lucky) and falls away sharply on both sides. One hiker put it this way, "If you fall, you're fucked." The trail is overgrown with razor sharp ferns which will cut your legs to ribbons if you're foolish enough to go up there wearing shorts, and if you wear long pants it will shred your Levis. Then there's the mud, which is extremely slippery (you really do not want to fall on this trail). All of this combines to make a hike on this trail sort of an endurance challenge. If you make it through to the end, you are completely and utterly thrashed, and nobody is waiting to give you a medal.

On a positive note, there's a lot of strawberry guava up there (brought to Oahu from Brazil two centuries ago), which bear tangy red fruit. If you hike up this trail for the sole purpose of getting a bag full of guava, you are clinically insane.

Johnny had an excellent view of the people foolish enough to challenge his trail (when you live next to a monster like this, you get possessive). Mostly he would just watch them go and hope for the best. On many occasions over fifty years of observation, things did not turn out well for many of these people.

Perhaps a few examples. The Ladies Auxiliary decided to take a little hike early one Saturday morning. There were approximately two dozen elderly ladies wearing dresses and leather shoes. He noted that no one carried water. Johnny thought "uh oh" but they were having such a fine time laughing and chatting as they started up the trail that he did not want to interrupt. Throughout the rest of the day, they would return in twos and threes bleeding, wheezing, and swearing at each other. Amazingly they all made it back - Johnny is pretty sure that not a single member of the Ladies Auxiliary got more than a mile.

There were a number of deaths, usually solo hikers. Friends of one carried a bench a quarter mile in and placed it on the edge of the trail overlooking Waialae Nui Valley. It is dedicated to the late Hawaiian Trail and Mountain Club hike leader Steve Becker and includes an admonition not to hike alone.

There have been literally hundreds of recues – slip & falls, heart attacks, fainting spells (surprisingly common among those who forgot to bring water), and broken bones. In the old days the fire trucks would stop in front of Johnny's driveway and a group of firemen would hike up and drag the victim(s) out on stretchers. This was usually a half-day ordeal since a lot of times they would have to repel down into the valleys on either side to retrieve the slippers & fallers and the occasional dead body.

Later, the Fire Department got a helicopter, which they use to locate and save those in need. Since Johnny has a large lawn in front of his place, the helicopter took to landing there every time there was a rescue. This became a popular spectator sport. When the Fire chopper was hovering around the trail, Johnny would call a few friends and break out the booze. Eventually the helicopter would hover over Johnny's house dangling a stretcher on a hundred-foot cable and gently drop the victim down on his lawn. Since this was occurring only a few dozen yards in front of his lanai, it made for quite a spectacular event.

Standard protocol required a standing ovation for the pilot once he'd dropped his load. The pilot, who was by now on a first name basis with Johnny, would usually waive or salute and bomb back outta there leaving fire and ambulance personnel in a swirling dust cloud to deal with the errant hiker. Since the stretcher has a tendency to spin around in flight, the person in it is pretty dizzy by the time he or she lands. Every once in a while, the rescuee would attempt to stand up under their own steam, but they would almost always wobble around, throw up and fall down. The most recent pukee misconstrued the applause and bowed deeply to Johnny and his friends.

So, just a brief word of advice - if you want to go hiking, unless you are with the Green Berets, Special Forces, or the Olympics, you may want to pick some other trail.

Chapter 45

Three Dogs and a Crazy Lady

It all began on May 3, 2018. That was the day lava started coming out of the ground in the otherwise idyllic Leilani Estates residential neighborhood on the Big Island of Hawaii.

Terry and Johnny were watching the morning news in Honolulu when they saw an alert that everyone living in Leilani Estates must immediately evacuate the area.

They called their friends Jay and Sara to make sure they had received the bulletin. They had not, questioned their sanity, and advised that they would "look into it." They called back a few minutes later and asked if it would be ok if they evacuated their house and moved a few miles over to Johnny & Terry's "for a spell." There was no way of knowing that this would turn out bad.

By way of background, Johnny & Terry's orchard house in Pahoa burned to the ground three years prior. The Fire Inspector said he thought it was caused either by the photovoltaic cells on the roof or the monstrous array of submarine batteries in the garage (they're supposed to be the best batteries to store PV energy and you can get 'em cheap since the Waikiki tourist submarines are required to change them annually for safety reasons).

So, Johnny and Terry were on the street so to speak. But their friends Jay and Sara took them in, and they stayed periodically at their home in Leilani for the better part of a year until they were able to wring a few dollars out of their insurance guy and buy a house in Hawaiian Beaches, about a mile away from their macadamia nut orchard and the charred remains of their previous home.

Their fire loss wasn't all bad – in fact, it was a step up. When you're living in the middle of a jungle you are "off the grid" so there is no electricity, no water, no gas, no cable, etc. They had to either make their own or haul all that stuff in there. Water was a particular pain since they had to hitch a trailer to their truck with a 200-gallon tank (since water weighs 8.34 pounds per gallon, a full tank weighs 1,668 pounds not including the trailer and truck) and haul it up out of the jungle (tires spinning) and down the road to the public water facility every few days. There are a lot of interesting people who hang around the free water place – guns and drugs are readily available as are numerous contagious diseases and wide assortment of insects.

Helpful people would periodically mention, "Hey, you should put gutters on your roof and catch water in a tank." Johnny had already tried that and suffered a series of illnesses including cholera, dysentery, malaria, typhoid, and salmonella.

So, they were ready for a new house – their timing was impeccable! For one thing, lava had just begun cascading down the mountain toward Pahoa and Hawaiian Beaches at the precise moment they started looking for a replacement house (this was a mild precursor to Fissure 8). Banks and insurance companies immediately withdrew from the market so the only way you could sell a house was for cash. Also, any potential buyer would have to be completely uninformed or a gambler willing to risk big money betting against Mother Nature. Johnny and Terry opted for a fast hand with Mama.

Johnny was working on the orchard, so Terry took the check from their reluctant insurance adjuster's cold damp hands and started waiving it around in Hawaiian Beaches. At that time there was a surge of panic selling and over 300 houses were listed at bargain basement prices (timing is everything). Naturally, Johnny had to mess with Terry a little bit. She found a dream house and Johnny found a really crappy one. Terry would say, "This is the one." Johnny would say

"Well I don't know – we could save a few dollars if we bought the fixer upper." She was hip to Johnny's ways however and had already put in an offer.

So, they got the dream house. Jeez, it had running water, electricity, gas, cable TV, flowers, an enclosed garage, a lawn, and all sorts of bells and whistles. In the end their traumatic house fire turned out pretty well. Not so much for our friends.

So, when their house was engulfed in lava, Johnny and Terry were happy to reciprocate since their house was vacant and would be for another month until they got back to the orchard. Had they known how this arrangement would turn out, they might have throttled back a little on the "happy."

Jay and Sara "took possession" of Johnny and Terry's home on the afternoon of May 3rd, bringing with them two huge recliners, three wild dogs, ten loaves of bread, twenty bags of potato chips, and a huge pile of crap. One of the recliners went in the front room, the other one in the spare bedroom after the two full size beds were stacked on top of each other in the corner to create enough space. Jay took the chair in front of the TV; Sara took the one in the bedroom where she had a distant view of the screen. She called it "the hole" and seemed to enjoy yelling at Jay to bring her things ("Get me some potato chips!"). The ten loaves of bread went in the freezer. You might ask why – J&T do not know but there was no room left for ice cream and vodka. The potato chips were stacked on top of the refrigerator for ready accessibility (Sara had a voracious appetite for potato chips which seem to spike her blood sugar and contribute mightily to her bad attitude and her severe case of diabetes. They told J&T to move their car because they were going to put the rest of their stuff in the garage.

Now, about the dogs. There are three of them. They are wild and apparently untrainable. Dusty, a large mongrel male who was banned from obedience school after the first class is the oldest, the largest, and the dimmest. Scout and Tucker are sisters from the same litter of large Whippets. They are totally unfit for anything beyond eating and defecating – if they were sent to obedience school, they would probably kill the instructor in the first five minutes. It is likely that all three dogs suffer from brain damage as well as some form of bowel irregularity that causes excess excretions all over anything they happen to be standing on or by.

So, what do you do if you have three wild dogs and you're living in somebody else's house? Their solution was (a) surround the lanai with chicken wire and fling shit over the fence with a shovel and (b) open the sliding glass doors off the lanai and let the dogs shit in the house.

So, by the time Johnny and Terry got back to Pahoa at the end of May, the house was trashed. Their guests saw nothing wrong with this because that's how they ran things at their house. Needless to say, this did not sit well with J&T.

Johnny walked in first, sat down on the couch, and was immediately mauled by three dogs that probably had not eaten in several days. Although the dog bites may have been playfully intended, blood flowed profusely, and the mayhem stopped just short of the emergency room.

Then it was Terry's turn. She partially opened one of the screen doors to pet the dogs who came roaring through the gap, knocking her aside. Johnny lost it. "Get those dogs outta here!" (Thoughtfully refraining from lacing his request with expletives). There was decided reluctance on the part of their guests, but they ultimately capitulated. However, a later effort to sneak them back in was thwarted by extremely foul language and wild gesticulation on Johnny's part.

The routine kind of settled down to where the twin sliding glass doors where left open, but the screen doors were randomly opened or closed. The dogs would get into howling fights in the house, and then blaze head long through the doors onto the lanai. Johnny mentioned that at some point the dogs might crash through the screen doors or worse, through the glass doors. The response was, "Don't worry, it's safety glass." Johnny, trying mightily to be a good host, let it slide.

The next day J&T returned to find both screen doors blown out. They were told that it was not the dogs' fault but the neighbor's chicken. Does this sound plausible to you? So, J&T asked that the screens be replaced and that the curtains be closed to prevent another mishap. This precipitated a game that went on for several weeks where J&T would close the drapes and the house guests would open them back up. It was almost as if they hoped the dogs would crash through the glass so they could file a lawsuit. J&T were getting close to the edge.

At about the same time, Civil Defense advised that the Leilani subdivision would be closed permanently and anyone wishing to retrieve anything from any homes still standing would be allowed to do so until high noon, at which time anyone found loitering would be subject to heavy fines and/or imprisonment. This was apparently an effort to discourage criminals (and all the people hanging around the free water place) from ransacking empty homes.

As it turned out, they were right about the looting. Not only did you have the criminals and the free water crowd, but also a large contingent of Witness Protection Program participants (Pahoa has one of the largest "Programs" in the nation) who stand out like neon lights in line at the Pahoa grocery store.

So, Johnny dutifully fired up the truck, Jay hitched a trailer to his and they caravanned into Leilani to see what was left. This turned out to be a surreal adventure snaking through barricaded roads and around huge steaming cracks in the earth. Amazingly, Jay's house was still standing, even though it was only a few hundred yards up a slight incline from Fissure 8, which was spewing lava 200 feet into the air at an estimated rate of 100 cubic yards per second. Jay's house was covered with rocks made of volcanic ash about the size of baseballs. These were falling from the sky with great regularity, apparently cooling down just enough before hitting the ground so as not to start a fire. You could wait a couple minutes, then pick one up and crush it in your hand (lots of bubbles, not much rock).

They spent several hours taking everything they could out of the house. They were breathing hard because they had to wear acid gas masks to protect against the cloud of sulfur dioxide that permeated the atmosphere. A half hour before the deadline, they pulled out. Just for the hell of it, they walked down the road toward Fissure 8. They passed a couple houses and came to a gigantic lava field (actually, it was more like a lava desert). And to their right looming almost overhead (sort of like standing on the sidewalk and looking up at a twenty-story building) was Fissure 8 fountaining into the sky and throwing large globs of molten rock in random directions. Add to this the sound of a large jet engine and you've got quite a spectacle. They backed off immediately and were fortunate not to get mowed down although several other people were splattered with lava over the course of the eruption (you do not want to get splattered with lava).

So, they hauled two trucks and a trailer full of "items" back to Hawaiian Beaches where Jay proceeded to put it all in J&T's one car garage (Sara was sitting on her fat ass eating potato chips in "the hole"). To his credit, Jay was amazingly able to stuff it all in there in multiple layers. He may not be able to get it back out of there, but he's a pretty industrious guy, so we'll see.

Now, about the crazy lady. Jay has been married to Sara for thirty some rocky years. She delighted in telling the story (a thousand times) how she was left at the altar of her almost first marriage (that guy was either prescient or lucky or both). Then there was a couple hundred tellings of how she constantly banged her next boyfriend on a boat in the Santa Monica harbor until they were asked to leave (too many waves). Jay would just hang his head and clench his teeth. How he was able to maintain his sanity through all this is a thing of utter amazement and probably would qualify him for sainthood if the Pope heard about his efforts.

J&T had known Jay and Sara for a decade. Jay is a steady guy and a good friend. Sara, not so much. During this ten-year period J&T winced a thousand times at her rude behavior and cutting remarks (mostly directed at anybody in ear shot). She describes herself as "a strong woman" and somehow apparently believes that this mischaracterization entitles her to be a mean-spirited nincompoop. But, notwithstanding this, J&T have always treated her differentially so as not to ruin their "friendship." Spending two months in close quarters with her had poisoned the well (and a significant portion of the Pacific Ocean) and revealed a vile unhappy person who should probably be occupying a room in the Kaneohe psychiatric ward. Does this seem too cruel? If you knew her you would probably want to reserve a whole hospital wing and surround it with barbed wire and armed guards.

You can only take so much. Getting together once in a while you can handle most anything. Living for a couple months on a 24/7 basis really brings out the true character of a person. In Sara's case, she let it all hang out. She took to wandering around the house in a ratty old coat mumbling a constant stream of unintelligible nonsense punctuated by "Ouch" for no apparent reason. Imagine listening to somebody babbling away nonstop and punctuating the drivel with "Ouch" every few minutes. J&T tried mightily to ignore it, but it got real old real fast.

Fortunately, Jay & Sara's insurance policy covered volcanic disasters and allowed a generous stipend for a rental house. It was clear to them all that J&T's house was too small for the circus they found themselves in. Fortunately, Jay found a larger house a couple miles down the road.

A week before they were to move to their new digs, the shit hit the fan.

Jay and Johnny were enjoying a light lunch of leftovers (Jay had the Mexican, Johnny had the Italian – food, not people). They were both topped off and ready to get on with the afternoon when Sara burst out of the kitchen, slapped a giant drum stick down in front of Jay and said, "Eat this." Jay said, "I'm full." A few moments later Sara came out with a load of spaghetti for Johnny who quickly mentioned he too was full.

That's when the bomb went off. Johnny politely asked Sara to wrap the leftovers back up and put them in the refrigerator so they could eat them tomorrow. Sara said, "Either you eat this shit now or I'm throwing it away."

Johnny responded, "Please, just put it back in the refrigerator for tomorrow."

That is when Sara looked at Johnny, put her fat hands on her fat hips and said, "DON'T FUCK WITH ME!"

That is when Johnny turned around, looked at Sara and said, "DON'T YOU FUCK WITH ME!" He tactfully left out "you worthless piece of shit."

So here they were, taking in their friends in their time of need, and what evolved from this humanitarian gesture? A chicken wire fence around their lanai, dog shit everywhere, and a crazy lady wandering around mumbling and screaming at the top of her lungs "DON'T FUCK WITH ME!"

They (Johnny, Terry, and Jay) spent the last week avoiding Sara who simmered in the "hole" by her nasty self. Any bond that may have existed was irretrievably broken. One of the happiest days in their lives was watching Sara pull away in her shitty little car with piles of crap in the back seat and a trunk full of Wonder bread and potato chips. Jeez!

Perhaps this story is too extreme. Or maybe Johnny was just having a bad day. In any case, he felt much better after he threw up.

Chapter 46

Board Cords and Black Holes

It didn't take long for Johnny to realize that surfing is dangerous. When you eat it (for the uninitiated, we're not talking about sandwiches here), you suffer the consequences. From the beginning of surfing history, that meant if you didn't get knocked unconscious by your board or the coral reef, you had to swim all the way in to retrieve said board. For all the guys between you and the beach, it meant, "look out" as loose boards will inevitably flip upside down and slide sideways at considerable speed toward the shore and anyone in the way.

Johnny experienced hundreds of unprovoked collisions in this way, particularly in the beginning phase of his surfing career when he was surrounded by equally inept but aspiring surfers who fell off on almost every wave. There was one time that really stood out at San Onofre. But first a little history.

Prior to 1971 the only legitimate access to the surf at San Onofre was membership in the San Onofre surf club. Each year a new membership sticker was glued to your windshield. It was not uncommon to see broken windshields full of stickers from older cars temporarily affixed to windshields of newer cars as a kind of badge and rite of passage.

A secondary obstacle was the fact that the whole coastline, including San Onofre, was part of Camp Pendleton Marine Base. Therefore, if you didn't have a San Onofre membership pass you had to have a military pass – otherwise, you had to sneak in from the Pacific Coast Highway (about a mile) carrying your board and your lunch. If you got caught the military police took your board away and sent it down to headquarters in Oceanside where you'd have to go to retrieve it. Sometimes they would beat you with a baton if you didn't move fast enough to surrender your board. The odds of getting caught and trashed were about 50-50. If you made it all the way to San Onofre, the guys at the gate would usually let you paddle out in recognition of the balls and the bravery it took to get there.

Marine brutality subsided considerably in 1971 when the US Marine Corp leased San Onofre to the State of California and restrictions on access were relaxed.

Well prior to this new 1970's love fest, Southern California Edison decided in 1964 to utterly trash the place by building a giant nuclear power plant (at a cost of nine billion dollars) consisting of two huge hemispherical containment buildings looming over San Onofre beach. These were supposed to contain unexpected releases of radioactive material and scared the bejesus out of everybody. The roads in that area were actually painted with giant white arrows and the words "ESCAPE ROUTE"). In 2013, there was an "incident" (fortunately, it did not explode) requiring an immediate shut down. It still sits there abandoned today. The owner of this monstrosity (Southern California Edison) prefers to say "decommissioned" and insists that it will be demolished "soon." Johnny apparently needs to cough – "BULLSHIT!"

But before all this, back in the summer of 1963, Johnny paddled out on a glorious San Onofre morning into fair size surf. When he got outside, he found the entire Dewey Weber surf team clustered in the take off zone. These guys were good. This was the moment Johnny realized how a poodle must feel running around on a freeway. And there, paddling out like the Emperor of San Onofre, was Dewey Weber himself. He had reason to gloat.

It is not generally known that when he was eight his mother took him to an audition at which he won the part of Buster Brown, a comic book character adopted by the Brown Shoe Company. When he was fourteen, Groucho Marx featured him on his national television show You Bet Your Life, as the three-time National Duncan Yo-Yo Champion. By the time he was eighteen he was a three-time high school wrestling champion and during college qualified for the Olympic wrestling team (although he was injured immediately before the Olympic event and was prevented from competing). Weber appeared in nearly every surfing movie in the late 1950's and 1960s including Slippery When Wet, Cat on a Hot Foam Board, and Walk on the Wet Side. An image of him surfing at Makaha became the symbol of the United States Surfing Association. AND, he had several surf shops and a huge team of riders.

So, Dewey was already well on his way. On top of all this, Dewey was an extraordinary party animal and a really heavy drinker. How he could drag himself out of bed with an epic hang over, slug down a half bottle of Jack and paddle out into formidable surf was truly amazing.

It was obvious Dewey was hurting and a little delirious, but he put his head down and kept paddling. At that moment, one of the members of his surf team took off on a particularly large wave and got his ass handed to him by Mother Nature. His board flipped and started sliding sideways at a rapid clip toward shore. All Dewey could do was sit up on his board and cover his head. He caught it straight in the face and went over backwards, later washing up on the beach in a pool of blood. Most people would have taken evasive action, diving off and heading for the bottom. Not Dewey. Some say he took it like a man. Johnny was thinking it's probably not a good idea to drink and surf as it apparently diminishes your survival instincts. Either way, the danger of a loose surfboard had been permanently seared into Johnny's brain.

Enter Mark Jennings, one of Johnny's high school friends. The year was 1962; the place was Doheny Beach where all the less accomplished surfers tended to congregate. They paddled out on a cold winter day (before wet suits) into what was then commonly referred to as "ankle snappers" (small surf). Mark had lingered on the beach but caught up a few minutes later. He lifted his leg out of the water and said, "Look at this."

He had tied a cloths line around his ankle and attached the other end through a hole in his fin. He said he was tired of swimming in for his board, so he invented this contraption. Johnny was not impressed and felt that this utter blasphemy impugned the integrity of the sport. That day Johnny lost his board several dozen times. Mark did not lose his once.

Mark continued for several years to use and refine his "board cord" even though he got a lot of heat from the guys about being a wussie.

In surfing lore, it is generally accepted that Pat O'Neil (the son of Jack O'Neill who invented the wet suit) first introduced a surfboard leash in 1971 – he called it a "leg rope." Pat's idea was to use surgical tubing attached to a surfboard with a suction cup. This crude device elicited heaps of scorn from the surfing community, so much so that when he entered the 1971 Malibu International surf contest wearing one (the guys called it "a goon leash"), he was disqualified from the event. Also, the surgical tubing was extremely stretchy and had a tendency to launch the surfboard back toward the surfer – that is how Pat's father Jack lost an eye.

The board leash, which Mark invented nine years prior to its public introduction, went on to prove itself and today 99.9% of all surfboards have one. But the guy who really invented it, Mark Jennings, deserves credit for being way ahead of the curve. Johnny did not realize how far, until he started reading about black holes.

Einstein's theories of relativity and the quantum physics that followed had predicted black holes, but almost all scientists doubted they existed. In 1971, a young astronomer named Charles Thomas Bolton was intrigued by a star called HDE226868. It's a blue super giant neutron star twenty times bigger and thousands of times brighter than the Sun.

He noticed that this star gave off enormous amounts of radiation of a type that is not generated by blue super giants. He noticed that HDE226868 was wobbling slightly, leading him to believe that he was looking at a binary system of two stars orbiting around each other. He called the second star Cygnus X-1. He calculated the speed of rotation at an incredible 200 times the speed of sound (at 0 degrees C the speed of sound is 741mph x 200 times is a rotational speed of 148,000mph which would definitely rip the rubber off any rim). He correctly deduced that the only way this was possible was if Cygnus X-1 was much smaller and much denser than a neutron star. He had discovered the first black hole.

Bolton was worried about going public with his discovery in the face of universal skepticism so he reached out to two groups of exceptionally well qualified astronomers, one in England and the other in the US. They both confirmed his findings. He published his paper, which was met with extreme skepticism. It took another twenty years for enough evidence to accumulate to prove that Bolton had, in fact, discovered the first black hole.

At a Poly High School reunion many decades after Mark and Johnny's graduation in 1963, cocktail conversation revealed that Mark was part of the US team. Who would have thought that Johnny's High School friend (who, incidentally had the hottest girlfriend in Southern California) would go on to invent the board cord AND collaborate on the discovery of the first black hole?

Mark is out there somewhere, but his whereabouts are unknown.

You go dude!

Chapter 47

The End is in Sight

"If you can read this, you're in range" (a welcoming sign on Dr. Miller's office door).

Johnny always thought that he was more or less immortal. Every time he hit a tree on his dirt bike, he was certain that he would be able to heal rapidly and get back in the saddle. Every time he crashed into a wall on the racquetball court, he was confident that he could shake off the concussion and walk back to the service line. Every time he ate it going over the falls on a big one, he was pretty sure the collision with the reef would be minor and that he'd eventually be able to float to the surface and paddle back out.

This sunny outlook on life took a turn recently when Johnny went to visit his urologist. Doctor Miller had been monitoring Johnny's prostate for several years. This entailed primarily reviewing the results of an annual blood test for a Prostate Specific Antigen (I don't know either).

Johnny had been skating along for years in the two to three zone (the good zone). Lately, however, his PSA score had moved up the ladder to four, then five (the beginning of the bad zone). You do not want to get to the much higher and more deadly "bozone." As a precautionary measure, the Doc recommended a "biopsy." This is a scientific euphemism for "I'm gonna ram a stick up your ass and rip out chunks of your prostate gland for microscopic examination."

Johnny was understandably apprehensive. He had picked up some lingo on the Internet, which he lamely attempted to apply to this situation "Doc, I think I'd like to do some 'watchful waiting.'" It wasn't meant to be a joke, but Dr. Miller laughed anyway. He said "Johnny, you're so close to the bozone that a biopsy is your only way out."

So, a biopsy was scheduled and the nurse filling in the calendar said, "You're going to love this." Johnny correctly deduced that she was putting him on and that she was actually alluding to the likelihood of pain. Johnny accordingly inquired about the type of anesthesia that would be employed. "Uh, this is an office procedure – no anesthetics. And by the way, don't forget to take these antibiotics (snooker sized white pills) to guard against infection." Johnny really did not want to hear this. "Well then, can I have a prescription for a dozen valium and two dozen vicodin?" The nurse allowed as how she'd have to check with the doctor.

Do you remember the TV show "Sienfeld?" There was this guy on there who ran a restaurant specializing in soup. They called him the soup Nazi because if he didn't like you, he would say "No soup for YOU!" Apparently, Johnny had offended somebody, because Dr. Miller's response was "No drugs for YOU!"

The biopsy was to be performed in two weeks. However, B-day arrived immediately and unexpectedly - in Johnny's mind the clock had not moved at all due to the time warping affects of stark terror.

He sat in the outer office feeling like a scared little schoolgirl. When his name was called, he jumped up and pretended unconvincingly that it was part of how he normally stood up. He marched head down toward the proverbial gallows, noting the comforting sign on the door (I'm in range?). They put him on a scale, which had some sort of malfunction, indicating 230 pounds, which is appropriate for a walrus but not a person. The nurse lamely attempted to make light of the situation "You'll be a little lighter a little later." Ha ha.

In the corner of Dr. Miller's office there is a foreboding leather bed with a television screen on the right side at one end for patient viewing. Johnny was asked to lie on his left side (butt toward the doctor, eyes on the screen).

Dr. Miller came in and picked up some kind of instrument. Johnny couldn't look directly at it but out of the corner of his eye he thought he glimpsed a shovel.

And then he said, "You're going to feel a little pressure."

Oh man, he had heard this before and knew it to be a straight up lie. He had reported for his first and only colonoscopy several decades earlier and found himself in a sort of locker room where he and another older gentleman were made to undress and slip into backless hospital gowns. After a little nervous small talk, his fellow traveler was summoned to the room where they perform the procedure.

Johnny was sitting on a bench pondering his next move when the screaming started – the kind you might expect to hear if someone was being tortured with sharp knives and red-hot pokers. The "yyy*aaaaaaahh*hs" and "ooo**oohhhhhh**s" continued for several minutes and did not bode well for the next person in line.

Then Johnny found himself assuming the position and listening intently to the proctologist as he said, "You're going to feel a little pressure" – you lying sack of shit.

So, reclining there in Dr. Miller's office on his left side staring at the monitor, Johnny knew he was in for a rough ride. Soon enough it became apparent that he'd drawn the baddest bronco in the barn.

From what he could make out, Dr. Miller had "inserted" the handle of the shovel up his ass (are we there yet?) until it appeared on the monitor, whereupon a needle emerged from the end and punctured the wall of his anal cavity and buried itself in Johnny's prostate. He had heard of drug addicts sharing needles and getting sick, but this was beyondo. The purpose of this questionable maneuver was to inject some kind of numbing agent in preparation for the main event. As an aside, the doctor cheerfully exclaimed, "Don't forget to take those antibiotics!"

They waited for a couple minutes for the Novocain to take effect, and during this time they mapped the gland with the computer and noted ten locations ripe for further investigation. It turned out these were where the arrows were going to go.

Then Dr. Miller said, "You're going to hear a clicking sound." By now Johnny was totally skeptical and prepared himself for a sonic boom. Another fatter needle appeared on the screen and positioned itself over the first bull's eye. Then, BLAM - the sound of a nail gun shooting 16d's into hardwood studs filled the room.

On the monitor, this needle (which appeared to be about the diameter of a garden hose) immediately retracted, taking with it a cylinder of meat and leaving a long hollow hole in Johnny's prostate gland – he envisioned it as something similar to the Pali Highway tunnel that accommodates cars, trucks and buses through the Koolau Mountain range.

Before he could register surprise, pain, or incredulity, Dr. Miller pulled the trigger again - BLAM. Then – BLAM, BLAM, BLAM, BLAM, BLAM, BLAM, BLAM, and BLAM. Johnny's prostate now resembled a wad of Swiss cheese, and Dr. Miller had a couple pounds of gland that he could send to a lab somewhere for analysis.

To add insult to injury, Johnny was directed to another part of the hospital for a blood test (can you believe it?) This was particularly egregious since every trip to the commode over the next few days resulted in a brilliant pool of red liquid, which resembled the kind of paint you might see on one of those Cholo wagons that bounce up and down at certain

East LA intersections. He knew, however, that it was type A positive and he thought he saw chunks of gland floating around in there, but that might just have been his imagination.

A week later, two things happened. The first was a call from the lab – an apologetic technician advised there had been a problem with the samples and that Johnny would have to provide some more. MOTHER FUCKER! Fortunately, they were referring to Johnny's blood samples and not the meat they'd removed from his prostate.

The second thing was a meeting with Dr. Miller to go over the results of the biopsy.

It would be nice to say that the results were negative. However, they were not. Dr. Miller put it nicely, "You have a pretty good batting average – you're eight for ten." He then proceeded to explain that eight of the ten samples came back positive for cancer. He rounded out the good news by noting that his Gleeson score was rather high, indicating a vigorous form of cancer. Thank you very much.

Johnny now had a ticket on the cancer train. First stop was a surgical theater where they inserted a hundred or so radioactive "seeds" directly into what was left of his prostate. Fortunately, they give you a general anesthetic to take the edge off an otherwise entirely uncomfortable procedure. In theory, the radioactivity in the seeds will burn up the cancer cells. They have a half-life of thirty days, so the level of radioactivity decreases rapidly over several months. They warn you, however, that for the first thirty days you should avoid lap dances and small children "because they may develop blisters."

As a precaution, they put Johnny back on the cancer train and deposited him at the oncology department at St. Francis hospital (where he had spent three months recuperating from an accident fifty years earlier). What comes around goes around. The waiting room was filled with people in advance stages of decline. It was a bit like that scene in Papillon where Steve McQueen, after months of starvation and torture, sticks his head out of the hole in his cell door only to encounter the guy in the next cell who asks him "How do I look?"

The doctors and nurses there were very nice, although Johnny could not shake the feeling that they were looking at him (and all the people in the waiting room) like the guy who holds the door open at the slaughterhouse.

It cannot be said that the experience was enjoyable, although it did not hurt. They put you on a slab surrounded by a donut like apparatus that slides forward until it is lined up with your smoking prostate. The donut spins slowly around, stopping periodically to administer a blast of radioactivity. The procedure takes about ten minutes. However, you have to do it every other day (except week ends) for five weeks.

In the end they pronounce you cured (maybe).

So much for immortality. It occurred to Johnny that his perspective on life had changed. Previously, he had viewed the journey from the standpoint of how far he'd come. Suddenly, he was viewing it from the standpoint of how far he had left to go.

The end is in sight. Wow, what a ride!

Chapter 48

Get Off the Bus Gus

Johnny had to fly over to the Big Island for the 320th time (40 years at approximately 8 flights per year = 320). If you count the return trip to Honolulu, that's 640 flights. If you count the wife that's 1,280 flights. If you count the dog, you're off the charts. The only good thing about it is a shit load of frequent flyer miles – enough to get back and forth to the mainland maybe about twice.

The purpose of this trip was to "mow the lawn" (all forty-four acres of it), spray herbicide (ditto), spread several tons of fertilizer (ditto) and a few dozen other things that are required if you are insane enough to be responsible for a macadamia orchard. At first it was fun, then it was work, and now it's a forty-pound anvil tied to his ankle. His friend Britton (previously known as Bob but now hiding out under an alias) would pick him up at the Hilo Airport and cart him twenty miles out to Pahoa but he had just landed a new (legal) job and was unavailable. So, Johnny had three options: (1) walk - it's a long way on foot, (2) Uber - it costs $50 or (3) take the Hele On Bus - it costs $1 if you're over sixty-five – Johnny was way past that (his wife says he's old as dirt). So naturally Johnny wandered over to the bus stop and waited for his dollar ride.

Now, the Hele On Bus is basically a Big Island community service for indigents. Hillary Clinton might describe it as a basket full of deplorables with wheels. So, when it finally showed up, Johnny walked on to a bus full of characters from the bar scene in Star Wars. Fortunately, he was able to find an empty seat somewhere in the middle of the bar. He fit right in.

Things went bad almost immediately. Johnny was situated directly behind a middle-aged lady talking on her cell phone. Approximately ten minutes into the ride a scruffy local guy with prison tattoos and a crazy look on his face came weaving up the aisle, stopped next to the lady, and said, "Give me that phone." She ignored him. He then said, "That's my phone – hand it over." She said, "It's my phone" whereupon he hauled off and punched her square in the face. Around the psycho ward they probably refer to him as "5150" but we'll call him Gus.

It had been fifty years since Johnny's last fight, but this egregious behavior could not be ignored. Normally you do not want to get into it with a surely looking dude half your age with a fanny pack that may contain a knife and/or a gun. Fortunately, Johnny had been on the wrestling team in high school and one of the things they taught you were the moves you were not allowed to employ in the ring for fear of inflicting injury or death. These maneuvers were numerous, and the outcome was predictably immense pain and/or an ambulance ride for the inflictee. The inflictor was immediately expelled from the match which was counted as a loss. However, the coach apparently anticipated that at some future date this knowledge might come in handy, so he spent a lot of time carefully demonstrating how to cripple people.

So, Johnny stood up, spun 'ol "Gus" around, cocked his right arm up behind his back, put him in a chock hold, and yanked. It was over immediately. Under these circumstances a person (any person) so rendered will do anything you want/ask/demand. Johnny was thankful for that and was thinking it might be a nice gesture to send a box of candy to his old coach.

Johnny perp walked 'ol screaming Gus down the aisle to the front and inquired of the driver if he should throw him off the bus. The driver gave him a look that said "Yeah, throw that miserable son of a bitch off the bus" but instead said "I already called the police - hold him until they get here so they can take him in and book him for assault and battery."

So, "Gus" got deposited down the stairs and kind of got mooshed up against the closed door. It was suggested that he not move. His right arm did not appear to be functioning properly.

Two police cars arrived. Simultaneously the girl with the swollen face came up behind Johnny and threw her cell phone over his shoulder at "Gus" just as the driver opened the door. "Gus" fell backwards to the pavement as the phone whizzed over his head. He got up and ran, right arm flopping around and cops in pursuit. Fortunately for him, the police in Hilo don't shoot fleeing suspects who appear to be unarmed and injured.

A half hour later the bus got back on the road, but not before most of the women passengers disembarked so they could walk the rest of the way to their destinations without getting involved in further mayhem. Most of them were grateful but scared. One lady said, "Good work, but I'm getting off here in case he's got friends on the bus or in the neighborhood."

Fortunately, "Gus" was such a despicable person he apparently had no friends. Johnny missed his next bus but did manage to get home five hours later. He reflected on the bus ride and concluded that it had been exhilarating.

PS – This all happened in the middle of the Covid epidemic. When Johnny called the wife, he casually mentioned that he'd been in a fight on a bus.   She exploded with a string of expletives that would make a sailor blush. "You fool, you could get Covid, what were you thinking?"   Johnny said "You should see the other guy. Love ya," hung up, and headed for the liquor cabinet.

Chapter 49

Three's The Charm

Well, forty-nine chapters later Johnny's running out of gas. There probably are a few interesting things that failed to make the cut, but there is one last thing that needs to be addressed.

As you go through life (Johnny's stuck at seventy-five), unwelcomed things happen to your body. In Johnny's case, you've got a Cadillac that fell on your face (bad) but which kept you out of Vietnam (good). You've got the five knee operations occasioned by spirited racquetball mishaps (bad) but which prevented you from experiencing the embarrassment of excelling at shaky ballroom dancing (good). Then you've got the broken thumbs from going over the handlebars on dirt bike crashes (bad) but which enable you to make everyone in the restroom laugh out loud as you try and button up your 501 jeans (laughter is always good). Then there's the time you crashed a borrowed bicycle into a Mexican curb at high speed and went over the handle bars (again) breaking your shoulder and freezing your arm so it could not be raised above a 90-degree angle (bad – hard to get a bottle of beer from the bar to your mouth) but which enabled you to mystify and amaze your doctor two years later when you caught a falling beam and rebroke your shoulder so it began functioning properly once again – (good). Then there are the miscellaneous head injuries from collisions with the reef occasioned by bad wipe outs (bad) but which made you smarter (good). Then, of course, there's the cancer which affected your prostate and many areas of your skin where melanomas' were excised like slices of pie (bad) but which went away after a little radiation and a few stiches (good).

But all this pales in comparison to the one thing that Johnny had to endure **three times** (you'll have to guess but here's a "tip" – it rhymes with "flip").

When Johnny hit sixty, he was in pretty good shape (relatively speaking). Everything seemed to be working pretty well and, although he had retired from racquetball and dirt bike racing, he was still surfing often and at a fairly high level. Since he lived in Hawaii, he was able to take advantage of some of the best surf in the world. This was no funky choppy 60-degree beach break - this was the good stuff!

He did, however, notice that on bigger sets he felt a twinge of pain as he stood up preparing to take the drop. As time went on the twinge blossomed and he noticed that it was starting to interfere with his ability to plant his forward foot on the deck in the right location. As any surfer knows, if your foot isn't in the right spot when you huck it over the ledge, you are most likely going to get a hydraulic beating.

There came a day, a beautiful soft offshore day, with South swell sets winding in at ten feet plus. It was a weekday, and the North Shore was flat, so many good surfers came on over to the South Shore to "get some." Most of those who made the trek went straight to Three's which is generally considered to be the best big wave surf spot on the South Shore (but don't tell anybody as it's crowded enough already).

This was all well and fine since not too many surfers had surfed Three's in conditions over ten feet and most were not familiar with the anatomy of the reef bottom which had the uncanny ability to shift the take-off zone in larger conditions. Whereas a sub-ten-foot swell will create a reeling right to left barrel with a far right take off, conditions above ten feet reverse the take off point the further out you go. So, if you saw a macker coming, you would normally paddle like crazy toward the horizon to the right to catch the wave. But (ah ha!) over ten feet you would have to paddle like crazy toward the horizon to the LEFT to where the really big ones form up and start

418

breaking. This is our little secret since it rarely gets over ten feet on the South Shore.

So, Johnny paddled out through the mob of really good surfers and waited for a big one. It wasn't long before a huge wave started to feather out to sea. The mob paddled like crazy toward the horizon to the right while Johnny nonchalantly paddled toward the horizon to the left. The wave was pushing fifteen feet as Johnny made the turn and started paddling for one hell of a take-off. He was the only person within fifty yards of where this wave would break.

As he was attempting to get to his feet, he experienced a kind of slaughterhouse related electric chair sort of piercing shock in his left side which had a crippling and wholly unwanted effect on his ability to stand up. All the surfers who were inside and to the right of this beauty were whistling and yelling and totally pissed off because they were going to miss the wave of the day and this guy (Johnny) was going to get it.

This is where the rubber met the road.

In his own mind, he was about to become the star of the Ed Sullivan Surf Show (sharing top billing with the Beatles) if only he could get to his feet. As the pain increased to the point where he would confess to murdering Santa

Claus if only it would abate, he realized that he was on the edge of really messing this up and would likely become a punk ass bitch in the eyes of the thirty or so surfers who each knew that if they were in his place they would drop in majestically and ride one of the finest waves of their life all the way to the beach where they would be carried to the bar on the shoulders of all the other surfers who missed the wave and had to buy the beer.

You know how when something really bad is going to happen, things have a tendency to shift into slow motion? Well, Johnny just shifted. At precisely the same moment he started screaming in pain (AAAAAAAAHHHHHHHHH) his left foot (which was attached by his left leg to his left hip which was apparently not functioning properly) completely missed the deck, thus precipitating the tip roll snowball wipe out of the century. As he skipped head over heels down the face of the wave he heard a chorus of derisive remarks from the audience, which was very angry about the prospect of this really large excellent wave going unridden because some minor league wannabe had fucked it up so badly.

In hindsight, Johnny could not blame them, although he did in fact have a valid excuse for his clumsy dismount.

About three quarters of the way down, the lip of this monster caught up with him and he began participating in what some surfers might call "a pile driver." This is where tons salt water (think Olympic swimming pool) falling at terminal velocity stuffs you into what is left of the deep blue sea. Johnny experienced a horrific hydraulic beating, which expelled whatever wind was left in his lungs.

Unfortunately, it wasn't quite over. Due to his other "troubles" he had forgotten to take into consideration the fact that at the end of this vertical mine shaft to hell there was...a reef. The irony was not lost on him. Here was his sweet little secret which had enabled him to catch many big ones over the years, and now it was waiting down there to say "hi" - which it did in spades.

The power of the white water mercifully dragged him quite a ways toward the beach before he was able to resurface and reoxygenate. This was good to the extent that the jeering crowd was left well out to sea. It also saved him the embarrassment of having to explain his poor performance, his broken board and all that blood.

The thing that really hurt was the realization that Johnny may never surf again.

As soon as he scabbed up, he made an appointment with an orthopedic surgeon. X-rays and gamma rays and all sorts of other rays were taken, and the doctor concluded that Johnny needed hip surgery ("tip", "flip", "**hip**"). He explained that the hip basically consists of a socket and a ball. Due to egregiously irresponsible physical "exercise" (Johnny seems to recall the doctor's exact words), the socket and the ball had worn out, thus causing extreme pain.

The Doctor's solution was a "hip replacement." This is where he gets a very sharp knife and cuts you vertically down the upper front part of your leg (they refer to this as an anterior incision) for about six or seven inches, which in other circumstances, such as a knife fight, would count as a loss. He then opens you up, digs the cup out of your hip and puts a new one in, saws the ball off the top of your femur, drives a spike (they call it a stem) down the inside of your hollowed out femur, screws a ball onto the top of the spike and snaps the ball into the cup and voila – you are a new man.

Johnny was a little skeptical, but the doctor said this is how doctors made hips work again. PLUS, there's a new ball and hip kit that was just introduced to the market by Johnson & Johnson, which is made out of steel specifically for clumsy athletes. The older ones were made out of ceramics and a type of plastic which had a tendency to break (if you fell off your dirt bike for instance). Unfortunately, Johnson & Johnson talked the FDA into approving the new hip without clinical trials. This bonehead maneuver (which neither Johnny nor the doctor were aware of) ultimately cost Johnson & Johnson hundreds of millions of dollars.

Johnny made the mistake of looking up "hip replacement" on You Tube. DO NOT LOOK UP HIP REPLACEMENT ON YOU TUBE! You will likely cancel the procedure and will probably throw up.

Given the alternatives, Johnny sucked it up, made a reservation, and submitted to his **first** hip replacement. It only took five or six weeks to get back up to speed. A short time later he climbed Mauna Loa with his nephew who was hanging with him in a desperate attempt to overcome alcohol addiction.

Unfortunately, the subtle dynamics of a new hip were, at least for Johnny, not the same as those required to surf well and he found himself more on the shore than in the water. He even got a blow-up raft, which he used once.

Johnny also noticed that said hip replacement operation had generated a couple unwelcomed side effects. For one, it started to hurt again a year later. The Talking Heads were talking "This is not my beautiful house, this is not my beautiful wife, this is not my beautiful painless hip!" Reflecting on the seventy-five-thousand-dollar bill he got for the pleasure of participating in the procedure, he did acknowledge that his health insurance chipped in seventy grand (good - although he kind of felt like he got shorted on the deal).

The other thing was that he started to lose his mind - not in a metaphorical sense but rather in an actual sense. It started to become difficult to finish sentences. Then it started to become difficult to start sentences. Then it became difficult to find the kitchen. Then the wife took away the keys (to the car AND to the house).

They dragged him down to the hospital psych ward and conducted a number of tests that included a lot of Johnny's blood being drawn and shipped to various laboratories spread out across the continental United States. They all came back negative except for two.

The doctor called him in and got right to it. "Well, you have a 16-blood count in cobalt and a 21 in chromium. These are really high numbers" (he refrained from saying "fantastically"). By way of explanation, cobalt and chromium are elements essential for human health but are toxic at high levels. Most people get small doses in their diet and in the environment. Some people are exposed to higher levels from industrial pollution, and (get this) **some people get toxic levels from wear and corrosion of metal hip implants.**

It turns out that cobalt and chromium are the constituent parts in a metal alloy with very high specific strength, which is commonly used in gas turbines, dental implants, and (oh dear) orthopedic implants.

The average Cobalt blood level in a normal human is between .7 and 3.4 whereas the average Chromium blood level in a normal human is between .5 and 2.5. What?

This was, shall we say, very bad news. The essence of further discussion was that these numbers were extremely very bad and needed to come down immediately. Aside from eating and defecating a lot of clay, the only real solution is to remove the source of contamination.

A few weeks later as Christmas approached, Johnny got a Christmas card from his doctor (at least he thought it was a Christmas card). As he opened it, he got one of those sensations which might accompany a letter from the last in a long list of colleges which you had desperately applied to and been rejected from.

The text was brief – "Dear Johnny, I regret to inform you that your hip implant has been recalled." **WHAT?!**

Who was it that said, "The crown lies heavy on the head?" Well, knowing that you need to undergo a **second** operation for a hip replacement is kind of like that except it's your soul they're talking about. Johnny's was crushed but he knew that there was really no other viable option (the prospect of consuming fifty pounds of clay a day with the associated plumbing repair expenses did not appeal). On the plus side, at least he might be able to find the kitchen again.

So he got back in the game so to speak, and lined up another operation. The count was zero and one and he was going to give it another Babe Ruth kind of try.

It would be wonderful to report that the second operation was a huge success, and that Johnny was able to retrieve his mind and surf off into the sunset. Unfortunately, it was the beginning of a ten-year ride on the Trauma Train.

What happened was that the doctor (who put in the first one) figured that since the grinding between the stainless-steel ball and cup had caused the "problem," he would simply cut Johnny open and swap out the offending parts. So, Johnny was stabbed again (a little bigger this time), the steel cup was popped out and a plastic one was popped back in, and the steel ball (which was screwed on to the spike in Johnny's femur) was unscrewed and a new ceramic one was screwed back on. Since the spike was apparently innocent, it was left in place. This was a terrible decision.

On the bright side, some of Johnny's friends suggested that he visit an attorney for a "consultation." It turned out that approximately 9,000 people worldwide had also had the "Johnny experience." There were lawsuits and mafia hits going on everywhere. A lawyer friend hooked Johnny up to a law firm in San Francisco that exclusively settled hip replacement issues one way or the other.

It only took a single phone call. The San Francisco lawyer (we'll call him "Mr. Paizano") said, "Yeh, we can help ya. We think we can get ya $250,000 cash since Johnson & Johnson probably doesn't want to go the other way. Here's the problem, you can either take a check right now or you can wait in line (a very long line) for a trial. There have only been two trials so far – the first guy got $7 million; the second guy got nothing. Waddayawanna do?"

Johnny cleared his throat and said, "I'll take a check please." And son of a gun, a couple weeks later he received a wire transfer for $250,000 (less a little something for Mr. Piazano). Johnny bought a new car for the little woman and a couple new surf boards just in case.

Now, for a little ride on the Trauma Train. The second hip replacement started to hurt a little bit. Johnny could not believe that he'd been played like this. But he opted to take a seat in the "happy car" toward the front of the train and poured himself a little drink. It turned out to be a ten-year ride on a bumpy set of tracks. The worst part of it was the "spiko-meter" which is an imaginary machine similar to a Giger counter which measures the degree of pain generated by the spike in Johnny's femur as it got looser and looser. You do not want to "red line" on the "spiko-meter." It only took five years – the second five years was brutally unimaginable.

The good news was that the levels of chromium and cobalt slowly declined to the point where Johnny was able to participate in a reasonably standard conversation and learned to type again (which was handy given his absurd decision to write The Johnny Chronicles).

The bad news was that the pain multiplied to the point where it was essentially unbearable (most professional athletes would break down in tears – can you imagine twenty-two guys plus a bunch of umpires wandering around on a football field blubbering?). Entering or exiting a car or a golf cart was excruciating in the fullest sense of the word. The wife was threatening to take the car keys away (again) and his golf handicap ballooned from eight to twenty-three. Even the girls did not want to play with him because they thought he was juicing it.

He finally went to see a doctor (a new one) who looked at his Xray and said, "How are you even able to walk?" Johnny replied that he stayed in the car most of the time and if he had to go to Costco or Home Depot, he leaned hard on a lumber cart.

The new doctor (we'll call him Dr. Kimo) had a reputation as the best orthopedic hip guy in Hawaii so Johnny latched on to him and he was kind enough to set up a **third** surgery (Three's The Charm) within a couple months (there were lots of people in that line).

It looked like there might be a smidgin of light at the end of the tunnel, but things got a little sketchy when they had their "pre-surgery consultation." To his credit, Dr. Kimo felt an obligation to lay it all out so Johnny had a clear understanding of what might, could, and would happen in a serious full hip replacement surgery of the type being contemplated.

While standard hip replacements are done about 70,000 times a year in the US, a "complete posterior arthroplasty hip revision" is up there on another orthopedic level. Johnny is not a doctor, and his attention span is probably not as long as it should be (given the chromium and cobalt and all), but this is what he understood in layman terms when Dr. Kimo let it all hang out:

1. This will require a "posterior" incision, which is much larger and deeper and different from the two previous "anterior" incisions he had undergone. The difference is that anteriorly you are just cutting through meat. Posteriorly, you are cutting through all sorts of important tissue with names like tensor fascia lata, iliotibial band and external rotators. This is necessary to really open up the barn (so to speak) to make room for a broad array of utensils and assistants. The time it takes to heal from all this is exponentially longer (three to six months vs four to six weeks).

2. A complete revision involves not only replacing the cup and ball, but also the

"stem" which is a type of stainless-steel spike with perforations all over that is jammed down into a hollowed-out femur bone and which, over time, bonds with the bone which grows into the little holes (sometimes they just use glue). The problem here is that it is only possible to remove it manually about 50% of the time. The other 50% requires a "bone saw" which is used to cut the femur vertically down both sides of the stem. The femur is then bent outward to break the bond with the stem. Sometimes the femur will break and have to be discarded in which case a replacement cadaver bone (i.e., a bone from a dead person) is shaped and inserted and held in place by a series of metal rings. This part of the operation is considerably more difficult, and time consuming and recovery time will probably stretch past next Christmas.

3. In certain cases, the interior of the femur may be infected. If this is the case, they will need to remove all the foreign material in the hip (spike, ball, and cup), and sew you up so they can treat the infection. The obvious problem with this scenario is that your leg will not be attached to anything but a bag of skin and will flop around wildly when you are

not confined to a stretcher or wheelchair.

4. If you encounter an infection or a belligerent spike requiring a bone saw party, the amount of "time on the table" is considerably longer and there is the prospect that the patient will bleed out. Multiple blood transfusions under these circumstances will likely be necessary - there may be complications and there are no guarantees.

5. You may end up walking with a limp since the scientific calibrations related to implanting a second different sized stem into a femur that was originally reshaped for some other stem are not as precise so you might be off one way or the other and might require a lift in one shoe or the other.

6. There were some other problems but Johnny was already on overload so it may be necessary to consult a medical journal.

So, Dr. Kimo said, "sign here" and the date for surgery was set.

The day of surgery arrived slowly. It must have been similar to a prearranged shoot out in the good old days where you knew somebody was going to die and you hoped it was not you, especially since you were a little rusty.

The sun came up on Monday morning – Johnny had not slept well but kept trying since he was not required to check in until 10 am with surgery around noon. The phone rang and 7:15 – it was Dr. Kimo's secretary explaining that the surgery before his was cancelled and they needed him at the hospital by 8:00 am to start prepping. This was a Mission Impossible kind of request since there are twelve miles of freeway between him and the hospital on which thousands of rush hour cars were stopped dead (well, let's just say "stopped").

The wife grabbed Johnny's little hospital bag (which contained a toothbrush, a pair of oversized shorts and a will), and jumped in the car. Johnny put his feet on the dashboard and violated quite a few traffic laws on his way down the hill and through the back streets of Honolulu. A mile from the hospital they came to a screeching halt at a crowded cross street packed with cars that did not move regardless of a green light or a red light. This happened for two consecutive stop light cycles. On the third one Johnny said, "Hang on cause I'm going up on the sidewalk and over or through whoever is blocking our way." Terry grabbed the "oh shit" bar and held on tight.

Fortunately, the guy sideways in front of them figured out what was about to happen and pulled over into the gutter just in time to let Johnny through – they checked into Queen's hospital at 8:02 am.

This is the part where you are "prepped." They put you in a gown with your butt hanging out, ask a million questions, take blood samples, hook you up to a saline drip, and somebody comes in with a rag full of chemicals and sponges you down. If you are allergic to the chemicals, you may balloon up to the size of a refrigerator but this is way better than getting an infection. A couple hours later they give you two Tylenols and roll you down the hallway to the OR (Operating Room not Oregon).

Johnny managed to completely blow this part. As they rolled him off the gurney and onto the operating table, he saw approximately a dozen nurses and doctors all dressed in white. One of them appeared to be holding a bone saw. To lighten the atmosphere, Johnny blurted out "Jeez, it looks like a bunch of penguins in here." Dead silence.

The anesthesiologist had fastened a blood pressure cuff to Johnny's arm and was staring in disbelief at the numbers, which read 225/109. Somebody said "Jeez, that's really high." Somebody else said "We're not doing this today." The party was over, and Johnny had set a new record for the least amount of time ever spent by a single patient in the OR.

This was totally embarrassing. Johnny had inconvenienced a dozen doctors and nurses who had spent hours getting ready to work their magic and make him well. He felt really bad about it. It turns out that some people have what they call "White Coat Syndrome" which is where anxiety about a medical environment causes your blood pressure to raise. The syndrome gets its name from doctors and medical staff who often wear white coats in professional settings. Studies have shown that people with White Coat hypertension have increased risk of stroke, heart attack, and heart failure. Since Johnny was off the charts, it was a good thing to postpone the operation and he is very grateful for this level of professional caution.

A few months later Johnny was able to convince Dr. Kimo's assistant to put him back on the list. In the meantime, he studied the issue of anxiety in the OR and discovered that a drug called Versed (Midazolam) is sometimes administered just prior to an operation to reduce anxiety. Johnny's request was granted, and the anesthesiologist administered a few milligrams. The next thing Johnny remembered was waking up in the recovery room three hours later at 120/80.

Dr. Kimo had pulled off a miracle. He was able to remove the stem manually without having to resort to other extreme measures. All aspects of the surgery went perfectly. Dr. Kimo called Terry immediately after to relate the good news – she said he sounded like a really happy guy. Johnny is very thankful and really happy also. He may have to see about a new surfboard.

He went to a post-op checkup a few weeks later to talk about rehabilitation therapy. Dr. Kimo asked, "Do you swim?" Johnny responded, "No, I surf." Dr. Kimo said "Me too!" I knew I liked this guy.

Epilogue

Johnny calculates that three-fourths of his life has sailed by. That means he still has a considerable amount of time left to get in trouble. And, who knows, he might write about that too. For now, he's just gonna bind this thing up, get it out there, and see how many people he can offend.

He's had the good fortune to hang with a lot of interesting people during his tenure so far on earth. They all mean something to him and influenced him in some way. Many of them appear in this book, although he has only used their first names (in most cases) so he can deny that he was talking about them when they sue him.

It may be of some interest to know where all these people are now. Unfortunately, Johnny has lost track of some of them. So, some of this information is approximately correct but in other cases it's just an educated guess.

Here goes:

Ronny from the Quarry - Served some time, got paroled, got shot and killed in Reno (Johnny Cash wrote a song about him – "shot a man in Reno just to watch him die").

Mike from the Quarry - Works for Riverside Board of Water Supply, last seen cruising through Tuxi's parking lot in a bitchin' 32 Duce Coupe.

Lester from De Anza - Beat to death in front of the De Anza Theater – assailant still at large.

Consuelo from De Anza – Graduated from cross-town rival Ramona High. Went on to college and law school. Currently Prosecuting Attorney, Riverside Criminal Court.

Glen, Johnny's brother from Perfect Vacation - Went on to become a mathematician creating formulas to fit curved surfaces together. Retired in LA – still goes to the gym every day.

Jackie, Johnny's sister (she is the smart one) from Perfect Vacation - Became a schoolteacher and later head of special education for San Diego County. Retired with her husband Jim in Ashland, Oregon where they ski, square dance, and fool around. Coincidentally, she had her first hip replacement a couple weeks ago.

Greg Noll "da Bull" from Biggest Wave – Moved to Alaska with wife Laura where he became a commercial fisherman. Retired and moved to Crescent City where he passed away on June 30, 2021. In one of his last interviews he said,

"In my mind, I never quit surfing. Surfing is a feeling that never leaves you..."

Brian from Biggest Wave - Alive and well in Hanalei with wife Caverly, sons Gavin and Quest, daughter Keala. Still surfs big Hanalei, successful real estate broker, all around great guy and is, among all of Johnny's surfing friends, the only man left who can still stand upright on a surfboard.

Kerry Jo from Biggest Wave - Living in Nova Scotia, wrote a book, which will probably be on the New York Times Best Seller List shortly.

Mike from Brothers - Resting peacefully in the deep blue sea.

Bob from Brothers – Bouncing, tending bar, still looking for Brian.

Wags from Brothers - Living with lovely wife Shara in Santa Barbara in new house he built after old house burned down in forest fire (had a half million left over – buys wine from the top rack at Costco). Plays the guitar like Eric Clapton, has a band and a record, still paddles out when the surf and the weather are right, and sports a low golf handicap.

Bill from Brothers - Also living in Santa Barbara with lovely wife Shiela. Got on the computer bandwagon before anybody knew what it was. Resides in a bitchin' barn he transformed into a beautiful home.

Tommy from Girl's League - Became a sheriff, ballooned to 400 pounds, went on TV show Biggest Losers, and came in second.

Suicide Six from Girl's League - Scattered to the wind.

Jerry from Motorcycle - Still lives in Riverside, runs a successful gas station and repair shop, gave up dirt bikes after one too many crashes.

Tucker from Cal Western – Went on to head his father's trailer company. Surfed all the way until he smoked his last big one, got on the Freeway, plowed into the rear of a parked semi, and died at the scene. He was a good guy.

Abdul Azziz from Cal Western – Hid for many years in a mud hut on the border between Afghanistan and Pakistan. Made the mistake of flipping the bird at a passing Special Forces helicopter - got the whole nine yards and then some.

Shaquilla from Menlo – Went on to become Mayor of Oakland.

Tony from Intoxication – Went on to manage a shoe store in San Bernardino. Visited Johnny once with his girlfriend Vicki. Noting a surfboard laying on the floor, Tony, a non-surfer, walked to the unstable skeg end, momentarily hung ten, then crashed and burned spectacularly. Vicki laughed for hours.

Ron from Kilo – Busted again for possession of a large quantity of cocaine with intent to distribute, fled to San Clemente, lived underground for ten years shaping boards and paying cash until a chance meeting in the surf with a friend from Hawaii who said, "Your case was dismissed ten years ago for lack of a warrant." Now a successful real estate mogul with a beautiful wife Jane and a beautiful house. ("And you may find yourself in a beautiful house, with a beautiful wife, and you may ask yourself, well...How did I get here?" - Talking Heads).

Buddy from Road Rage – Drowned in his own pool.

Pokii from Pali Cruiser – Lives in Hau'ula with his lovely wife Mary Ann. Sells hot dogs to tourists from a stand on the beach in Waikiki – makes more money than God.

Susan – Divorced Johnny and moved to California with the kids and her alcohol addiction.   Bought a ranch next to Hell's Angel's President Sonny Barger in Grants Pass, Oregon. Tried valiantly to remain sober but ultimately succumbed.   In her will she bequeathed everything to Johnny. She was a good woman.

Mark from Mauna Kea 200 – Although he had a weak heart, he continued to ride hard, and was often put away wet.   On a Sunday afternoon after a long ride with Johnny and friends he died on the couch.   He was a wonderful guy.

Earl from Mauna Kea 200 – Living in Honolulu and running a series of Bridal Chapels which are big things for Japanese tourists and very profitable for those in the business.

Rick from Golf at Punaluu – Retired and living in Kona with his lovely Hawaiian wife Claire. Traded coconut trees for a membership in Big Island Country Club – plays daily, rarely loses.

Matthew Makani ma la'au (Wind Through the Trees), Johnny's son from Matt's Wedding – Became a chef, mechanic, builder, and all-around handyman.   Moved to Christmas Valley, Oregon where he lives with his lovely girlfriend Elisha and their handsome young son Nickola.

Anna Pukana la (Sunrise), Johnny's twin daughter, lives in Texas with her husband Jeff, and is enjoying the good life. Still gets cross when Johnny calls her Ingrid.

Ingrid Pa'ana a ka 'la (Sunshine), Johnny's other twin daughter, lives just down the hill in Palolo Valley with her husband Spencer – they run a commercial fishing operation and bring in big Ahi and Mahi just about every day. Still gets cross when Johnny calls her Anna.

Gerrit from Geezer Golf – That son of a bitch is still running around Honolulu bumming people out. He once recounted a conversation he had with a fellow employee who said, "You're not the kind of guy who gets heart attacks, you're the kind of guy who gives them."

Dave & Lisa from Napa Valley – Happily married and living in a lovely home in Napa. Runs a contracting business, lives a good life, and occasionally takes the Missus to Tahoe where he cleans up at the poker table and she cleans up at the slot machines.

Jay & Sara from Three Dogs and a Crazy Lady – Moved from close proximity to Hawaii's Fissure 8 to the mainland in close proximity to Mount Saint Helens. Waiting for the next eruption.

Tyler & Amy from the Wedding – It didn't work out and they divorced a year after the wedding. Tyler went on to run the Information Technology Department at the University of Omaha. In a brief fall from the wagon, he failed to show for several weeks and was fired whereupon he remotely shut down the entire computer system of the University and was charged with some sort of felony, which was later dropped if he promised not to do it again. He is now clean and sober.

Mark Jennings from Board Cords and Black Holes – he's out there somewhere, probably working on the next big thing.

Terry – She's my sweetie, my wife, and the love of my life. I will love her forever. Plus, she gave me back the keys!

Johnny – Recovering from his third hip replacement, looking forward to the fourth. Continues to get into trouble (an 18-year-old mind and a 75-year-old body will do that to you).

Aloha.

Acknowledgments

Writing is hard. I don't know how professional writers do it. I started this book in 2005. By 2009 I was totally winded and decided to put it down although I kept a hard copy. In 2016 I had some encouragement and dove back in. Every year after that I wrote a little more. Covid came in 2020 so I decided to sprint to the finish line. It's now 2021 and I'm just about there (sixteen years and thousands of miles from the starting line).

The other thing about writing is it requires that you bare your soul to a certain extent, which is embarrassing, particularly when you're writing about egregious transgressions of which I have many. So, this may well be my first and last book, but you never know. I had thought about publishing it posthumously to avoid ridicule and jail time, but what the hell.

There are a few people who were instrumental in getting Johnny off the couch and on the computer where books are born, and I would like to thank them:

Pat Zell - Pat is a darling girl with many talents including the ability to drink more Chardonnay in one night than the French Foreign Legion. It was both difficult and enjoyable to try and keep up. Johnny had made vague threats involving the writing of a book (the wine was talking). In a likely effort to shut him up, Pat presented him with a book about how to write books. She had called his bluff and is, therefore, largely responsible for pushing Johnny off the ledge. So, if you're looking for somebody to blame, call Pat. She lives in Oregon. Fortunately for her, she's unlisted.

Karla Graham-Wilson – Karla was his faithful secretary for many years and was particularly adept at shielding Johnny from the lunatics who surrounded him at the office. She was extraordinarily convincing and therefore able to lie with impunity every time someone came looking for him while he was out surfing ("He's at a board meeting"). She lives in Honolulu with her husband Al, an avid golfer and bona-fide maniac. Carla gave Johnny a pencil as big as an Italian sausage and a blank notebook as a retirement gift and is, therefore, also culpable. As luck would have it, she is also unlisted.

Bill & Joan Rose – Friends and surfers from high school, they shared many of the same tribulations. Fifty-three years later we reconnected on the Internet and, guess what, Bill was writing a novel also. We started trading chapters (his were better than mine). But it got me motivated and resulted in many enjoyable weeks of pounding away on the old typewriter. Bill passed away shortly after his book was published so in a couple of ways, he beat me to the finish line. He was a good friend and a good man.

Ingrid Pa'ana a ka 'la Hisatake (Sunshine) – Jumping from writing a book to getting it published would have been an impossible leap for me. The rules for publishing are almost beyond comprehension and I'm pretty sure half the instructions are in some other language. Fortunately, Ingrid not only understands that language but also thrives on it. She is my Executive Producer and is singularly responsible for publishing **The Johnny Chronicles.** Mahalo Sweetheart!

Theresa Razon Peterson – The love of my life who I met late in life. I was a 64-year-old aimless divorcee making the turn at Makaha Resort and she was a sweet young thing serving up beer and hot dogs. I asked her "What's a girl like you doing in a place like this?" She was nice enough not to disparage me for such a lame line or ignore me all together. Instead, she explained that she'd retired early from her job as an insurance adjuster in San Francisco and decided to (1) come to Hawaii to visit with her son Dave who owns a house in Waianae and (2) learn to play golf. Working at Makaha was perfect because she could play golf for free. I asked if I could play with her some time. She looked into my eyes and said, "You can play with me any time you like." I am by nature a shy guy, but I went around behind the counter and gave her a big ol' kiss. She moved in immediately thereafter and we were married several years later, but not before I tortured her with quips like, "Do you really want to marry me?" She would respond in the affirmative, and I would say, "That's good to know because I don't handle rejection very well." So, when Billy Rose got me back on my writing bicycle, Terry encouraged me to write as often and as long as I liked. As a special bonus, she volunteered to proofread the whole thing, which was quite a job. This was especially sweet since there are a million things of a constructive nature that I probably should have been doing around the house, but I had a good excuse to dilly-dally. So, thank you Terry – I love you.

Cast of Characters – All the people referenced in this book are or were or may be real (within the meaning of the Prologue). Most of them are still alive and kicking (in a real or ethereal sense) and are largely responsible for making Johnny's life a beautiful thing.

Mahalo Plenty!